THINK LIKE A LAWYER

Legal Reasoning for Law Students
and Business Professionals

E. SCOTT FRUEHWALD

AMERICAN BAR ASSOCIATION
Section of Legal Education
and Admissions to the Bar

Printed in the United States of America.

17 16 5 4 3

Cataloging-in-Publication Data is on file with the Library of Congress.

ISBN 978-1-62722-141-2

Discounts are available for books ordered in bulk. Special consideration is given to state bars, CLE programs, and other bar-related organizations. Inquire at Book Publishing, ABA Publishing, American Bar Association, 321 N. Clark Street, Chicago, Illinois 60654-7598.

www.ShopABA.org

I dedicate this book to the memory of my mother, Mary Jo Fruehwald, who sought the best possible education for my brother and me.

CONTENTS

PREFACE

As instructors, we all are changing the way our
students think about the world, and we are interested
in assisting the change in a productive way.
BRIAN P. COPPOLA[1]

I. THE PROBLEM WITH LEGAL EDUCATION

Law schools do not adequately prepare lawyers for practice. In recent years, numerous books and articles have discussed this obvious fact.[2] A study funded by the Law School Admissions Council concluded that "students' case reading and reasoning skills do not improve as a result of law school instruction."[3] Similarly, Professor Benjamin Spencer has remarked, "Unfortunately, the law school of today is not optimally designed to prepare students for practice."[4] In addition, "[T]he Great Recession has led clients and thus law firms to have less capacity to subsidize the on-the-job training of law graduates that they had been expected to provide, revealing deficiencies in the ability of law schools to adequately prepare a sufficient number of their students to handle legal matters for clients."[5] Students sense the deficiencies in their legal education: The 2011 Survey of Law Student Engagement found that "[f]orty percent of students felt their legal education had contributed only some or very little to their acquisition of job or work-related knowledge and skills."[6]

Contemporary legal education is a modified version of the method developed by Christopher Columbus Langdell at Harvard University in the nineteenth century.[7] Characteristics of this method include large classes taught by the Socratic method, appellate cases as the major materials of study, professors being drawn from academia rather than practice, an emphasis on doctrine over practical skills, and evaluation of professors based mainly on their scholarly writings rather than on their teachings.[8] While there have been some modifications in this method, such as adding legal writing courses and clinics to the law school curriculum, law schools are still focused on teaching doctrine and rewarding scholarship.[9]

The Carnegie Report, which criticized traditional legal education, designated three "apprenticeships" for educating today's lawyers: (1) the "cognitive apprenticeship," which focuses on expert knowledge and modes of thinking, (2) the "apprenticeship of practice," which educates students in "the forms of expert practice shared by competent practitioners," and (3) the "apprenticeship of identity and purpose," which "introduces students to the purposes and attitudes that are guided by the values for which the professional community is responsible."[10]

The doctrinal approach of the Langdellian tradition satisfies the cognitive approach, but it does a poor job with the other two approaches.[11] As one scholar has asserted concerning education in general, "Although thinking always occurs within a domain of knowledge, the usual methods that are used for teaching content matter are not optimal for teaching the thinking skills that psychologists and other educators want students to use in multiple domains because instruction in most courses focuses on content knowledge (as might be expected) instead of the transferability of critical-thinking skills."[12]

II. THE PURPOSE OF THIS BOOK

This book's purpose is to better prepare law students and lawyers for the apprenticeship of practice by providing them with a firm foundation in legal reasoning, showing them how to apply legal reasoning skills to facts, and teaching them legal problem solving.[13] I will do this by focusing explicitly on the different types of legal reasoning and the types of mini-skills needed to develop the different types of legal reasoning.[14] Traditional legal education has claimed that it teaches students to "think like a lawyer." However, traditional legal education rarely specifies what thinking like a lawyer means. This book will talk explicitly about what goes into thinking like a lawyer, such as rule-based reasoning (deductive reasoning), synthesis (inductive reasoning), analogical reasoning, distinguishing cases, and policy-based reasoning.

This book will also discuss the mini-skills that are necessary to develop the types of legal reasoning and, thus, create expert legal problem solvers.[15] Daniel Kahneman has observed that the acquisition of expertise in any field requires the acquisition of many mini-skills.[16] Likewise, a group of researchers has noted, "If students lack critical component skills—or their command of these skills is weak—their performance on the overall task suffers."[17] Professor Kahneman has declared, "Studies of chess masters have shown that at least 10,000 hours of dedicated practice (about 6 years of playing chess five hours a day) are required to attain the highest levels of performance. During these hours of intense concentration, a serious chess player becomes familiar with thousands of configurations, each consisting of an arrangement of related pieces that can threaten or defend each other."[18] Similarly, a concert pianist must spend years practicing scales, octaves, chords, pedaling, interpretation, etc. The same is true of the law.[19] To reuse a joke about how to get to Carnegie Hall, how does one develop a skilled lawyer? Practice, practice, practice. To become an expert, a person must "constantly . . . push her- or himself, or be prompted by a coach, beyond current abilities."[20] Also, to become an expert, the learner must know what to practice.[21] Consequently, this book has many exercises intended to develop students' legal mini-skills.

In addition, this book has chapters on combining these mini-skills so that the reader can become a complete problem solver. "If the task is highly complex and can be easily divided into component parts [mini-skills], students often learn more effectively if the components are practiced temporarily in isolation, and then progressively combined."[22] The learners must then also practice the integrated skills in combination to develop fluency.

III. GENERAL PRINCIPLES OF MASTERING LAW

The first step in mastering law is to become an engaged learner. Professor Kahneman distinguishes between engaged and lazy thinkers.[23] He asserts: "Those who avoid the sin of intellectual sloth could be called 'engaged.' They are more alert, more intellectually active, less willing to be satisfied with superficially attractive answers, more skeptical about their intuitions."[24]

He asserts that laziness is "a reluctance to invest more effort than is strictly necessary."[25] A goal of this book is to develop engaged learners.

An engaged learner is a self-regulated learner. "Self-regulated learning refers to one's ability to understand and control one's learning environment."[26] "Self-regulation is a self-directive process and set of behaviors whereby learners transform their mental abilities into skills and habits through a developmental process that emerges from guided practice and feedback."[27] Self-regulated learning "involves the active, goal-directed, self-control of behavior, motivation, and cognition for academic tasks by an individual student."[28] Similarly, "self-regulated learners "are intrinsically motivated, self-directing, self-monitoring, and self-evaluating."[29] Self-regulated learners are inquisitive, are open to new ideas, and take risks. They do not settle for the first answer, but always consider alternatives. They "recognize when a skill is needed and [they have] the willingness to apply it."[30] Self-regulated learners know themselves. They admit when they are confused, and they try to clear up their confusion before proceeding.[31] Most important, self-regulated learners have learning strategies, and they focus more on mastery than on grades.[32]

Self-regulated learning involves three recursive stages: forethought, performance, and reflection.[33] In other words, think about doing the task, perform the task, and reflect on what you have done. Most students only do the performance stage. However, legal employers expect law school graduates to be self-regulated learners.[34]

Self-regulated learners have developed their inner voice (inner critic). The inner voice is the "voice people hear when they are engaged in the learning process—the voice that will tell them what they have to do to accomplish a task, what they already know, what they do not know, how to match their previous learning to the new situation, when they don't understand what they are reading or learning, and how to evaluate their learning. It is this internal reflection and conscious control of the learning process that goes to the heart of metacognition."[35] Stated differently: "Metacognition refers to the self-monitoring by an individual of his own unique cognitive processes."[36] Imagine a concert pianist using his inner voice while performing.

Another way to become an engaged learner is to develop certain habits. The first is to become an engaged reader. The first step in becoming an engaged reader is to always read with a purpose. The second habit you should develop is to be a self-reflective learner (part of being a self-regulated learner). Self-reflective learners can learn on their own, and they develop the ability to reflect on what they have learned and analyze ideas, their own and others'. I will present other habits and skills that you can use to become an engaged learner throughout this book.

IV. USING THIS BOOK

The chapters in this book will present the different types of legal reasoning, the mini-skills that are related to those types of legal reasoning, and how to use these mini-skills in combination. Chapter One discusses the types of legal reasoning. In Chapter Two, I will teach you how to be an engaged reader and analyze cases—skills that are needed before you can learn the other mini-skills in detail. Chapter Three concerns reasoning by analogy, which involves showing how your case is like a precedent case. Chapter Four examines rule-based reasoning and its connection to syllogisms. Chapter Five involves synthesizing cases, which is an important skill in establishing the law. Chapter Six investigates statutory interpretation, which is a type of rule-based reasoning that fills in the details with analogies. Chapter Seven brings the prior chapters together by demonstrating how the different types of legal reasoning relate to the small-scale paradigm (how to organize a simple analysis). Chapter Eight fills in this paradigm by examining how to respond to opposing arguments and distinguish cases. Finally, Chapter Nine serves as a capstone to this book with its presentation of advanced problem solving and creative thinking.

I have written this book for several audiences. First, law students can use this book independently to learn legal mini-skills. I have written it so that students can progressively build their reasoning and analytical skills. Second, it is intended as a text for legal methods and legal writing courses. Third, doctrinal professors can use it in any first-year courses as a supplement on legal reasoning. Fourth, I hope it is valuable to academic support professors. Fifth, I intended it for lawyers who want to improve their legal reasoning and analytical skills. Finally, I hope that this book can help law students and lawyers become lifelong, self-regulated learners.

While I have written the chapters to be read sequentially, a teacher using this book may want to focus on individual chapters. While there are cross-references among chapters for clarity, the chapters are mainly self-contained so that they can be used individually.

Note: It is important that you have a legal dictionary by your side when you read this book. Engaged learners look up all words they do not know.

Note on the exercises: One of the purposes of this book is to allow law students to learn legal skills independently. I want students to be able to get immediate feedback on their learning. Consequently, I have put answers to some of the exercises at the end of each chapter. Please don't look at the answers until you have completely thought through an exercise. Be an engaged learner, not a lazy one! (Note: I have not given answers to all the exercises.)

EXERCISE PREFACE-1

Learning requires self-reflection and self-assessment. Keep a journal as you read through this book and do the exercises. Record what you have learned about legal reasoning and legal analysis. Do you understand these concepts fully? Write about how your thought processes have changed. Note the problems you have had in doing the exercises, and think about how you would help others learn legal reasoning. At the end of each chapter, evaluate your progress in developing your legal reasoning skills. (The purpose of this exercise is to develop your self-evaluation skills and your inner voice.)

NOTES

1. Brian P. Coppola, Progress in Practice: Using Concepts from Motivational and Self-Regulated Learning Research to Improve Chemistry Instruction, 63 NEW DIRECTIONS FOR TEACHING AND LEARNING: UNDERSTANDING SELF-REGULATED LEARNING 87, 94 (1995).

2. E.g., A. Benjamin Spencer, The Law School Critique in Historical Perspective, 69 WASH. & LEE L. REV. 1949 (2012); David Segal, What They Don't Teach Law Students: Lawyering, N.Y. TIMES (Nov. 19, 2011) (http://www.law.com/jsp/

article.jsp?id=1202509595910&slreturn=1); New York State Bar Ass'n, *Report of the Task Force on the Future of the Legal Profession,* http://www.nysba.org/AM/Template.cfm?Section=Task_Force_on_the_Future_of_the_Legal_Profession_Home&Template=/CM/ContentDisplay.cfm&ContentID=48108, *38 (2011) ("Too many law students and recent graduates are not as well prepared for the profession as they might be."); Erwin Chemerinsky, *Rethinking Legal Education,* Harv. C.R.C.L. L. Rev. 595 (2008) ("[T]here is no way to reform legal education in any meaningful way without giving law students far more experience in the practice of law." *Id.* at 597); *see generally* William M. Sullivan et al., Educating Lawyers: Preparation for the Profession of Law (Jossey-Bass 2007) (hereinafter The Carnegie Report); Roy Stuckey et al., Best Practices in Legal Education (Clinical Legal Educ. Ass'n 2007).

3. Dorthy H. Evensen et al., Developing an Assessment of First-Year Law Students' Critical Case Reasoning and Reasoning Ability: Phase 2, http://www.lsac.org/lsacresources/Research/GR/GR-08-02.pdf, *1 (Law School Admissions Council 2009).

4. Spencer, *supra* note 2, at 1958.

5. *Id.* at 1955.

6. Karen Sloan, *Students Happy with Law School Experience, with Caveats,* Nat. L.J. (http://www.law.com/jsp/nlj/PubArticleNLJ.jsp?id=1202538236462&slreturn=1) (Jan. 12, 2012).

7. Spencer, *supra* note 2, at 1973–81.

8. *Id.* at 1973–79.

9. *Id.* at 2015–54.

10. The Carnegie Report, *supra* note 2, at 28.

11. *Id.* at 25, 79.

12. Diane F. Halpern, *Teaching Critical Thinking for Transfer across Domains: Dispositions, Skills, Structure Training, and Metacognitive Monitoring,* 53 Am. Psych. 449, 451 (1998). Similarly, as Nancy Schultz has stated: "The limited focus of most law school classes on derivation of rules and policy considerations from appellate decisions cannot begin to approximate the thinking process of the competent attorney. Teaching students to think like attorneys loses much of its meaning if that thinking is not placed in the context of what lawyers actually do." Nancy L. Schultz, *How Do Lawyers Really Think?,* 42 J. Legal Educ. 57, 64 (1992).

13. This book will employ principles of cognitive psychology. As Professor Halpern has argued, "It is clear that a successful pedagogy that can serve as a basis for the enhancement of thinking will have to incorporate ideas about the way in which learners organize knowledge and internally represent it and the way these representations change and resist change when new information is encountered. Despite all of the gains that cognitive psychologists have made in understanding what happens when people learn, most teachers do not apply their knowledge of cognitive psychology." Halpern, *supra* note 12, at 451. Much of the learning theory in this book is based on DUANE F. SHELL ET AL., THE UNIFIED LEARNING MODEL: HOW MOTIVATIONAL, COGNITIVE, AND NEUROBIOLOGICAL SCIENCES INFORM BEST TEACHING PRACTICES (Springer 2010).

14. The Carnegie Report stressed the need for making skills explicit. THE CARNEGIE REPORT, *supra* note 2, at 11, 26; *see also* Nelson P. Miller & Bradley J. Charles, *Meeting the Carnegie Report's Challenge to Make Legal Analysis Explicit: Subsidiary Skills to the IRAC Framework*, 59 J. LEGAL EDUC. 192 (2009); Anthony Niedwiecki, *Lawyers and Learning: A Metacognitive Approach to Legal Education*, 13 WIDENER L. REV. 33, 58 (2006) [hereinafter Niedwiecki, *Lawyers and Learning*]; Halpern, *supra* note 12, at 454 ("Thinking skills need to be explicitly and consciously taught and then used with many types of examples so that the skill aspect and its appropriate use are clarified and emphasized.").

15. BEST PRACTICES has asserted, "Law schools cannot help students cultivate practical wisdom or judgment unless they give students opportunities to engage in legal problem-solving activities." BEST PRACTICES, *supra* note 2, at 150. Similarly, the CARNEGIE REPORT has argued, "Practice requires not the distanced stance of the observer and critic but engagement with situations." CARNEGIE REPORT, *supra* note 2, at 87–88.

16. DANIEL KAHNEMAN, THINKING, FAST AND SLOW 238 (Farrar, Straus & Giroux 2011).

17. SUSAN AMBROSE ET AL., HOW LEARNING WORKS: & RESEARCH-BASED PRINCIPLES FOR SMART TEACHING 100 (Jossey-Bass 2010). These authors added, "[E]ven a small amount of focused practice on key component skills had a profound effect on overall performance." *Id.* at 101.

18. KAHNEMAN, *supra* note 16, at 101.

19. As BEST PRACTICES points out, "It takes time to develop expertise in legal problem-solving. Problem-solving skills can be developed only by actually working

through the process of resolving problems. Developing problem-solving expertise requires repetitions of 'training' as against the hard world of consequences, of repeated success and failure, and some inductive efforts at understanding what works and what does not, what seems important and what does not." Best Practices, *supra* note 2, at 142. *See also* Timothy W. Floyd, Oren R. Griffin & Karen J. Sneddon, *Beyond Chalk and Talk: The Law Classroom of the Future*, 38 Ohio N. U. L. Rev. 257, 266 (2011) ("Practicing or rehearsing improves retention, especially when it is distributed practice. By distributing practices, the learner associates the material with many different contexts rather than the one context afforded by mass practice.").

20. Keith Oatley & Maja Djikic, *Writing as Thinking*," 12 Rev. Gen. Psych. 9, 13 (2008).

21. *Id.*

22. Ambrose et al., *supra* note 17, at 102.

23. Kahneman, *supra* note 16, at 46.

24. *Id.*

25. *Id.* at 31. Similarly, Halpern writes, "It is important to separate the disposition or willingness to think critically from the ability to think critically. Some people may have excellent critical-thinking skills and may recognize when the skills are needed, but they also may choose not to engage in the effortful process of using them. This is the distinction between what people can do and what they actually do in real-world contexts." Halpern, *supra* note 12, at 452.

26. Teaching Excellence in Adult Literacy, Just Write! Guide, https://teal.ed.gov/resources, *29 (Teal 2012). This book contains an excellent introduction to self-regulated learning at *29–31.

27. *Id.*

28. Barry J. Zimmerman, *Developing Self-Fulfilling Cycles of Academic Regulation: An Analysis of Exemplary Instruction Models, in* Self-Regulated Learning: From Teaching to Self-Reflective Practice 1 (Dale H. Schunk & Barry J. Zimmerman eds., Guilford Pubs. 1998); *see also* Floyd et al., *supra* note 19, at 268; Niedwiecki, *Lawyers and Learning, supra* note 14, at 41–42; Just Write! Guide, *supra* note 26, at 29 ("Specifically, self-regulated learning consists of three components: **cognition, metacognition,** and **motivation**."). The Just Write! Guide states, "The cognition component includes the skills and habits that are necessary to encode, memorize, and recall information as well as think critically. Within the metacognition

component are skills that enable learners to understand and monitor their cognitive processes. The motivation component surfaces the beliefs and attitudes that affect the use and development of both the cognitive and metacognitive skills." *Id.*

29. Gerald F. Hess, *The Legal Educator's Guide to Periodicals on Teaching and Learning*, 67 UMKC L. REV. 367, 385 (1998).

30. Halpern, *supra* note 12, at 452.

31. Michael Hunter Schwartz, *Teaching Law Students to Be Self-Regulated Learners*, 2003 MICH. ST. DCL L. REV. 447, 472.

32. *Id.* at 453–54, 471. Professor Schwartz's article is worth reading in detail. Of course, an engaged learner would look at sources cited in the footnotes without being told.

33. *Id.* at 454. I will give more details on becoming a self-regulated learner in Chapter Two.

34. *Id.* at 471. In addition, minorities and immigrants who are self-regulated learners are successful, while those who are not self-regulated learners are not. *Id.* at 474–75.

35. Anthony Niedwiecki, *Teaching for Lifelong Learning: Improving the Metacognitive Skills of Law Students through More Effective Formative Assessment Techniques*, 40 CAP/ U. L. REV. 149, 159 (2011).

36. Niedwiecki, *Lawyers and Learning*, *supra* note 14, at 35. The authors of the JUST WRITE! GUIDE explain, "Metacognition refers to awareness of one's own knowledge—what one does and doesn't know—and one's ability to understand, control, and manipulate one's cognitive processes. It includes knowing when and where to use particular strategies for learning and problem solving as well as how and why to use specific strategies. Metacognition is the ability to use prior knowledge to plan a strategy for approaching a learning task, take necessary steps to problem solve, reflect on and evaluate results, and modify one's approach as needed." JUST WRITE! GUIDE, *supra* note 26, at 32. They continue: "The metacognitive component is comprised of declarative knowledge (knowledge about oneself as a learner—the factors that influence performance), procedural knowledge (knowledge about strategies and other procedures), and conditional knowledge (knowledge of why and when to use a particular strategy). Adults often struggle to articulate their knowledge or to transfer domain-specific knowledge to a new setting. The goal of self-regulated learning is for these strategies to first become visible and eventually automated for the adult learner." *Id.* at 30.

CHAPTER ONE

THE FIVE TYPES OF LEGAL REASONING

CHAPTER GOALS

1. To introduce the reader to the five types of legal reasoning.
2. To help the reader recognize the five types of legal reasoning when the reader sees them in an argument or case.
3. To introduce the reader to making policy arguments.

The first step in understanding legal reasoning explicitly is to learn the five types of legal reasoning.

1. Rule-Based Reasoning

Rule-based reasoning is the most important type of legal reasoning. In rule-based reasoning, you take a rule (a statute, a case holding, or an administrative regulation) and apply it to a set of facts. (This is a type of deductive reasoning—reasoning from the general to the specific.) Rules have at least three parts: "(1) a set of elements, collectively called a test; (2) a result that occurs when all the elements are present (and the test is thus satisfied); and (3) . . . a causal term that determines whether the result is mandatory, prohibitory, discretionary, or declaratory."[1] In addition, some rules have "one or more exceptions that, if present, would defeat the result, even if all the elements are present."[2] An example of a rule would be that intentional infliction of emotional harm occurs if (1) the defendant's conduct is outrageous, (2) the defendant's conduct is intentional, and (3) the defendant's conduct causes (4) severe emotional distress. The rule would be satisfied if the facts of the present case satisfy all the elements of the rule. For example, if an ex-boyfriend calls an ex-girlfriend several times in the middle of the night to harass her (outrageous conduct; intentional conduct) and this causes (causation) her severe emotional distress (an emotional breakdown), intentional infliction of emotional harm has taken place.

2. Reasoning by Analogy

Reasoning by analogy involves finding similarities (comparison—the specific to the specific). Reasoning by analogy in the law occurs when one argues that the facts of the precedent case are like the facts of the present case, so the rule of the precedent case should apply to the present case. (The facts of case A are like the facts of case B, so the rule from case A should apply to case B.) Here is an example of reasoning by analogy: The rule that one who keeps a wild animal, like a tiger, on her property is strictly liable for any damage caused by that animal also applies to pit bull owners because a pit bull, although not a wild animal, is inherently dangerous, just like a wild animal. The two cases are rarely exactly the same; reasoning by analogy is a question of degree. The writer must convince the reader that the facts of the two cases are similar enough that the rule from the precedent case should apply to the present case.

3. Distinguishing Cases

Distinguishing cases (contrasting) is the opposite of reasoning by analogy. In distinguishing cases, one argues that the facts of the precedent case are not like the facts of the present case, so the rule from the precedent case does not apply to the present case. (The facts of case A are not like the facts of case B, so the rule from case A should not apply to case B.) For example, a toy poodle is not like a wild animal because toy poodles are not inherently dangerous, so the rule from the wild animal cases that an owner of a wild animal should be strictly liable for any damage caused by that wild animal should not apply to owners of toy poodles.

4. Reasoning by Policy

With policy-based reasoning, the writer argues that applying a particular rule to a case would create a precedent that is good for society. For instance, in early products liability cases, lawyers argued for strict liability when a product injured a consumer because manufacturers could better spread the cost of injuries than consumers. Policy-based reasoning can also be combined with reasoning by analogy. For instance, one can argue that the policy behind the rule in the precedent case also applies to the present case, so the rule from the precedent case should also apply to the present case.

5. Inductive Reasoning

Inductive reasoning is reasoning from the specific to the general. Lawyers use inductive reasoning to synthesize rules. In other words, lawyers take the holdings from several cases and by synthesizing those cases, they come up with a general rule. To synthesize a rule, look at both the similarities and the differences among the facts of the precedent cases. Also, look at the reasoning behind the holdings.

EXAMPLE

Case 1 holding: A person who owns a tiger that escapes and causes personal injury is strictly liable for that personal injury.

Case 2 holding: A person who owns a tiger that escapes and causes property damage is strictly liable for that property damage.

Case 3 holding: A person who owns a pit bull that escapes and causes personal injury is strictly liable for that personal injury.

Case 4 holding: A person who owns a toy poodle that escapes and causes personal injury is not strictly liable for that personal injury.

Synthesized rule: A person who owns an inherently dangerous animal that escapes and causes personal injury or property damage is strictly liable for that personal injury or property damage.

Reasoning: Tigers, which are wild animals, and pit bulls, which are often bred to be aggressive, are inherently dangerous, while toy poodles are not. When two innocent parties are involved, the law usually holds the party liable that keeps dangerous things, like wild animals, even if the individual is not at fault. The rule applies to both personal injury and property damage.

EXERCISE 1-1

Label the following types of legal reasoning.

1. A contract requires an offer and an acceptance to be binding. In this case, the plaintiff's letter of July 15 was an offer, and the defendant's phone call on July 16 accepted that offer.
2. *Smith* held that someone who grabs a hat out of another person's hand can be liable for battery. In our case, the defendant grabbed a plate out of our client's hand, which is like grabbing a hat out of a person's hand. Therefore, the defendant should be liable for battery.
3. If this court adopts strict liability for defective products, it would make proving liability easier for plaintiffs.
4. Case A held that grabbing a hat out of someone's hand could be a battery. Case B held that grabbing a plate out of someone's hand could be a battery. Case C held that grabbing a plate off the table in front of someone was not a battery. Case D held that ripping a shirt off of someone could be a battery. **Rule:** To constitute a battery, the object taken from the plaintiff must be touching the plaintiff's person.
5. Case A held that it would adopt strict liability for product liability cases because it would make proving liability easier for plaintiffs. Proving liability in airplane disasters is similarly difficult for plaintiffs. Therefore, this court should apply strict liability to airplane disasters.
6. In case A, the court held that when a defendant signed a contract in a jurisdiction, that jurisdiction could assert personal jurisdiction over that defendant. In case B, the defendant did not sign the contract in the jurisdiction. **Held:** There is no jurisdiction in case B.
7. Under a state statute, a will is valid if it is signed by the testator in the presence of two witnesses who then sign the will. John Dunne, the testator, signed the will in the presence of Bill Williams and Jackie Hendrix, both of whom also signed the will. **Held:** The will is valid.

8. To establish false imprisonment, (a) the plaintiff must prove the defendant intended to confine the plaintiff within boundaries fixed by the defendant, (b) the defendant's act must directly or indirectly result in the plaintiff's confinement, and (c) the plaintiff must be conscious of the confinement or must be harmed by it. The store detective asked Martha to remain in the detective's office while he investigated whether Martha had shoplifted the sweater. Martha agreed to stay. **Held:** There was no false imprisonment because Martha could have left at any time.

9. In *Rodriguez*, the court held that a school could restrict the speech of high school students because such restrictions are often necessary to keep order. In *Griffin*, the court did not apply this rule to college students because discipline is not as much of a problem on college campuses.

10. Under a statute, a court will hold a contract term unconscionable if the term is unfair to the plaintiff and the plaintiff lacks bargaining power. In *Gold*, the court held that a waiver of warranty in an automobile contract was unconscionable because the term was unfair to the plaintiff and because the plaintiff lacked bargaining power with the defendant, a large corporation. *Silver* involved the sale of a used automobile in a contract between neighbors that contained an "as is" clause. **Held:** The "as is" clause is not unconscionable because there was no disparity of bargaining power.

EXERCISE 1-2

Identify the type of legal reasoning at each bold letter.

In case 1, an exotic animal lover kept a tiger on his property, being very careful to make sure it did not escape. The tiger escaped and bit a neighbor, causing him to incur $500 in health care costs. The court held that the tiger's owner is liable for the damages under strict liability on the ground that one who owns a wild animal that escapes and causes personal injury should be liable regardless of fault, because the owner brought the animal into the neighborhood knowing it was dangerous. (**A**) In case 2, a person owned a pit bull. The pit bull escaped despite the fact that the owner was very careful to keep it caged, and it bit a neighbor, causing her to incur $500 in hospital bills. The court held that the pit bull's owner was strictly liable for the personal injuries because a pit bull is like a tiger. (**B**) In case 3, Grandma owned a sweet French poodle named Fluffy, which had never even growled at another person. When a loud helicopter flew overhead, Fluffy became frightened, causing him to bite a neighbor, who incurred $500 in medical bills. The court held that Grandma was not liable for the neighbor's medical expenses on the grounds that she had no reason to know that Fluffy might bite someone, that someone who has no reason to know of a danger should not be held strictly liable, and that a French poodle is not like a pit bull or a tiger. (**C**) Based on cases 1, 2, and 3: An owner of an animal who has reason to know that animal might be dangerous can be held strictly liable for personal injury caused by that animal. (**D**)

Legal arguments resemble the types of arguments we use every day. When you hear an argument (a commercial, a political speech, a friend trying to convince another friend to go to the movies), you should think about the type of argument being used.

EXERCISE I-3

Find a copy of Martin Luther King's letter from a Birmingham jail on the Internet or in a book. Do you find this document persuasive? Why? What kinds of arguments does King use? Note how the letter reads like a legal argument in many ways. In addition to your point of view, read the letter from the viewpoint of a Southern black clergyman in the 1960s. Is the letter persuasive to this audience? Next, read the letter from the point of view of the general public in the 1960s. Is the letter persuasive to them? Are there other viewpoints you can use in reading the letter?

EXERCISE I-4

You are a freshman in college who is living with your parents. You want to go to Florida for spring break with your friends. Write an argument to convince your parents that they should let you go. Label the arguments you use. Read your argument out loud. Would you be convinced if you were the parents? Assume you are a parent, and design a test to determine whether a child is ready to be left home alone. Design a test to determine whether a teenager is ready to drive a car (from the parent's view point, not the DMV's). Design a test to determine whether a college student is ready to go on spring break. Design a test to help a person decide whether she should go to law school.

Habit: When reading cases, always consider the type of argument the court is using! Is the argument convincing to you?

EXERCISE 1-5
Policy Exercises

When courts face a new issue, they often decide it based on policy. Of course, policy reasoning is a part of most cases. The following exercises require you to make decisions based on policy.

1. In the 1970s, X Corporation built a plant in a rural area. The plant created pollution, but no one complained because it was surrounded by farmland. Over the years, the area around the plant became more populated. In 2008, developers built a subdivision with 1,000 expensive homes next to the plant. When the new homeowners moved in, they discovered that smoke from the plant "smelled funny." The homeowners want the plant to eliminate the smell or shut down. It would cost $10 million to eliminate the smell. Assume the plant complies with all laws and there is no danger to health. Argue both sides—that the plant should shut down and that it shouldn't be required to do anything. (The builder of the homes has gone bankrupt.) Is there a compromise?

2. You are an attorney. The rules of professional conduct require that attorneys be honest with the court and with opposing counsel. They also require zealous representation of your client. You and your partner are litigating a case against Lying Lucy. You know that Lucy and her attorney are lying to the court, but you can't prove it. Your partner wants to match Lying Lucy and her attorney lie for lie. What do you say to your partner?

3. Sometimes the law requires a judge to make a decision that goes against her inner principles. What do you think a judge should do in such a situation?

CHAPTER WRAP-UP

Do you think you understand the different types of legal reasoning? Can you recognize them in a case? If not, you should read cases in your casebooks and identify the types of legal arguments used before moving on to the next chapter. Can you make a policy argument?

Preview: Chapters Three, Four, Five, and Eight will deal with the types of legal reasoning in detail by helping you develop the mini-skills of reasoning by analogy, rule-based reasoning, synthesizing cases, and distinguishing cases, respectively. However, first you will need to study two important mini-skills in detail in Chapter Two: how to become an engaged reader and how to analyze cases.

Answers
EXERCISE I-1

1. Rule-based reasoning (deductive reasoning), 2. Reasoning by analogy, 3. Reasoning by policy, 4. Inductive reasoning (rule synthesis), 5. Reasoning by analogy using policy, 6. Distinguishing cases, 7. Rule-based reasoning, 8. Rule-based reasoning (in this case, the rule does not apply because one of the required elements is not met), 9. Distinguishing cases based on policy, 10. Rule-based reasoning

EXERCISE I-2

A. Reasoning by policy (the court didn't have a precedent on this issue, so it was forced to make its decision based on policy); B. Reasoning by analogy (a pit bull is like a tiger because it is a dangerous animal, so the rule from case 1 applies to case 2); C. Reasoning by policy and distinguishing cases (a poodle is not like a tiger or a pit bull, so the rule from cases 1 and 2 should not apply to case 3); D. Inductive reasoning (rule synthesis; you are taking the holdings from the three cases and coming up with a broad rule that is consistent with all three cases)

EXERCISE I-5

1. The plant owners would argue that they were there first and that the subdivision came to the problem. Anyway, they are not doing anything to endanger health. The property owners would argue that the pollution is affecting their enjoyment of the property and that personal uses are more important than industrial uses. Homeowners need places to live. A compromise would be if the property owners each paid the plant owners $10,000 to eliminate the smell. While at first this might seem unfair, the facts said the homes were expensive. Ten thousand dollars each is probably not much when compared with the value of the homes.

2. A student once came to me with this question when I was teaching a legal ethics class. My answer was that the fact that the opposing counsel was cheating did not justify the attorney's cheating. While this may create problems for a client, there nothing an attorney can do if he cannot prove the cheating. Attorneys have a duty to the court and the public to be honest. While one cheating attorney hurts this process, if everybody cheated, our court system would break down. We can only hope the cheating attorney will get caught in later cases. Attorneys do get caught and punished, even if they escape some of the time.

3. You are on your own.

NOTES

1. Richard K. Neumann, Jr., Legal Reasoning and Legal Writing: Structure, Strategy, and Style 16 (Aspen Pub. 2005).

2. *Id.*

CHAPTER TWO

READING AND ANALYZING CASES

CHAPTER GOALS

1. To help the reader understand the steps in becoming an engaged reader.
2. To help the reader become an engaged reader.
3. To show the reader how to analyze cases.
4. To help the reader develop mastery in case analysis.
5. To further develop the reader's skill in recognizing the five types of legal reasoning by applying this skill to more difficult cases.
6. To show the reader how to "mine" cases.

Before learning in detail the mini-skills that are related to the types of legal reasoning, it is necessary to master two other important mini-skills: how to become an engaged reader and how to analyze cases.

I. HOW TO BECOME AN ENGAGED READER

You need to be an engaged reader when you read cases (or other legal materials).[1] However, some law professors have observed that many students seem to read cases without thinking.[2] Reading is thinking. If you read the case casually or in a bored manner, you will not remember what you have read. You should read a case to learn, not just to get through it.

Reading is a process. You should read cases in the same manner you undertake other self-regulated learning.[3] Engaged readers divide reading into three stages: forethought, performance, reflection. These stages are not rigidly linear; you should return to an earlier stage if you are having problems understanding what you are reading.

The forethought stage involves all thought processes you undertake before you start reading.[4] (Expert readers do these processes automatically; apprentice readers must gradually develop their skills in these processes so that they become automatic.) These thought processes are "task perception, self-efficacy, self-motivation, goal setting, and strategic planning."[5] In the task stage (first forethought substage), you should perceive and react to the task.[6] First, identify and classify the task by perceiving its skill domain and the subject.[7] For reading cases, the skill domain is reading, and the subject of the task is reading a case in a particular area, such as torts or civil procedure. Also in the task stage, the reader should react to the task by determining how much the reading interests the reader, establishing the relevance of the reading, and relating the reading to prior knowledge.[8]

Putting a case into context is an important part of the task first forethought stage. First, make sure you know the parties, the date of the opinion, the level of the court, the procedure below (if any), and the jurisdiction. Most important, context means reading the case within a narrative—as a real-world story. As the Carnegie Report has noted, "Actual legal practice is heavily dependent upon expertise in narrative modes of reasoning. . . . It follows that the formation of the habits of mind needed for legal practice also demand fluency in both the engaged mode of narrative thinking characteristic of everyday practice and the detached mode of analytical thinking emphasized in case-dialogue teaching."[9] While reading cases, always think about the law's connection to the facts and how each case relates to other cases.

In the second forethought substage, the reader "assesses her efficacy for accomplishing the task."[10] Self-efficacy is "the belief that one is capable of identifying, organizing, initiating, and executing a course of action that will bring about the desired outcome."[11] Readers should know their skill and experience levels, and they should believe they can improve those levels. Students who have positive attitudes and confidence in themselves learn more. If you are not confident in your self-efficiency, you can do other pre-reading tasks, such as reading in a legal treatise or an encyclopedia concerning the case's subject matter.

Self-motivation is a key to effective learning.[12] A student who *wants* to read something is more motivated than a student who *has* to read something. Of course, most reading in law school is mandatory, but a student who is also interested in learning will do better in law school and will not give up when the task is difficult. Ways to help self-motivation include replacing negative self-talk (usually from prior learning experiences) with "positive self-instruction and a sense of self as an effective learner" and developing new habits.[13] Developing metacognitive strategies (ways to monitor one's thinking) also helps motivation because using them builds confidence.[14] The best way to develop metacognitive strategies is to focus on your process of learning (think about thinking).[15] "Self-questioning, reflective journal writing, and discussing their thought processes with other learners" are techniques that learners can use to develop their metacognitive processes.[16]

Based on the efficacy and self-motivation analyses, the reader then sets goals (purposes) for the reading (the desired outcome).[17] The goals can be mastery goals, such as a goal that "focuses on acquiring the skills or the knowledge that are the subject matter of study," or performance goals, which focus on grades or other indices of performance.[18] An example of a mastery goal is "I will read this case to learn the law on enforceability of covenants not to compete so that I can apply it to other situations." A mastery goal generally results in more learning than a performance goal. The goals of the reading should "include the standards by which the student will measure success, are specific to the task, are short term, and are neither too easy nor too hard."[19]

The reader should have a "real-world" purpose (similar to a goal) when reading.[20] Why you are reading the case? Be as specific as possible when establishing your purpose. Are you reading it to write an objective memo? Are you a law clerk who is reading it to explain it to the judge? Are you reading it as part of a synthesis of the law? Having a purpose focuses you and makes the reading more interesting.

The final step in the forethought stage is developing a reading strategy (how you will approach the reading) based on the earlier substages.[21] "Reading strategies are 'set[s] of mental processes used by a reader to achieve a purpose.'"[22] Think about the steps you will take in reading the case and the tools you will use. If you are a novice legal reader, it might help to write down your reading strategy. Of course, a large part of a strategy for reading cases is to incorporate the case analysis techniques set forth in the following section. (I have presented a reading strategy for cases in the activity substage paragraphs below.)

The performance stage is the actual reading. This stage encompasses three processes: (1) "attention focusing," (2) "the activity itself," and (3) "the self-monitoring the student performs as she implements her strategies and starts to learn."[23] Attention focusing helps make the reading productive. Self-regulated readers are able to focus their attention.[24] Having a strategy, purpose, and goal when reading helps to focus attention. Moreover, the reader should avoid multitasking while reading because it reduces attention.[25]

In the activity substage, you should first skim the case to obtain a general sense of what it is about (including deciding what is important and what is irrelevant), then read the case carefully. Use the tools of critical thinking: "interpretation, analysis, evaluation, inference, explanation, and self-regulation."[26] You should read and understand every word and how words, sentences, and paragraphs fit together. Be prepared to shift between larger and smaller concepts to check the consistency of the big picture you are creating.[27] Finally, "[b]ecause of its ambiguity, [reading] needs a lot of inference-making, interpretation and reading between the lines."[28]

You should also be a recursive reader. If you don't understand something, read it again or go back to an earlier passage. Persistence is a characteristic of self-regulated learners;[29] they don't let obstacles stop them. Also, always look up words you do not understand. Consider how well you are thinking about the material (internal feedback).[30] In other words, self-monitoring (using your inner voice) is simultaneous with the activity stage. As one author has written, "Critical thinking also involves evaluating the thinking process—the reasoning that went into the conclusion one arrived at or the kinds of factors considered in making a decision."[31]

You should evaluate the case as you are reading it (engage the text and use your inner voice/critic). Think about the structure of the case:[32] Is the judge discussing the facts, the reasoning, or the outcome? What type of legal reasoning is the judge using? "Talk back" to the text.[33] Question a case's reasoning and outcome and think about alternative reasoning and outcomes (interrogate/debate the text), including drawing inferences from the text. (For example, you could think about the case from the viewpoint of a law professor. What questions would a law professor ask the students if she were teaching a class on the case?) Engaged readers write down their questions and comments. If you mark a passage in the text, make sure you know why you marked that passage. Engaged readers also connect the case with prior knowledge.

The final stage in legal reading is the post-reading or reflective stage. In this stage, readers critically reflect on what they've read and consider the implications of the reading, again using their inner voice.[34] Did you fully understand the reading? If not, read it again. Did it take longer to read the case than it should have? If so, why? Did you have enough context (background) before you read the case? How did your reading strategy work? What did you get from the reading, and how does this relate to your prior knowledge? How did you feel after you read the case? Did you feel better because you learned something? Self-regulated readers feel better about themselves because they learned something while reading and accomplished their mastery goals.[35] In addition, self-regulated readers do not blame others for their lack of learning. Consequently, they are more successful because they realize they are responsible for their own learning and failures.[36]

Similarly, don't beat yourself up if you don't understand something, don't know something, or have made a mistake. All humans make mistakes. You should admit it when you've made a mistake, but don't get overly emotional about it. Instead, think about how you can improve. You should only get mad at yourself if you have not tried hard enough.

Concerning implications of the reading, can you improve your reading process or your reading strategy? Substantively, how did the case you read change your concept of the area of the law? How can the case apply to different sets of facts (hypothesizing)?

SUMMARY OF THE ENGAGED READING PROCESS

I. Forethought
    A. Task perception
    B. Self-efficacy

C. Self-motivation

D. Goal setting

E. Strategic planning

II. Performance

A. Attention focusing

B. The activity itself

C. Self-monitoring

III. Reflection

A. Reflection on reading

B. Reflection on the reading process

Do not move on to the next section until you fully understand the above.

II. ANALYZING CASES

The next legal mini-skill is written case analysis. I prefer "analysis" to the traditional "case briefing" because analysis means to break into parts to understand and because case briefing has often become a mechanical exercise. Case analysis is like analyzing "car parts, then put[ting] them all together again so the car can run."[37] Case analysis is certainly not a mechanical exercise; it is not just placing the parts of a case into the right boxes. Its purpose is to help a lawyer understand the law as set forth in a case and why the court ruled that way. With that knowledge, the lawyer is able to combine that case with other law so that the synthesized law can be applied to a particular set of facts (see Chapter Five). Write out the case analysis because writing it out in your own words helps you better understand the case.

When done correctly, case briefing turns reading cases into an active task. It provides a framework or schema for understanding law.[38] "One of the most important functions of a good case brief schema is to force students to consider their own thoughts and reactions to the case."[39] It helps students "be conscious of their own thinking."[40] Written case analysis allows students to "chunk" information (connect related ideas), thus saving space in working memory and permitting them to remember complex patterns.[41]

The most important part of case analysis is to read the case carefully to determine how all the parts fit together. If you use your speed-reading skills in law school, you will not learn how to properly read a case. You should reread the case several times; reading for content is a recursive process. Also, think about what every word means. You should also think about how the judge has structured the case.

There are four main parts to a case: the issue, the facts, the reasoning, and the holding.

ISSUE: The issue (or issues) is what the outcome of the case hinges upon. An issue is usually a combination of the law and the facts. In other words, if certain conduct or behavior occurs, what is the result? In stating the issue, a student should generally frame it as narrowly as possible to focus his or her attention on the details of the case.

EXAMPLES
1. Is a newspaper ad for a sale on computers that states prices and that "quantities are limited" an offer under contract law?
2. Does Arkansas have jurisdiction over a defendant who has never been to Arkansas and who signed a contract in Mississippi, when the contract only involves performance in Mississippi?

Pointer: Cases are won and lost on the details.

FACTS: Courts do not produce law based on hypotheticals; they work with facts. Consequently, to understand how and why a court has ruled a particular way, a lawyer must thoroughly understand the facts. The most important are the material facts—those facts that help determine the outcome. A key skill is being able to determine what is material and not material to the outcome.

Lawyers must also understand other aspects of the facts. It is important to be aware of who the parties are in relationship to the case. Are the parties a husband and wife in a divorce? Parties to a contract? Parties involved in a traffic accident?

A lawyer must also understand the procedural posture of the case—where the case is in the litigation and how it got there. Because standards differ depending on the procedural posture of the case, it is important to know whether an appeal is from a motion to dismiss or a summary judgment. The standard for a motion to dismiss is taking the facts as stated in the complaint as true and asking if the plaintiff has a claim upon which relief can be granted, while the summary judgment standard is whether the moving party can establish that there is no issue of material fact and that the moving party is entitled to a judgment as a matter of law. Can you see the differences in the two standards? Make sure you fully understand the differences. (This applies to any legal concept.)

Pointer: In real life, an attorney gets a jumble of facts, and he or she must organize and analyze those facts to determine which are material.

Pointer: Try to visualize the facts, to see them as a story.

REASONING: Reasoning is how and why the court came up with the holding. This is the most important part of the legal analysis because it helps teach students to understand legal reasoning. To understand the court's reasoning, a student should determine how the court applied the law to the facts. A student should not do this superficially ("the court used policy") but should analyze the court's reasoning in detail. In doing so, the student should consider which type (or types) of legal reasoning the court used.

Pointer: "Why" is the most important question in the law. It is not enough to understand what the court held; to develop legal reasoning skills, the student must understand why. Develop the habit of asking why.

HOLDING: The holding is the court's legal decision; it answers the issue. As with the issue, a student should include both the law and the facts in the holding and frame it as narrowly as possible.

EXAMPLES

1. A newspaper ad for a sale on computers that states prices and that "quantities are limited" is not an offer because such an advertisement does not indicate the intent to be bound. (Note that this holding includes why the court ruled the way it did.)

2. Arkansas does not have personal jurisdiction over a defendant who has never been to Arkansas and who signed a contract in Mississippi if the contract only involves performance in Mississippi because the defendant has not established minimum contacts with Arkansas. (Does this holding include the reasoning?)

After completing your case analysis, you need to evaluate it (reflection stage). Does your case analysis accurately reflect the case? Does it reflect why you did the analysis? (Initially, you analyze cases to learn legal reading and prepare for class. Later, you analyze cases to learn the law.) Is your issue (or issues) the real issue in the case? Does your issue combine the law and the facts? Have you stated the issue narrowly to reflect the details in the case? Have you identified the material facts? Do you see how they relate to the issue? Have you analyzed the reasoning *in detail*? Do you understand why the court ruled the way it did? Have you identified the types of legal reasoning the court used? Have you properly identified the holding (or holdings)? Have you written the holding narrowly to reflect the details in the case? Do you understand how the court went from the issue through the facts and reasoning to the holding? Can you think of any other questions you should ask about your case analysis?

One obtains from the holding a rule that can be used to analyze new problems. A rule is "a statement that explains how the law tells us to decide the particular legal issue."[42] More specifically: "A rule should meet three criteria. First, it should be simply stated—concise enough for the reader to grasp easily. Second, it should be readily applied—unambiguous because the terms have defined, non-circular meanings, specific enough to give guidance for a new set of facts, but not too narrow to be useful. Third, it should be consistent with the cases and law in the jurisdiction—if applied to the existing cases, the rule would accurately predict the outcome of each."[43]

One can distinguish between the "inherited" rule ("the rule of law the opinion inherits from prior authorities") and the "processed" rule ("the complete rule as it appears when the opinion concludes") (the holding).[44] "[T]o formulate a rule from a case, start by identifying (1) the inherited rule that governs the legal issue [in that case], (2) the facts relevant to the rule of law, (3) the new information the opinion gives about the rule, and (4) the court's decision about the rule's application to the parties before it."[45] It is very important to understand how the court went from the inherited rule to the processed rule; this is the essence of legal reasoning. To understand how the court did this, look carefully at the reasoning and analyze it in detail.

Habit: Develop the habit of being a detail-oriented reader.

One can read rules and holdings narrowly or broadly. In other words, one can obtain from a case a rule that is limited to similar facts or a broad standard that can apply to many situations. Whether an attorney adopts a narrow or broad rule depends on how he or she intends to use it. Which helps best in the attorney's new situation? Cases are open to interpretation, and it is a part of the advocate's role to adopt the interpretation that best helps the client. Of course, that interpretation must be reasonable, and the lawyer must be ready to defend the interpretation in front of the court.

Habit: Develop the habit of being able to support your arguments.

Pointer: If a case you are reading has a concurrence or a dissent, you should also analyze that concurrence or dissent, especially how and why the opinion came to the same conclusion based on differing reasoning or how and why it came to a different conclusion. The best way to develop your legal reasoning ability is to determine how different judges come to different conclusions based on the same facts. This will also help you deal with the fact that law is often ambiguous.

Pointer: Discuss and criticize the cases you read with your classmates. This type of interaction sharpens your reading skills. If you can explain something to someone else, you understand it. Study groups can be very helpful if you use them effectively.

EXERCISE II-1

What are the material facts in the following cases? Why are they important? What is the issue? Read these scenarios as if you were advising a lawyer you work for.

1. **Law:** To establish personal jurisdiction with a state, the defendant must establish minimum contacts that are related to the lawsuit and that show that the defendant purposely availed himself of the benefits and protections of that state's laws. **Facts:** This case involves the breach of a construction contract. The plaintiff wants to sue in Alabama. The defendant contracted to build a shopping center for the plaintiff in Tuscaloosa, Alabama, by January 1, 2011, which the defendant failed to do. The plaintiff is a resident of Alabama, and the defendant is a

resident of Georgia. The plaintiff has sued for $2 million. The contract was negotiated and executed in Georgia to be performed in Alabama. Last year the defendant and his family vacationed on the Alabama coast. The defendant's son and daughter are both currently enrolled at the University of Alabama. The defendant attended Auburn in the 1980s.

2. **Ethics rule:** An attorney shall keep a separate account in which to deposit client funds, and he shall deposit all client funds in that separate account. **Facts:** Anthony is accused of violating this rule. On July 20, he received a check made out to him that was payment to a client for breach of contract, and he immediately called his client to tell her that he would mail her a check that day. Anthony deposited the check in his account because he forgot to bring a deposit slip for the client escrow account and could not remember the number of that account. Anthony then immediately wrote a check to his client for the full amount and mailed it to the client at the post office next door. Anthony has never been accused of an ethical violation before.

3. **Law:** To recover for negligent infliction of emotional harm, the plaintiff must establish that she witnessed the accident in which her child was killed. **Facts:** Plaintiff's son was riding in a neighbor's convertible when he was killed in an accident for which the defendant was negligently liable. At the time of the accident, the plaintiff was in her car about a block away. She saw something, but she did not see the accident clearly. When she pulled up to the scene of the accident, she saw her child lying on the ground motionless. She could tell that her child had been badly injured. Later, at home, she saw a video of the accident on television.

4. **Law:** The first person to have control of a wild animal is the owner of that animal. **Facts:** While hiking in the woods, John found a wounded deer that had run away from a hunter. John carried the deer to his truck. He nursed the deer back to health and kept it in a fenced meadow behind his house. Martin, who had shot the deer, heard about John rescuing it, and he demanded that John give him the deer. Assume that Martin could prove that he shot the deer. Also, assume that John had no intention of getting a deer when he set out on the hike.

5. **Law:** A person who pulls an object from another person's hands can be liable for battery. **Facts:** Martha hates Peggy. She decided to embarrass

Peggy at lunch one day by pouring milk down the back of her blouse. Martha then pulled a towel out of Peggy's hands as she was drying off. She whirled the towel around Peggy's head, getting more milk on her. She called Peggy names, and she threatened to beat her up after school. The blouse was Peggy's favorite.

EXERCISE II-2

1. Analyze the following case, using the four categories set forth above. Read the case as if you were going to use it to write an objective memo.
2. What is the main type of reasoning that the court uses?
3. Does the court use any other type of reasoning?
4. Why did the court uphold the will when it was clear that Mrs. Kroll intended to revoke it? Is this a good policy?
5. Why didn't the court adopt the general meaning of cancellation— "any act which would destroy, revoke, recall, do away with, overrule, render null and void, the instrument"?

Reminder: Develop the habit of looking up any terms you don't know in a legal dictionary. (Learning the language of the law is a key part of becoming a lawyer.)

163 Va. 492 (1934)
SALLY J. THOMPSON, ET AL.
v.
JENNIE BOWEN ROYALL, ET AL.
Supreme Court of Virginia.
September 20, 1934.
HUDGINS, J., delivered the opinion of the court.

The only question presented by this record is whether the will of Mrs. M. Lou Bowen Kroll had been revoked shortly before her death.

The uncontroverted facts are as follows: On the 4th day of September, 1932, Mrs. Kroll signed a will, typewritten on five sheets of legal cap paper; the signature appeared on the last page duly attested by three subscribing witnesses. H. P. Brittain, the executor named in the will, was given possession of the instrument for safekeeping. A codicil typed on the top third of one sheet of paper dated September 15, 1932, was signed by the testatrix in the presence of two subscribing witnesses. Possession of this instrument was given to Judge S. M. B. Coulling, the attorney who prepared both documents.

On September 19, 1932, at the request of Mrs. Kroll, Judge Coulling and Mr. Brittain took the will and the codicil to her home, where she told her attorney, in the presence of Mr. Brittain and another, to destroy both. But instead of destroying the papers, at the suggestion of Judge Coulling, she decided to retain them as memoranda, to be used as such in the event she decided to execute a new will. Upon the back of the manuscript cover, which was fastened to the five sheets by metal clasps, in the handwriting of Judge Coulling, signed by Mrs. Kroll, there is the following notation: "This will null and void and to be only held by H. P. Brittain, instead of being destroyed, as a memorandum for another will if I desire to make same. This 19 Sept 1932"

"M. LOU BOWEN KROLL."

The same notation was made on the back of the sheet on which the codicil was written, except that the name S. M. B. Coulling was substituted for H. P. Brittain; this was likewise signed by Mrs. Kroll.

Mrs. Kroll died October 2, 1932, leaving numerous nephews and nieces, some of whom were not mentioned in her will, and an estate valued at approximately $200,000. On motion of some of the beneficiaries, the will and codicil were offered for probate. All the interested parties including the heirs at law were convened, and on the issue, devisavit vel non, the jury found that the instruments dated September 4 and 15, 1932, were the last will and testament of Mrs. M. Lou Bowen Kroll. From an order sustaining the verdict and probating the will, this writ of error was allowed.

For more than 100 years, the means by which a duly executed will may be revoked have been prescribed by statute. These requirements are found in section 5233 of the 1919 Code, the pertinent parts of which read thus:

No will or codicil, or any part thereof, shall be revoked, unless . . . by a subsequent will or codicil, or by some writing declaring an intention to revoke the same, and executed in the manner in which a will is required to be executed, or by the testator, or some person in his presence and by his direction, cutting, tearing, burning, obliterating, canceling, or destroying the same, or the signature thereto, with the intent to revoke.

The notations dated September 19, 1932, are not wholly in the handwriting of the testatrix, nor are her signatures attested by subscribing witnesses; hence, under the statute they are ineffectual as "some writing declaring an intention to revoke." The faces of the two instruments bear no physical evidence of any cutting, tearing, burning, obliterating, canceling, or destroying. The only contention made by appellants is that the notations, written in the presence and with the approval of Mrs. Kroll on the back of the manuscript cover in the one instance and on the back of the sheet containing the codicil in the other, constitute "canceling" within the meaning of the statute.

Both parties concede that to effect revocation of a duly executed will, in any of the methods prescribed by statute, two things are necessary: (1) The doing of one of the acts specified, (2) accompanied by the intent to revoke —the animo revocandi. Proof of either, without proof of the other, is insufficient.[46]

The proof established the intention to revoke. The entire controversy is confined to the acts used in carrying out that purpose. The testatrix adopted the suggestion of her attorney to revoke her will by written memoranda, admittedly ineffectual as revocations by subsequent writings, but appellants contend the memoranda, in the handwriting of another, and testatrix's signatures are sufficient to effect revocation by cancellation. To support this contention, appellants cite a number of authorities who hold that the modern definition of cancellation includes "any act which would destroy, revoke, recall, do away with, overrule, render null and void, the instrument."

Most of the authorities cited who approve the above, or a similar meaning of the word, were dealing with the cancellation of simple contracts or other instruments that require little or no formality in execution. However, there is one line of cases that apply this extended meaning of "canceling" to the revocation of wills. The leading case so holding is *Warner v. Warner's Estate*, 37 Vt. 356. In this case, proof of the intent and the act were a notation on the same page with and below the signature of the testator, reading: "This will is hereby cancelled and annulled. In full this the 15th day of March in the year 1859," and written lengthwise on the back of the fourth page of the foolscap paper, upon which no part of the written will appeared, were these words: "Cancelled and is null and void. (Signed) I. Warner." It was held this was sufficient to revoke the will under a statute similar to the one here under consideration.

In *Evans's Appeal*,[47] the Pennsylvania court approved the reasoning of the Vermont court in *Warner's Estate, supra*, but the force of the opinion is weakened when the facts are considered. It seems there were lines drawn through two of the three signatures of the testator appearing in the Evans will, and the paper on which material parts of the will were written was torn in four places. It therefore appeared on the face of the instrument, when offered for probate, that there was a sufficient defacement to bring it within the meaning of both obliteration and cancellation.

The construction of the statute in *Warner's Estate, supra*, has been criticized by eminent text writers on wills, and the courts in the majority of the states in construing similar statutes have refused to follow the reasoning in that case.[48]

The above, and other authorities that might be cited, hold that revocation of a will by cancellation within the meaning of the statute contemplates marks or lines across the written parts of the instrument, or a physical defacement, or some mutilation of the writing itself, with the intent to revoke. If written words are used for the purpose, they must be so placed as to physically affect the written portion of the will, not merely on blank parts of the paper on which the will is written. If the writing intended to be the act of canceling does not mutilate or erase, or deface, or otherwise physically come in contact with any part of written words of the will, it cannot be given any greater weight than a similar writing on a separate sheet of paper, which identifies the will referred to just as definitely as does the writing on the back. If a will may be revoked by writing on the back, separable from the will, it may be done by a writing not on the will. This the statute forbids.

The learned trial judge A. C. Buchanan, in his written opinion, pertinently said:

The statute prescribes certain ways of executing a will, and it must be so executed in order to be valid, regardless of how clear and specific the intent. It also provides certain ways of revoking and it must be done so in order to a valid revocation, regardless of intent. As said in Will of Ladd, 60 Wis. 187, 18 N.W. 734, 50 Am. Rep. at pp. 362-3:

> The difficulty with the rule contended for is that it gives to the words written in pencil, although not attested, witnessed, nor executed in the manner prescribed by statute, the same force as though they had been so attested, witnessed and executed, for the purpose of proving that the act of putting the words there was with the "intention" of revoking the will. It is the language, the expression by written words alone, which is thus sought to be made effectual; whereas the statute in effect declares that such written words shall have no force or effect as such unless executed, attested and subscribed as required.

The same reasoning led the Illinois court to the same conclusion in Dowling v. Gilliland, [122 N.E. 70 (Ill. 1919)], where it is said:

> The great weight of authority is to the effect that the mere writing upon a will which does not in any wise physically obliterate or cancel the same is insufficient to work a destruction of a will by cancellation, even though the writing may express an intention to revoke and cancel. This appears to be the better rule. To hold otherwise would be to give to words written in pencil, and not attested to by witnesses nor executed in the manner provided by the statute, the same effect as if they had been so attested.

The same rule seems to prevail in New York, Massachusetts, and North Carolina. The Georgia cases are to the same effect, although it does not appear that the Georgia statute is the same as ours.

A different rule seems to be followed in Tennessee, as shown by *Billington v. Jones*,[49] but the court there points out that Tennessee has no statute on the subject and says the same thing is true in Connecticut, where *Witter v. Mott*, 2 Conn. 67, was decided.

The attempted revocation is ineffectual, because testatrix intended to revoke her will by subsequent writings not executed as required by statute, and because it does not in any wise physically obliterate, mutilate, deface, or cancel any written parts of the will.

For the reasons stated, the judgment of the trial court is affirmed.

EXERCISE II-3

1. Analyze the following case. Read it as if you were a judge in a later case who wanted to use it as precedent for a novel question of law in your state.
2. Will the plaintiff win when the trial court reconsiders the case based on this opinion?
3. The facts of this case are no more complicated than those of *Thompson*. Why is the reasoning much more complicated?
4. What is the most important type of legal reasoning used by the court?
5. Does the court use rule-based reasoning?
6. Does the court use policy-based reasoning?
7. How does the court distinguish *Fifield*?
8. How does the court distinguish *Adams*?
9. How does the court deal with the dangers from creating this new broad cause of action?
10. What is the inherited rule and what is the processed rule?

24 Cal. 3d 799 (1979)

J'AIRE CORPORATION, Plaintiff and Appellant,

v.

CRAIG A. GREGORY, Defendant and Respondent.

Supreme Court of California

August 13, 1979

BIRD, C.J.

Appellant, a lessee, sued respondent, a general contractor, for damages resulting from the delay in completion of a construction project at the premises where appellant operated a restaurant. Respondent demurred successfully and the complaint was dismissed. This court must decide whether a contractor who undertakes construction work pursuant to a contract with the owner of premises may be held liable in tort for business losses suffered by a lessee when the contractor negligently fails to complete the project with due diligence.

I

The facts as pleaded are as follows. Appellant, J'Aire Corporation, operates a restaurant at the Sonoma County Airport in premises leased from the County of Sonoma. Under the terms of the lease, the county was to provide heat and air-conditioning. In 1975 the county entered into a contract with respondent for improvements to the restaurant premises, including renovation of the heating and air-conditioning systems and installation of insulation.

As the contract did not specify any date for completion of the work, appellant alleged the work was to have been completed within a reasonable time as defined by custom and usage.[50] Despite requests that respondent complete the construction promptly, the work was not completed within a reasonable time. Because the restaurant could not operate during part of the construction and was without heat and air-conditioning for a longer period, appellant suffered loss of business and resulting loss of profits.

Appellant alleged two causes of action in its third amended complaint. The first cause of action was based on the theory that it was a third-party beneficiary of the contract between the county and respondent. The second cause of action sounded in tort and was based on negligence in completing the work within a reasonable time. Damages of $50,000 were claimed.

Respondent demurred on the ground that the complaint did not state facts sufficient to constitute a cause of action.[51] The trial court sustained the demurrer without leave to amend and the complaint was dismissed. On appeal, only the sustaining of the demurrer to the second cause of action is challenged.

II

In testing the sufficiency of a complaint, a reviewing court must assume the truth of all material allegations in the complaint,[52] including the allegations of negligence and cause in fact. The only question before this court is whether a cause of action for negligent loss of expected economic advantage may be maintained under these facts.

Liability for negligent conduct may be imposed only where there is a duty of care owed by the defendant to the plaintiff or to a class of which the plaintiff is a member.[53] A duty of care may arise through statute or by contract. Alternatively, a duty may be premised upon the general character of the activity in which the defendant engaged, the relationship between the parties, or even the interdependent nature of human society.[54] Whether a duty is owed is simply a shorthand way of phrasing what is "the essential question—whether the plaintiff's interests are entitled to legal protection against the defendant's conduct."[55]

This court has held that a plaintiff's interest in prospective economic advantage may be protected against injury occasioned by negligent as well as intentional conduct. For example, economic losses such as lost earnings or profits are recoverable as part of general damages in a suit for personal injury based on negligence.[56] Where negligent conduct causes injury to real or personal property, the plaintiff may recover damages for profits lost during the time necessary to repair or replace the property.[57]

Even when only injury to prospective economic advantage is claimed, recovery is not foreclosed. Where a special relationship exists between the parties, a plaintiff may recover for loss of expected economic advantage through the negligent performance of a contract, although the parties were not in contractual privity.[58]

In each of the above cases, the court determined that defendants owed *In hade*/ plaintiffs a duty of care by applying criteria set forth in *Biakanja v. Irving*.[59] Those criteria are (1) the extent to which the transaction was intended to affect the plaintiff, (2) the foreseeability of harm to the plaintiff, (3) the degree of certainty that the plaintiff suffered injury, (4) the closeness of the connection between the defendant's conduct and the injury suffered, (5) the moral blame attached to the defendant's conduct, and (6) the policy of preventing future harm.[60]

Applying these criteria to the facts as pleaded, it is evident that a duty was owed by respondent to appellant in the present case. (1) The contract entered into between respondent and the county was for the renovation of the premises in which appellant maintained its business. The contract could not have been performed without impinging on that business. Thus respondent's performance was intended to, and did, directly affect appellant.

(2) Accordingly, it was clearly foreseeable that any significant delay in completing the construction would adversely affect appellant's business beyond the normal disruption associated with such construction. Appellant alleges this fact was repeatedly drawn to respondent's attention. (3) Further, appellant's complaint leaves no doubt that appellant suffered harm, since it was unable to operate its business for one month and suffered additional loss of business while the premises were without heat and air-conditioning. (4) Appellant has also alleged that delays occasioned by the respondent's conduct were closely connected to, indeed directly caused, its injury. (5) In addition, respondent's lack of diligence in the present case was particularly blameworthy, since it continued after the probability of damage was drawn directly to respondent's attention. (6) Finally, public policy supports finding a duty of care in the present case. The willful failure or refusal of a contractor to prosecute a construction project with diligence, where another is injured as a result, has been made grounds for disciplining a licensed contractor.[61] Although this section does not provide a basis for imposing liability where the delay in completing construction is due merely to negligence, it does indicate the seriousness with which the Legislature views unnecessary delays in the completion of construction.

In light of these factors, this court finds that respondent had a duty to complete construction in a manner that would have avoided unnecessary injury to appellant's business, even though the construction contract was with the owner of a building rather than with appellant, the tenant. It is settled that a contractor owes a duty to avoid injury to the person or property of third parties.[62] As appellant points out, injury to a tenant's business can often result in greater hardship than damage to a tenant's person or property. Where the risk of harm is foreseeable, as it was in the present case, an injury to the plaintiff's economic interests should not go uncompensated merely because it was unaccompanied by any injury to his person or property.

To hold under these facts that a cause of action has been stated for negligent interference with prospective economic advantage is consistent with the recent trend in tort cases. This court has repeatedly eschewed overly rigid common law formulations of duty in favor of allowing compensation for foreseeable injuries caused by a defendant's want of ordinary care.[63] Rather than traditional notions of duty, this court has focused on foreseeability as the key component necessary to establish liability: "While the question whether one owes a duty to another must be decided on a case-by-case basis, every case is governed by the rule of general application that all persons are required to use ordinary care to prevent others from being injured as the result of their conduct. . . . [F]oreseeability of the risk is a primary consideration in establishing the element of duty."[64] Similarly, respondent is liable if his lack of ordinary care caused foreseeable injury to the economic interests of appellant.

In addition, this holding is consistent with the Legislature's declaration of the basic principle of tort liability, embodied in Civil Code section 1714, that every person is responsible for injuries caused by his or her lack of ordinary care.[65] That section does not distinguish among injuries to one's person, one's property, or one's financial interests. Damages for loss of profits or earnings are recoverable where they result from an injury to one's person or property caused by another's negligence. Recovery for injury to one's economic interests, where it is the foreseeable result of another's want of ordinary care, should not be foreclosed simply because it is the only injury that occurs.

Respondent cites *Fifield Manor v. Finston* (1960)[66] for the proposition that recovery may not be had for negligent loss of prospective economic advantage. *Fifield* concerned the parallel tort of interference with contractual relations.[67] In that case, a nonprofit retirement home that had contracted with Ross to provide him with lifetime medical care sued a driver who negligently struck and killed Ross. The plaintiff argued it had become liable under the contract for Ross's medical bills and sought recovery from the driver on both a theory of direct liability and one of subrogation. Recovery was denied.

The critical factor of foreseeability distinguishes *Fifield* from the present case. Although it was reasonably foreseeable that defendant's negligence might cause injury to Ross, it was less foreseeable that it would injure the retirement home's economic interest. Defendant had not entered into any relationship or undertaken any activity where negligence on his part was reasonably likely to affect plaintiff adversely. Thus, the nexus between the defendant's conduct and the risk of the injury that occurred to the plaintiff was too tenuous to support the imposition of a duty owing to the retirement home.[68] In contrast, the nexus in the present case between the injury that occurred and respondent's conduct is extremely close. *Fifield* does not entirely foreclose recovery for negligent interference with prospective economic advantage.

Respondent also relies on *Adams v. Southern Pacific Transportation Co.* (1975).[69] In *Adams*, plaintiff employees were held unable to sue the railroad whose cargo of bombs exploded, destroying the factory where they worked. It should be noted that the court of appeal in *Adams* clearly believed that plaintiffs should be permitted to maintain an action for negligent interference with prospective economic interests. It reluctantly held they could not, only under the belief that *Fifield* precluded such recovery. Adhering to the *Fifield* rule, the court of appeal in *Adams* did not determine whether the railroad owed plaintiffs a duty of care.[70] In the present case, plaintiff's injury stemmed directly from conduct intended to affect plaintiff and was more readily foreseeable than the damage to the employer's property in *Adams*. To the extent that *Adams* holds that there can be no recovery for negligent interference with prospective economic advantage, it is disapproved.

The chief dangers that have been cited in allowing recovery for negligent interference with prospective economic advantage are the possibility of excessive liability, the creation of an undue burden on freedom of action, the possibility of fraudulent or collusive claims, and the often speculative nature of damages.[71] Central to these fears is the possibility that liability will be imposed for remote consequences, out of proportion to the magnitude of the defendant's wrongful conduct.

However, the factors enumerated in *Biakanja* and applied in subsequent cases place a limit on recovery by focusing judicial attention on the foreseeability of the injury and the nexus between the defendant's conduct and the plaintiff's injury. These factors and ordinary principles of tort law, such as proximate cause, are fully adequate to limit recovery without the drastic consequence of an absolute rule which bars recovery in all such cases.[72] Following these principles, recovery for negligent interference with prospective economic advantage will be limited to instances where the risk of harm is foreseeable and is closely connected with the defendant's conduct, where damages are not wholly speculative, and the injury is not part of the plaintiff's ordinary business risk.

III

Accordingly, this court holds that a contractor owes a duty of care to the tenant of a building undergoing construction work to prosecute that work in a manner which does not cause undue injury to the tenant's business, where such injury is reasonably foreseeable. The demurrer to appellant's second cause of action should not have been sustained. The judgment of dismissal is reversed.

EXERCISE II-4
Visual Reading

Find several editorial cartoons in the newspaper or on the Internet. Write out what the cartoonist is saying in the cartoon.

III. MINING CASES

While analyzing cases is important in developing students' reasoning skills, the main purpose of case analysis is to provide the raw material (the law) for objective memoranda and persuasive documents. I like to call this process "mining cases." In mining cases, the attorney takes everything he or she can from the cases that will be useful in presenting the law in an analysis (small-scale paradigm; see Chapter Seven). This is like mining for ore. A miner takes everything that is useful from the mine, separating the valuable material from the material that is not useful. Of course, what is valuable and what is not useful in a case depends on its use—the problem being analyzed. In other words, you should mine the case according to your purpose in reading the case.

There is more to be mined in a case than the rule. A case can also used as a source for the rule explanation and rule illustration. (See Chapter Seven for the definition of these terms.) Miners try to squeeze everything out of the ore that is valuable; a lawyer should do the same thing with cases.

EXERCISE II-5

Mine everything you can from the *J'Aire* case.

CHAPTER WRAP-UP

Do you feel comfortable reading and analyzing cases? What can you do to improve these skills? What are the most important things to do when reading cases? Did you fully understand the cases you read in this chapter? If you had trouble at first, what did you do to improve your understanding? What is the hardest part of analyzing cases? What is the most important part of analyzing cases? Why? Does it help your learning if you read a case for a purpose (such as explaining it to your boss before she meets with a client)? If you can't answer these questions, reread the chapter before moving on.

Answers
EXERCISE II-1

1. **Facts:** The key to determining the material facts is to first look at the law. What elements are required to establish jurisdiction? Here, there are two conjunctive requirements (both parts must be satisfied): The defendant must establish minimum contacts that are related to the subject matter of the lawsuit and that show the defendant purposely availed itself of the benefits and protections of that state's laws. The lawsuit involved breach of contract. Consequently, the facts that last year the defendant and his family vacationed on the Alabama coast, the defendant's son and daughter are both currently enrolled at the University of Alabama, and the defendant attended Auburn in the 1980s are not material facts because they are not related to the lawsuit. At first, the fact that the plaintiff sued for $2 million might seem relevant because it is related to the lawsuit, but it is not, because it is not a contact to Alabama. The facts that the contract was negotiated and executed in Georgia and to be performed in Alabama are material facts because they are related to the subject matter of the lawsuit, and they might help establish whether the defendant purposely availed himself of the benefits and protections of Alabama law. Where the parties are domiciled might at first seem material; however, the fact that a plaintiff is domiciled in the forum cannot, by itself, create jurisdiction over a defendant.

Issue: Has the defendant established minimum contacts with Alabama by a contract that was negotiated and executed in Georgia and to be performed in Alabama?

2. **Facts:** The only fact that is really material is that Anthony deposited the check in his account, which is a violation of the rule. Nothing else in the facts directly relates to the rule. The rest of the facts may be important as background to help you understand the case, but that doesn't make them material. You may have an intuition that Anthony was not really doing anything wrong because he immediately mailed the check to the client, but the rule does not allow for exceptions. However, this intuition is good because in the real world you will want to look for case law that helps you interpret the rule. The fact that Anthony has never committed an ethics violation before might turn out to be a mitigating factor in punishment, but you won't know this until you do more research.

    Issue: Has an attorney violated an ethics rule that requires him to deposit all client funds in a separate client account when he deposits a check in his own account, because he forgot to bring a deposit slip for the other account and could not remember the number of the other account, and then immediately writes a check for the full amount and goes to the post office next door to mail it to the client? (I have included some of the facts in the issue that I said were nonmaterial above because they might turn out to be material with further research).

3. **Facts:** The rule requires that the plaintiff witness the accident. Therefore, the material facts are those that relate to whether she actually witnessed the accident. What she saw at the scene of the accident when she drove up and later saw on television are not material to the issue. (Of course, they could be material to other issues in the case.) Can you decide the outcome of the issue based on what you have been given? Which would help you more—more law or more facts?

    Issue: Can a plaintiff recover for negligent infliction of emotional harm from witnessing an accident in which her child was killed, when the plaintiff was in her car about a block away at the time and saw something, but she did not see the accident clearly?

4. **Facts:** Control of a wild animal is the key. Accordingly, those facts that show whether John or Martin had control of the deer are the relevant

ones. The fact that Martin shot the deer, which then ran away, does not show control. John did have control. The fact that Martin had no intention to shoot a deer on his hike is irrelevant.

Issue: Does a person have control of an animal for the purpose of ownership when he shoots a deer, but the deer escapes? (Of course, there are alternative ways of phrasing this issue, which is true of most issues. For example, if a person finds a wild deer and keeps it in a fenced-in part of his property, does he own that deer?)

5. **Facts:** The only material fact to the rule is that Martha pulled the towel out of Peggy's hands. The other facts may be relevant to other rules, but they are not relevant to this one.

   Issue: Can a person be liable for battery when she pulls a towel out of another person's hands?

EXERCISE II-2

1. **Issue:** Did the testator revoke her will by cancellation under the revocation statute by having her lawyer write on the back of the will and the back of her codicil in her presence: "This will null and void and to be held only by H. P. Brittain, instead of being destroyed, as a memorandum for another will if I desire to make same"? (Notice that I framed the issue narrowly. This is because small changes in the facts can change the outcome.)

   Facts: The testator had made a will and codicil. Later, she told her attorney in the presence of another man to destroy them in order to revoke them. Rather than destroying the papers, at the suggestion of her lawyer, she decided to retain them as memoranda, to be used if she decided to execute a new will. Upon the will and the codicil, there is the following notation: "This will [codicil] null and void and to be held only by H. P. Brittain, instead of being destroyed, as a memorandum for another will [codicil] if I desire to make same."

   The testator died, leaving several nieces and nephews, some of whom were not mentioned in the will, and an estate of approximately $200,000. Some of the beneficiaries under the will and codicil offered them for probate. A jury found the will and codicil were valid, and they were probated.

Holding: The testator did not revoke her will by having her lawyer write "This will null and void," because that act did not constitute cancellation under the statute.

Reasoning: Revocation of wills in Virginia is governed by a statute, which states, "No will or codicil, or any part thereof, shall be revoked, unless . . . by a subsequent will or codicil, or by some writing declaring an intention to revoke the same, and executed in the manner in which a will is required to be executed, or by the testator, or some person in his presence and by his direction, cutting, tearing, burning, obliterating, canceling, or destroying the same, or the signature thereto, with the intent to revoke." Revocation of a will requires (1) the doing of one of the acts specified (2) accompanied by the intent to revoke. Since there was no question the testator intended to revoke her will, the only issue was whether she performed one of the acts set forth in the statute. The only possible act could be cancellation. Because the statute did not define cancellation, the court was forced to look at cases and treatises for the definition. The weight of authority held

> that revocation of a will by cancellation within the meaning of the statute, contemplates marks or lines across the written parts of the instrument, or a physical defacement, or some mutilation of the writing itself, with the intent to revoke. If written words are used for the purpose, they must be so placed as to physically affect the written portion of the will, not merely on blank parts of the paper on which the will is written. If the writing intended to be the act of cancelling, does not mutilate, or erase, or deface, or otherwise physically come in contact with any part of written words of the will, it cannot be given any greater weight than a similar writing on a separate sheet of paper, which identifies the will referred to, just as definitely, as does the writing on the back. If a will may be revoked by writing on the back, separable from the will, it may be done by a writing not on the will.

This rule exists because "to hold otherwise would be to give to words written in pencil, and not attested to by witnesses nor executed in the manner provided by the statute, the same effect as if they had been so attested." Based on this definition, the court found that the testator had not canceled the will because the writing did not "in any wise physically obliterate, mutilate, deface, or cancel any written parts of the will."

2. Rule-based reasoning, because the court is applying a statute, which is a rule

3. The court uses reasoning by analogy to help define cancellation. It also uses policy-based reasoning ("to hold otherwise would be to give to words written in pencil, and not attested to by witnesses nor executed in the manner provided by the statute, the same effect as if they had been so attested") to help justify its decision. Finally, it distinguishes cases. Look carefully at how the court distinguishes the conflicting authority.

4. Because the formalities are important in creating and revoking wills. These formalities force the testator to consider the seriousness of what she is doing.

5. Because there is a more specific meaning of cancellation in wills law. Students should be careful to have the proper definition of a term when analyzing cases.

EXERCISE II-3

1. **Issue:** Whether a contractor who undertakes construction work pursuant to a contract with the owner of a premises may be held liable in tort for business losses suffered by a lessee when the contractor negligently fails to complete the project with due diligence. (It is okay to use the court's statement of the issue, as long as that is the best statement of the issue.)

   Facts: Appellant, a lessee, sued respondent, a general contractor, for damages resulting from the delay in completion of a construction project at the premises where appellant operated a restaurant (renovation of the heating and air-conditioning systems and installation of insulation). Appellant could not operate during the repairs, and it lost profits. Respondent demurred successfully and the complaint was dismissed.

   Holding: A contractor owes a duty of care to the tenant of a building undergoing construction work to prosecute that work in a manner that does not cause undue injury to the tenant's business, where such injury is reasonably foreseeable.

Reasoning: Liability for negligent conduct may be imposed only where there is a duty of care owed by the defendant to the plaintiff or to a class of which the plaintiff is a member. A duty may be premised upon the general character of the activity in which the defendant is engaged, the relationship between the parties, or even the interdependent nature of human society. A plaintiff's interest in prospective economic advantage may be protected against injury occasioned by negligent as well as intentional conduct. Where a special relationship exists between the parties, a plaintiff may recover for loss of expected economic advantage through the negligent performance of a contract, although the parties were not in contractual privity (cases involved negligent preparation of a will). Defendants owe plaintiffs a duty of care based on (1) the extent to which the transaction was intended to affect the plaintiff, (2) the foreseeability of harm to the plaintiff, (3) the degree of certainty that the plaintiff suffered injury, (4) the closeness of the connection between the defendant's conduct and the injury suffered, (5) the moral blame attached to the defendant's conduct, and (6) the policy of preventing future harm. Applying these criteria to the facts as pleaded, it is evident that a duty was owed by respondent to appellant in the present case: (1) The contract entered into between respondent and the county was for the renovation of the premises in which appellant maintained its business. The contract could not have been performed without impinging on that business. Thus respondent's performance was intended to, and did, directly affect appellant. (2) Accordingly, it was clearly foreseeable that any significant delay in completing the construction would adversely affect appellant's business beyond the normal disruption associated with such construction. Appellant alleges this fact was repeatedly drawn to respondent's attention. (3) Further, appellant's complaint leaves no doubt that appellant suffered harm, since it was unable to operate its business for one month and suffered additional loss of business while the premises were without heat and air-conditioning. (4) Appellant has also alleged that delays occasioned by the respondent's conduct were closely connected to, indeed directly caused, its injury. (5) In addition, respondent's lack of diligence in the present case was particularly blameworthy, since it continued after the probability of damage was drawn directly to respondent's attention. (6) Finally, public policy supports finding a duty of care in the present case.

2. We cannot answer this question. A demur is like a motion to dismiss. (You should have looked up this term.) Under a motion to dismiss, the court decides whether there is a cause of action, taking the facts pleaded in the complaint as true. On remand, the plaintiff will have to prove facts that establish the cause of action.

3. Because the court is establishing a new cause of action, and it takes more to convince the reader. (Judges have to convince their readers just like attorneys do. A judge's readers include the parties, the attorneys, and the public.)

4. Reasoning by analogy. The key argument is that California allows recovery for negligent drafting of wills. Negligent delay in completing a construction project is substantially similar to the negligent drafting of a will, so a plaintiff can recover for negligent delay in completing a construction project. The facts of case A are like the facts of case B, so the rule from case A applies to case B. In other words, the court has created a broad duty based on a narrow line of wills cases. This is why the court needs additional reasoning to be convincing.

5. The court uses rule-based reasoning to back up its analogy to wills cases. It states a test based on the wills cases, then applies the test to the facts. This is a very clear example of rule-based reasoning; study it carefully.

6. The court extensively uses policy arguments to back up its analogy. For example, "Whether a duty is owed is simply a shorthand way of phrasing what is 'the essential question—whether the plaintiff's interests are entitled to legal protection against the defendant's conduct.'"

> The willful failure or refusal of a contractor to prosecute a construction project with diligence, where another is injured as a result, has been made ground for disciplining a licensed contractor.[73] Although this section does not provide a basis for imposing liability where the delay in completing construction is due merely to negligence, it does indicate the seriousness with which the Legislature views unnecessary delays in the completion of construction." . . . "To hold under these facts that a cause of action has been stated for negligent interference with prospective economic

advantage is consistent with the recent trend in tort cases. This court has repeatedly eschewed overly rigid common law formulations of duty in favor of allowing compensation for foreseeable injuries caused by a defendant's want of ordinary care.

7. Based on foreseeability. In *Fifield*, while it was reasonably foreseeable that defendant's negligence might cause injury to Ross, it was less foreseeable that it would injure the retirement home's economic interest. Defendant had not entered into any relationship or undertaken any activity where negligence on his part was reasonably likely to affect plaintiff adversely. Thus, the nexus between the defendant's conduct and the risk of the injury that occurred to the plaintiff was too tenuous to support the imposition of a duty owing to the retirement home.[74] In contrast, the nexus in the present case between the injury that occurred and the respondent's conduct is extremely close. *Fifield* does not entirely foreclose recovery for negligent interference with prospective economic advantage.

8. "[P]laintiff's injury stemmed directly from conduct intended to affect plaintiff and was more readily foreseeable than the damage to the employer's property in *Adams*." More important, "to the extent that *Adams* holds that there can be no recovery for negligent interference with prospective economic advantage, it is disapproved."

9. Through the requirement of foreseeability, the test, and traditional notions of proximate cause.

10. Inherited rule: "that intended beneficiaries of wills could sue to recover legacies lost through the negligent preparation of the will." Processed rule: "A contractor owes a duty of care to the tenant of a building undergoing construction work to prosecute that work in a manner which does not cause undue injury to the tenant's business, where such injury is reasonably foreseeable." Broader reading of processed rule: California allows recovery for negligent interference with prospective economic advantage.

EXERCISE II-5

The whole case can be used as a rule illustration (I define terms such as "rule illustration" in Chapter Seven).

The standard for testing the sufficiency of the complaint.

General standards for liability for negligent conduct.

The standard for liability for prospective economic advantage.

A special relationship standard in wills cases. (These cases can be used as rule illustrations.)

A test for determining a duty of care and application of that test to a specific set of facts (the facts of *J'Aire*).

A comparison to recent trends in torts cases (good for public policy in the rule explanation).

A look at tort policy in California statutes.

Distinguishable cases.

A discussion of foreseeability.

A discussion of possible problems with the new standard.

The holding.

Pointer: Not everything in a case will be valuable for analysis of your problem. In addition, other cases may have material that works better for your facts. However, you should always "mine" your cases completely before discarding the waste so that you don't miss anything.

NOTES

1. Professors Zabihi & Pordel have declared: "[T]he process of reading is not a static process; rather it is a dynamic one." Reza Zabihi & Mojtabe Pordel, *An Investigation of Critical Reading in Reading Textbooks: A Qualitative Analysis*, 4 INT'L EDUC. STUD. 80, 81 (2011). Professor Oates has determined "that students who do better on exams read differently than those who don't." Laurel C. Oates, *Beating the Odds: Reading Strategies of Law Students Admitted through Alternative Admissions Programs*, 83 IOWA L. REV. 139, 148 (1997); *see also* Leah M. Christensen, *Legal Reading and Success in Law School: An Empirical Study*, 30 SEATTLE U. L. REV. 603 (2007) [hereinafter Christensen, *Legal Reading*] ("Students who take the time and effort to read critically and to resolve their confusion before moving on have more success with legal reading." *Id.* at 643).

2. Michael Hunter Schwartz, *Teaching Law Students to Be Self-Regulated Learners*, 2003 MICH. ST. DCL L. REV. 447, 453–54, 472.

3. *See* Preface.

4. Schwartz, *supra* note 2, at 455.

5. *Id.*

6. *Id.* at 456.

7. *Id.*

8. *Id.*

9. WILLIAM M. SULLIVAN ET AL., EDUCATING LAWYERS: PREPARATION FOR THE PROFESSION OF LAW 109 (Jossey Bass 2007) [hereinafter THE CARNEGIE REPORT]. This can be accomplished in law school through simulations.

10. Schwartz, *supra* note 2, at 456.

11. SUSAN A. AMBROSE ET AL., HOW LEARNING WORKS: 7 RESEARCH-BASED PRINCIPLES FOR SMART TEACHING 76–77 (Jossey Bass 2010).

12. Self-regulated learners "also monitor progress as they work through the task, managing intrusive emotions and waning motivation as well as adjusting strategies processed to foster success." Teaching Excellence in Adult Literacy, JUST WRITE! GUIDE, https://teal.ed.gov/resources, *29 (Teal 2012). These authors continue, "Self-regulated students are those students who are metacognitively, motivationally, and behaviorally active in their own learning processes and in achieving their own goals." *Id.*

13. *Id.* at 30.

14. *Id.* at 33.

15. *Id.*

16. *Id.*

17. Schwartz, *supra* note 2, at 457.

18. *Id.*

19. *Id.*

20. James Stratman posits that students understand more when they read with a "real world purpose" (as a judge, an advocate, etc.) rather than merely preparing for class. James F. Stratman, *When Law Students Read Cases: Exploring Relations between Professional Legal Reasoning Roles and Problem Detection*, 34 DISCOURSE PROCESSES 57 (2002). *See also* Christensen, *Legal Reading*, *supra* note 1, at 614.

21. Schwartz, *supra* note 2, at 457; Peter Dewitz, *Legal Education: A Problem of Learning from Text*, 23 N.Y.U. L. REV. L. & SOC. CHANGE 225, 228 (1997)

(Strategic readers "set a purpose for reading, self-question, search for important information, make inferences, summarize, and monitor the developing meaning."). Professor Christensen notes that low-performing students employ default reading strategies (basic reading strategies: moving through the text in a linear manner, paraphrasing, rereading, noting certain structural elements of the text, underlining text, making margin notes) much more than high-performing students. Christensen, *Legal Reading*, *supra* note 1, at 644. "Strategies help make explicit the routines and techniques employed by effective learners so that all learners can be more effective." Just Write! Guide, *supra* note 12, at 39.

22. Christensen, *Legal Reading*, *supra* note 1, at 608.

23. Schwartz, *supra* note 2, at 458.

24. *Id.* at 458–59.

25. Daniel Kahneman, Thinking, Fast and Slow 31–38 (Farrar, Straus & Giroux 2011).

26. Zabihi & Pordel, *supra* note 1, at 82; *see also* Diane F. Halpern, *Teaching Critical Thinking for Transfer across Domains: Dispositions, Skills, Structure Training, and Metacognitive Monitoring*, 53 Am. Psych. 449, 450–51 (1998) ("Critical thinking is purposeful, reasoned, and goal-directed. It is the kind of thinking involved in solving problems, formulating inferences, calculating likelihoods, and making decisions.").

27. Brian P. Coppola, *Progress in Practice: Using Concepts from Motivational and Self-Regulated Learning Research to Improve Chemistry Instruction*, 63 New Directions for Teaching and Learning: Understanding Self-Regulated Learning 87, 92 (1995).

28. Zabihi & Pordel, *supra* note 1, at 81.

29. Coppola, *supra* note 27, at 92.

30. Schwartz, *supra* note 2, at 460.

31. Halpern, *supra* note 26, at 451.

32. Professors Oatley and Djikic write, "Novice readers concentrate at the word and sentence level, as compared with experts who think about larger-scale structures and their possible meanings." Keith Oatley & Maja Djikic, *Writing as Thinking*, 12 Rev. Gen. Psych. 9, 13–14 (2008). For expert readers, "[r]eading a paragraph involves finding the main idea of the paragraph and how it is related to other paragraphs. Structural reading can be used to locate the main paragraphs in a text. Having understood the main ideas in a paragraph, good readers are able

to connect them meaningfully to their own situations and experiences." Zabihi & Pordel, *supra* note 1, at 82.

33. Christensen, *Legal Reading*, *supra* note 1, at 609.

34. Schwartz, *supra* note 2, at 460–61.

35. *Id.* at 462.

36. *Id.* at 481.

37. Judith Welch Wegner, *Reframing Legal Education's "Wicked Problems,"* 61 RUTGERS L. REV. 867, 898 (2009).

38. Leah M. Christensen, *The Psychology behind Case Briefing: A Powerful Cognitive Schema*, 29 CAMPBELL L. REV. 5, 13 (2006) [hereinafter Christensen, *Case Briefing*]. Professors Oatley and Djikic write, "Thinking involves translation of some aspect of the world into a schema, which [is] called a mental model. Manipulation of such a model can produce a new state, and this manipulation is thinking. Then retranslation can occur of the derived state of the model back into terms of the world, for instance into action or words." Oatley & Djikic, *supra* note 32, at 9. In other words, thinking "is to take a problem in the world and operate on a mental version—a model of some kind—within which it is possible to make inferences." *Id.* at 10.

39. Christensen, *Case Briefing*, *supra* note 38, at 17.

40. *Id.*

41. *Id.* at 18.

42. LINDA HOLDEMAN EDWARDS, LEGAL WRITING: PROCESS, ANALYSIS, AND ORGANIZATION 15 (1996).

43. Paul Figley, *Teaching Rule Synthesis with Real Cases*, 61 J. LEGAL EDUC. 245, 247 (2011).

44. EDWARDS, *supra* note 42, at 39.

45. *Id.*

46. Malone v. Hobbs, 1 Rob. (40 Va.) 346, 39 Am. Dec. 263; 2 Minor Ins. 925. I am using the same citation format used by the cases here and throughout this book.

47. 58 Pa. St. 238.

48. JARMAN ON WILLS (6th ed.) 147, note 1; SCHOULDER ON WILLS (5th ed.), sec. 391; REDFIELD ON THE LAW OF WILLS (4th ed.) 323–25; 28 R.C.L. 180; 40 Cyc. 1173; Dowling v. Gilliland, 286 Ill. 530, 122 N.E. 70, 3 A.L.R. 829; Freeman's notes to Graham Burch, 28 Am. St. Rep. 339, 351; Will of Ladd, 60 Wis. 187, 18 N.W. 734, 50 Am. Rep. 355; Howard v. Hunter, 115 Ga. 357, 41 S.E. 638, 639, 90

Am. St. Rep. 121; Sanderson v. Norcross, 242 Mass. 43, 136 N.E. 170; Gay v. Gay, 60 Iowa 415, 14 N.W. 238, 46 Am. Rep. 78; Brown v. Thorndike, 15 Pick. (Mass.) 388; Noesen v. Erkenswick, 298 Ill. 231, 131 N.E. 622.

49. 108 Tenn. 234, 66 S.W. 1127, 56 L.R.A. 654, 91 Am. St. Rep. 751.

50. CIV. CODE § 1657.

51. CODE CIV. PROC., § 430.10, subd. (e).

52. Serrano v. Priest (1971), 5 Cal. 3d 584, 591 [96 Cal. Rptr. 601, 487 P.2d 1241].

53. Richards v. Stanley (1954), 43 Cal. 2d 60, 63 [271 P.2d 23].

54. *See* Valdez v. J.D. Diffenbaugh Co. (1975), 51 Cal. App. 3d 494, 505 [124 Cal. Rptr. 467].

55. Dillon v. Legg (1968), 68 Cal. 2d 728, 734 [69 Cal. Rptr. 72, 441 P.2d 912, 29 A.L.R. 3d 1316], *quoting from* PROSSER, LAW OF TORTS (3d ed. 1964), pp. 332–33. *See also* PROSSER, LAW OF TORTS (4th ed. 1971), pp. 324–27; FLEMING, AN INTRODUCTION TO THE LAW OF TORTS (1967), pp. 43–50.

56. Connolly v. Pre-Mixed Concrete Co. (1957), 49 Cal. 2d 483, 489 [319 P.2d 343]; Neumann v. Bishop (1976), 59 Cal. App. 3d 451, 462 [130 Cal. Rptr. 786].

57. Reynolds v. Bank of America (1959), 53 Cal. 2d 49, 50–51 [345 P.2d 926].

58. Biakanja v. Irving (1958), 49 Cal. 2d 647 [320 P.2d 16, 65 A.L.R. 2d 1358], Lucas v. Hamm (1961), 56 Cal. 2d 583 [15 Cal. Rptr. 821, 364 P.2d 685], and Heyer v. Flaig (1969), 70 Cal. 2d 223 [74 Cal. Rptr. 225, 449 P.2d 161] held that intended beneficiaries of wills could sue to recover legacies lost through the negligent preparation of the will. (*See also* PROSSER, LAW OF TORTS (4th ed. 1971), p. 952.)

59. *Supra*, 49 Cal. 2d at p. 650.

60. *See also* Connor v. Great Western Sav. & Loan Ass'n (1968), 69 Cal. 2d 850, 865 [73 Cal. Rptr. 369, 447 P.2d 609, 39 A.L.R. 3d 224].

61. BUS. & PROF. CODE § 7119[2].

62. *See* Stewart v. Cox (1961), 55 Cal. 2d 857, 862–63 [13 Cal. Rptr. 521, 362 P.2d 345].

63. *See, e.g.*, Dillon v. Legg, *supra*, 68 Cal. 2d at p. 746 [liability for mother's emotional distress when child was killed by defendant's negligence]; Rowland v. Christian (1968), 69 Cal. 2d 108, 119 [70 Cal. Rptr. 97, 443 P.2d 561, 32 A.L.R. 3d 496] [liability of host for injury to social guest on premises]; *cf.* Brown v. Merlo (1973), 8 Cal. 3d 855 [106 Cal. Rptr. 388, 506 P.2d 212, 66 A.L.R. 3d 505] [liability of automobile driver for injury to nonpaying passenger]; Rodriguez v. Bethlehem

Steel Corp. (1974), 12 Cal. 3d 382 [115 Cal. Rptr. 765, 525 P.2d 669] [liability for loss of consortium].

64. Weirum v. RKO General, Inc. (1975), 15 Cal. 3d 40, 46 [123 Cal. Rptr. 468, 539 P.2d 36], fn. omitted.

65. *See* Rowland v. Christian, *supra*, 69 Cal. 2d at p. 119.

66. 54 Cal. 2d 632 [7 Cal. Rptr. 377, 354 P.2d 1073, 78 A.L.R. 2d 813].

67. *See* PROSSER, LAW OF TORTS (4th ed.), *supra*, at p. 952.

68. *Id.* at p. 637.

69. 50 Cal. App. 3d 37 [123 Cal. Rptr. 216].

70. 50 Cal. App. 3d at p. 47.

71. *See, e.g.*, PROSSER, LAW OF TORTS (4th ed.), *supra*, at p. 940 and Note, *Negligent Interference with Economic Expectancy: The Case for Recovery* (1964), 16 STAN. L. REV. 664, 679–93, neither of which considers these fears to justify denial of recovery in all cases.

72. *See* Dillon v. Legg, *supra*, 68 Cal. 2d at p. 746.

73. BUS. & PROF. CODE § 7119.

74. *Id.* at 637.

CHAPTER THREE

REASONING BY ANALOGY

CHAPTER GOALS

1. To help the reader understand reasoning by analogy.
2. To help the reader make arguments based on reasoning by analogy.
3. To teach the reader how to write analogical arguments.

I. UNDERSTANDING ANALOGIES

The English common law is based on reasoning by analogy. The common law developed case by case. A judge would decide a case. Then a new case would arise that had similar, but not exactly the same, facts. The judge would then decide whether the facts of the two cases were similar enough to apply the rule from the first case (precedent) to the second case. If he applied the rule to the new case, he would be reasoning by analogy based on the facts. If he did not, he would be distinguishing cases (discussed in Chapter Eight). Thus, the common law continued developing through reasoning by analogy and distinguishing cases. While statutes and administrative law added to English and American law, reasoning by analogy and distinguishing cases remain important methods of legal reasoning today.

As mentioned in Chapter One, the structure of reasoning by analogy is simple. The facts (or reasoning) of case A are like the facts (or reasoning) of case B, so the rule from case A applies to case B. Reasoning by analogy is a question of degree. (This is a part of the law's ambiguity.) Are the facts of case A close enough to the facts of case B to convince the court that the rule from case A should be applied to case B? Thus, the key task for the advocate is to convince the court that the analogy is valid. If you can do that, you win. In addition, always consider how the other side will try to distinguish the case, so that you can make your analogy even stronger.

While reasoning by analogy is often considered a legal skill, we use it every day in real life. Assume you are eating in a new restaurant and you want fusilli carbonara. The restaurant has fusilli with pesto sauce and spaghetti carbonara. Which one do you order? You will probably choose spaghetti carbonara because it is closer to fusilli carbonara. Spaghetti and fusilli are both pastas that taste similar, but pesto sauce and carbonara sauce are very different.

Take a more complicated example. You are in charge of decorating a men's clothing store's window. Your current display has expensive men's suits and vests. Your manager wants to add appropriate items from a new shipment to the window display. The shipment includes designer shoes, jeans, designer wallets, silk ties, and cruise shirts. Which ones do you add to your display? I would add the designer shoes, designer wallets, and silk ties, but not the jeans or cruise shirts. The designer shoes, designer wallets, and silk ties are for sophisticated businessmen, as are expensive men's suits and vests, while the jeans and cruise shirts are not. Can you think of a different basis for the analogy? Maybe you can't here, but you should always test your analogies to see if they are convincing and if there is a more persuasive alternative.

EXERCISE III-1
General Analogies
Choose the best analogy.

1. Coffee is to a coffeepot as
   a. wine is to a wineglass.
   b. tea is to a teapot.
   c. water is to a canteen.
   d. orange juice is to an orange.

2. Day is to night as
    a. afternoon is to midnight.
    b. right is to wrong.
    c. 3:00 a.m. is to noon.
    d. sun is to moon.
3. A man is to a woman as
    a. a buck is to a doe.
    b. black is to white.
    c. a girl is to a woman.
    d. a beard is to long hair.
4. Baseball is to basketball as
    a. a duck is to water.
    b. football is to soccer.
    c. day is to night.
    d. swimming is to ice-skating.
5. The sun is to light as
    a. a singer is to a song.
    b. a star is to the sky.
    c. a planet is to Earth.
    d. the moon is to dark.
6. A boy is to a man as
    a. a child is to a woman.
    b. a cat is to a mouse.
    c. a colt is to a stallion.
    d. a filly is to a mare.
7. A pillow is to a head as
    a. a light bulb is to a lamp.
    b. a sheet is to a bedpost.
    c. paper is to scissors.
    d. a table is to a dish.
8. Lemon is to sour as
    a. sugar is to sweet.
    b. fruit is to citrus.
    c. dusk is to dawn.
    d. candy is to sour.

9. Gilbert is to Sullivan as
    a. Beethoven is to Bach.
    b. Rimsky is to Korsakov.
    c. Mozart is to Mancini.
    d. Hammerstein is to Rodgers.
10. Milwaukee is to beer as
    a. Chicago is to Illinois.
    b. Louisville is to baseball bats.
    c. Detroit is to lemons.
    d. St. Louis is to wine.
11. Battery is to torts as
    a. archery is to sports.
    b. criminal law is to property.
    c. murder is to assault.
    d. jurisdiction is to civil procedure.
12. Feline is to cat as
    a. equine is to horse.
    b. Fido is to dog.
    c. bovine is to mouse.
    d. a fur coat is to a mink.

EXERCISE III-2
General Analogies
Think up analogies similar to those in Exercise III-1. You should do this every day for fifteen minutes for two to four weeks to develop your ability to work with analogies. Make sure you consider the degree of similarity.

EXERCISE III-3
Legal Analogies
Choose the best answer for the following. Base your answer *only* on the information you are given. Make sure you understand why it is the best analogy.

1. A hunter negligently shot John's Great Dane. John would like to recover damages from the hunter. Which of the following rules would be most helpful to John's case?
   a. A wild animal is the property of the one who captures it.
   b. One who trespasses on another's property is liable for any damage caused by the trespass.
   c. A person is liable for negligently damaging lawn furniture belonging to another.
   d. A person is liable for intentionally causing damage to another person's pet.

2. In the state of Hysteria, rape is defined as forced sexual intercourse with another, and statutory rape is defined as sexual intercourse with a person under the age of eighteen. Fred, nineteen, was arrested for statutory rape because he had sexual intercourse with Marcia, seventeen, who consented. John thought Marcia was nineteen. Which of the following rules would be most helpful to Fred's defense?
   a. A person under the age of eighteen cannot be convicted of statutory rape.
   b. Consent is a defense to the alleged rape of an adult.
   c. A mistake of fact is defense to murder.
   d. A person who did not intend to kill another, but committed homicide through gross negligence, cannot be convicted of murder.

3. Mary wrote a pop song and registered it with the copyright office the next day. A year later, Jo wrote the identical song without having heard Mary's song. Jo registered the song with the copyright office a week later. Jo's song immediately became a monster hit. Mary sued Jo for copyright infringement. Which of the following rules would most help Mary's case?
   a. The person who first invents a machine and applies for a patent obtains an exclusive patent on that machine.
   b. A plaintiff must register a book before she can bring a copyright infringement action.
   c. A patent is valid for only seventeen years.
   d. Subconscious copying is still copyright infringement.

4. Mark was a knife thrower at a carnival. Linda volunteered to allow Mark to throw knives at her as a part of his act. One of the knives came dangerously close to Linda's head, and she sued Mark for assault. Assault is defined as making one apprehensive of a harmful touching. Which of the following would most help Mark's case?

   a. There is no battery without a harmful touching.

   b. A person who is unconscious cannot recover for an assault.

   c. There is no false imprisonment if a person can return the way she came.

   d. Consent is a defense to battery.

5. Larry owned a commercial fishing lake. Bob stored toxic chemicals on his property, which was next to Larry's. One day, through no fault of Bob, the chemicals seeped out of their containers and spilled into Larry's lake, killing his fish and ruining his business. Which of the following rules would help Larry create an argument that Bob is liable for the damage?

   a. A person is liable for damage he negligently causes to the property of another.

   b. A person is liable for damage caused by the use of explosives on his property, even if he is not at fault.

   c. A person is liable for intentionally killing an animal belonging to another.

   d. A manufacturer is liable for personal injury caused by one of its products, even if the manufacturer is not at fault.

6. Plaintiff was injured in a traffic accident. He would like to put into evidence photographs of his injuries taken shortly after the accident. Defendant does not want these photographs admitted because of their shock value. Which of the following rules would most help Defendant?

   a. Photographs that are not relevant to the issues in a lawsuit are inadmissible.

   b. A witness may testify only from personal knowledge.

   c. Originals of a document must be submitted unless the proponent explains why they cannot be produced.

   d. A filmed re-creation of an accident cannot be admitted into evidence because of its prejudicial effect.

7. A Jewish group wanted to set up a holocaust memorial in a public park. In addition to pictures of conditions at concentration camps, the memorial included a Star of David and other religious symbols. The town council refused to allow construction of the memorial, declaring it violated the Establishment Clause of the Constitution. The Jewish group filed suit in federal court. If the memorial does not violate the Establishment Clause, the court will rule in favor of the Jewish group. Which of the following rules would most help the Jewish group?

   a. If a forum is opened to one group for purposes of expression, it must be opened to all groups, even if the group has a religious purpose.

   b. A manger scene on public property does not violate the Establishment Clause if it also includes secular items.

   c. A school can let students out of school early on Fridays to attend religious services without violating the Establishment Clause.

   d. The presence of "In God We Trust" on U.S. coins does not violate the Establishment Clause.

8. Your law firm wants to sue a defendant in Alabama. The defendant, a resident of California, defamed your client over the Internet by a posting on a blog she wrote in California. Which of the following most helps you establish personal jurisdiction in Alabama?

   a. The court allowed personal jurisdiction over a resident of Alabama.

   b. The court allowed personal jurisdiction over an out-of-state defendant because the defendant signed a contract in the forum state.

   c. The court allowed personal jurisdiction over an out-of-state defendant because the defendant committed a tort in the forum state.

   d. The court allowed personal jurisdiction over a defendant, a Florida resident, in Ohio because a magazine published in Florida caused harm to the defendant in Ohio.

9. Your client wants to pierce the corporate veil (always look up all terms you do not know) against a corporation's president and principal shareholder. In this case, the president frequently used the corporate jet for personal business. Which of the following helps you the most?

   a. A corporate officer can be criminally liable if she commits a crime on the corporation's behalf.

b.   A corporate officer can be held liable for fraud if she defrauds the corporation.

c.   A corporate officer or shareholder can be liable if the officer or shareholder uses corporate funds as collateral for a personal loan.

d.   A corporate officer or shareholder can be liable for giving prospective clients gifts if such gifts are prohibited by the corporation's rules.

10. The only issue in your client's case involving intentional infliction of emotional distress is whether your client's injuries are severe. After the incident, your client could not work for six months, and she had to consult a psychiatrist before returning to work. Which answer best supports your case?

a.   A court allowed recovery for intentional infliction of emotional distress when the plaintiff had serious trouble sleeping and recurrent nightmares when he was able to sleep.

b.   A court allowed recovery for intentional infliction of emotional distress when a collection agency caused the plaintiff to be fired from his job.

c.   A court allowed recovery for emotional damages because a woman saw her child killed by a car.

d.   A court allowed recovery for intentional infliction of emotional distress when a woman had to be institutionalized for two years because she saw the plaintiff shoot her husband and two children.

EXERCISE III-4

Read the following case and determine whether it is an appropriate analogy for the cases that follow. Assume you are trying to find appropriate cases for a brief.

Williams v. Walker-Thomas

350 F.2d 445 (D.C. Cir. 1965)

Appellee, Walker-Thomas Furniture Company, operates a retail furniture store in the District of Columbia. During the period from 1957 to 1962, each appellant in these cases purchased a number of household items from Walker-Thomas, for which payment was to be made in installments. The terms of each purchase were contained in a printed form contract, which set forth the value of the purchased item and purported to lease the item to appellant for a stipulated monthly rent payment. The contract then provided, in substance, that title would remain in Walker-Thomas until the total of all the monthly payments made equaled the stated value of the item, at which time appellants could take title. In the event of a default in the payment of any monthly installment, Walker-Thomas could repossess the item.

The contract further provided that "the amount of each periodical installment payment to be made by [purchaser] to the Company under this present lease shall be inclusive of and not in addition to the amount of each installment payment to be made by [purchaser] under such prior leases, bills or accounts; and all payments now and hereafter made by [purchaser] shall be credited pro rata on all outstanding leases, bills and accounts due the Company by [purchaser] at the time each such payment is made." The effect of this rather obscure provision was to keep a balance due on every item purchased until the balance due on all items, whenever purchased, was liquidated. As a result, the debt incurred at the time of purchase of each item was secured by the right to repossess all the items previously purchased by the same purchaser, and each new item purchased automatically became subject to a security interest arising out of the previous dealings.

On April 17, 1962, appellant Williams bought a stereo set of stated value of $514.95. She defaulted shortly thereafter, and appellee sought to replevy all the items purchased since December, 1957. The Court of General Sessions granted judgment for appellee. The District of Columbia Court of Appeals affirmed, and we granted appellants' motion for leave to appeal to this court.

Appellants' principal contention, rejected by both the trial and the appellate courts below, is that these contracts, or at least some of them, are unconscionable and, hence, not enforceable. In its opinion in *Williams v. Walker-Thomas Furniture Company*,[1] the District of Columbia Court of Appeals explained its rejection of this contention as follows:

> Appellant's second argument presents a more serious question. The record reveals that prior to the last purchase appellant had reduced the balance in her account to $164. The last purchase, a stereo set, raised the balance due to $678. Significantly, at the time of this and the preceding purchases, appellee was aware of appellant's financial

position. The reverse side of the stereo contract listed the name of appellant's social worker and her $218 monthly stipend from the government. Nevertheless, with full knowledge that appellant had to feed, clothe and support both herself and seven children on this amount, appellee sold her a $514 stereo set.

We cannot condemn too strongly appellee's conduct. It raises serious questions of sharp practice and irresponsible business dealings. A review of the legislation in the District of Columbia affecting retail sales and the pertinent decisions of the highest court in this jurisdiction disclose, however, no ground upon which this court can declare the contracts in question contrary to public policy. We note that were the Maryland Retail Installment Sales Act, Art. 83 §§ 128-153, or its equivalent, in force in the District of Columbia, we could grant appellant appropriate relief. We think Congress should consider corrective legislation to protect the public from such exploitive contracts as were utilized in the case at bar.

We do not agree that the court lacked the power to refuse enforcement to contracts found to be unconscionable. In other jurisdictions, it has been held as a matter of common law that unconscionable contracts are not enforceable. While no decision of this court so holding has been found, the notion that an unconscionable bargain should not be given full enforcement is by no means novel. In *Scott v. United States*,[2] the Supreme Court stated:

> If a contract be unreasonable and unconscionable, but not void for fraud, a court of law will give to the party who sues for its breach damages, not according to its letter, but only such as he is equitably entitled to. . . .

Since we have never adopted or rejected such a rule, the question here presented is actually one of first impression.

Congress has recently enacted the Uniform Commercial Code, which specifically provides that the court may refuse to enforce a contract it finds to be unconscionable at the time it was made.[3] The enactment of this section, which occurred subsequent to the contracts here in suit, does not mean that the common law of the District of Columbia was otherwise at the time of enactment, nor does it preclude the court from adopting a similar rule in the exercise of its powers to develop the common law for the District of Columbia. In fact, in view of the absence of prior authority on the point, we consider the congressional adoption of § 2-302 persuasive authority for following the rationale of the cases from which the section is explicitly derived. Accordingly, we hold that where the element of unconscionability is present at the time a contract is made, the contract should not be enforced.

Unconscionability has generally been recognized to include an absence of meaningful choice on the part of one of the parties together with contract terms that are unreasonably favorable to the other party. Whether a meaningful choice is present in a particular case can only be determined by consideration of all the circumstances surrounding the transaction. In many cases the meaningfulness of the choice is negated by a gross inequality of bargaining power. The manner in which the contract was entered into is also relevant to this consideration. Did each party to the contract, considering his obvious education or lack of it, have a reasonable opportunity to understand the terms of the contract, or were the important terms hidden in a maze of fine print and minimized by deceptive sales practices? Ordinarily, one who signs an agreement without full knowledge of its terms might be held to assume the risk that he has entered a one-sided bargain. But when a party of little bargaining power, and hence little real choice, signs a commercially unreasonable contract with little or no knowledge of its terms, it is hardly likely that his consent, or even an objective manifestation of his consent, was ever given to all the terms. In such a case, the usual rule that the terms of the agreement are not to be questioned should be abandoned, and the court should consider whether the terms of the contract are so unfair that enforcement should be withheld.

In determining reasonableness or fairness, the primary concern must be with the terms of the contract considered in light of the circumstances existing when the contract was made. The test is not simple, nor can it be mechanically applied. The terms are to be considered "in the light of the general commercial background and the commercial needs of the particular trade or case." Corbin suggests the test as being whether the terms are "so extreme as to appear unconscionable according to the mores and business practices of the time and place." 1 Corbin, *op. cit.* We think this formulation correctly states the test to be applied in those cases where no meaningful choice was exercised upon entering the contract.

Because the trial court and the appellate court did not feel that enforcement could be refused, no findings were made on the possible unconscionability of the contracts in these cases. Because the record is not sufficient for deciding the issue as a matter of law, the cases must be remanded to the trial court for further proceedings.

Other Cases

1. A parking lot has a waiver of liability on the back of its parking stub. Plaintiff wants to sue the parking lot because she got robbed in the lot and the lighting was not working.
2. Big Corporation A buys one hundred airplanes from Big Corporation B, an airplane manufacturer. The contract keeps a security interest in all the planes until Big Corporation A pays for all the planes. Big Corporation A makes payment on ninety-nine planes but fails to make the last payment on the last plane. Big Corporation B sues to repossess all the planes.
3. Martina and Juan Montez, both surgeons, go on a luxury Alaska cruise with the Big Cruise Company. They both get very ill because of food prepared improperly onboard. Their cruise contract contains a waiver of all liability against the cruise company. They want to sue the cruise company.
4. Wanda bought a used Yugo from Dirty Harry's Used Cars. Wanda recently lost her job, and she has only a sixth-grade education. The sales contract has a clause that states: "If buyer fails to make any payment, after thirty days' notice, seller can repossess the car and sue for additional monies owed under this contract." After making payments for six months, Wanda can no longer make the payments. Dirty Harry repossesses the car and sues for the remainder of the payments under the contract.
5. Debbie bought a used VW from Dirty Harry's Used Cars. The sales contract has a clause that states in bold print on the front of the contract: "This car is being sold As Is. No warranties or representations are

made by the seller to the buyer, so take a good look at the car before you buy it. If the car breaks down, you have to pay to repair it, not us. If you don't like this, buy your car somewhere else." The car broke down an hour after Debbie bought it, and she wants to sue Dirty Harry.

6. Roger was a retailer of coal who sold coal to a home owner in Louisville, Kentucky. He bought his coal from Corbin Mining Company, the largest coal-mining company in Kentucky and one of the few mining companies in the Southeast that sold coal to small companies like Roger's. The contract provided that Corbin would supply Roger with ten million tons of coal a month at $10,000 a ton for five years (a fair price). Shortly after Roger and Corbin entered into the contract, Louisville banned the burning of coal by homeowners and small businesses. Roger wants to get out of the contract based on unconscionability.

EXERCISE III-5

Read the following case and determine whether it is an appropriate analogy for the cases that follow. Assume you are trying to find appropriate cases for a brief.

Green v. Sumaski[4]

We begin with a brief review of the facts of the instant case, which reveal a somewhat typical unlawful detainer action. On September 27, 1972, landlord Jack Sumaski commenced an unlawful detainer action in San Francisco Small Claims Court seeking possession of leased premises and $300 in back rent. The tenant admitted nonpayment of rent but defended the action on the ground that the landlord had failed to maintain the leased premises in a habitable condition. The court awarded possession of the premises to the landlord and entered a money judgment for $225 against the tenant.

The tenant then appealed the decision to San Francisco Superior Court, where a de novo trial was held pursuant to section 117j of the Code of Civil Procedure. In testimony at trial, the petitioner and his roommate detailed a long list of serious defects in the leased premises that had not been repaired by the landlord after notice and that they claimed rendered the premises uninhabitable. Some of the more serious defects described by the tenants included (1) the collapse and nonrepair of the bathroom ceiling, (2) the continued presence of rats, mice, and cockroaches on the premises, (3) the lack of any heat in four of the apartment's rooms, (4) plumbing blockages, (5) exposed and faulty wiring, and (6) an illegally installed and dangerous stove. The landlord did not attempt to contest the presence of serious defects in the leased premises, but instead claimed that such defects afforded the tenant no defense in an unlawful detainer action. The superior court agreed with the landlord's contention and ruled for the landlord, holding that the "repair and deduct" provisions of Civil Code § 1941 et seq. constituted the tenant's exclusive remedy under these circumstances.

The tenant thereafter sought a hearing in this court. Because of the state-wide importance of the general issues presented, we exercised our discretion and issued an alternative writ of mandate, staying the execution of judgment conditioned upon the tenant's payment to court of all rent that had accrued since the superior court judgment and all future rent as it became due.

At common law, the real estate lease developed in the field of real property law, not contract law. Under property law concepts, a lease was considered a conveyance or sale of the premises for a term of years, subject to the ancient doctrine of caveat emptor. Thus, under traditional common law rules, the landlord owed no duty to place leased premises in a habitable condition and no obligation to repair the premises. These original common law precepts perhaps suited the agrarianism of the early Middle Ages, which was their matrix; at such time, the primary value of a lease lay in the land itself, and whatever simple living structures may have been included in the leasehold were of secondary importance and were readily repairable by the typical "jack-of-all-trades" lessee farmer. Furthermore, because the law of property crystallized before the development of mutually dependent covenants in contract law, a lessee's covenant to pay rent was considered at common law as independent of the lessor's covenants.

In recent years, however, a growing number of courts have begun to reexamine these "settled" common law rules in light of contemporary conditions, and, after thorough analysis, all of these courts have discarded the traditional doctrine as incompatible with contemporary social conditions and modern legal values. The recent decisions recognize initially that the geographic and economic conditions that characterized the agrarian lessor-lessee transaction have been entirely transformed in the modern urban landlord-tenant relationship. Today, the typical city dweller, who frequently leases an apartment several stories above the actual plot of land on which an apartment building rests, cannot realistically be viewed as acquiring an interest in land; rather, he has contracted for a place to live.

In the past, California courts have increasingly recognized the largely contractual nature of contemporary lease agreements and have frequently analyzed such leases' terms pursuant to contractual principles. Our holding in this case reflects our belief that the application of contract principles, including the mutual dependency of covenants, is particularly appropriate in dealing with residential leases of urban dwelling units.

In addition, the increasing complexity of modern apartment buildings not only renders them much more difficult and expensive to repair than the living quarters of earlier days, but also makes adequate inspection of the premises by a prospective tenant a virtual impossibility; complex heating, electrical, and plumbing systems are hidden from view, and the landlord, who has had experience with the building, is certainly in a much better position to discover and to cure dilapidations in the premises. Moreover, unlike the multi-skilled lessee of old, today's city dweller generally has a single, specialized skill unrelated to maintenance work. Likewise, the expense of needed repairs will often be outside the reach of many tenants. Finally, urbanization and population growth have wrought an enormous transformation in the contemporary housing market, creating a scarcity of adequate low-cost housing in virtually every urban setting, which has left tenants with little bargaining power.

These enormous factual changes in the landlord-tenant relationship have been paralleled by equally dramatic changes in the prevailing legal doctrines governing commercial transactions. Modern legal decisions have recognized that the consumer in an industrial society should be entitled to rely on the skill of the supplier to ensure that goods and services are of adequate quality. For the most part, the modern urban tenant is in the same position as any other normal consumer of goods. Consequently, a tenant may reasonably expect that the product he is purchasing is fit for the purpose for which it is obtained, that is, a living unit. It is just such reasonable expectations of consumers that the modern "implied warranty" decisions endow with formal legal protection.

Finally, the landlord in a companion case contends that even if we should uphold such a warranty, we could never permit a tenant to raise a landlord's breach of it in an unlawful detainer action. Relying initially on the fact that the *Hinson* decision [a precedent used by *Green*] itself involved a declaratory judgment action and not an unlawful detainer action, the landlord maintains that the trial court's refusal to permit the defense of a "warranty of habitability" in the instant case fully conforms with *Hinson*. We cannot agree. [Court's reasoning omitted.]

For the reasons discussed at length above, we believe that the traditional common law rule has outlived its usefulness; we agree with the *Hinson* court's determination that modern conditions compel the recognition of a common law implied warranty of habitability in residential leases.

Other Cases

1. Pat, a medical student, rents an apartment close to campus from Greedy Property, Inc. The apartment has numerous problems, including a broken lock on the back door, water dripping from the apartment above, a foul odor, and a broken window. Pat would like to withhold rent based on a warranty of habitability until the landlord makes repairs.

2. During Christmas weekend, the heat in Manny's apartment didn't work for three days. He wants to withhold rent based on the warrant of habitability.

3. The kitchen sink in Jorge's apartment drains slowly, and the landlord has not fixed it despite numerous phone calls by Jorge. He wants to withhold rent based on the warranty of habitability.

4. Ada lives in a walk-up apartment on the third floor. The lighting on the stairs and in the hallway has been broken for several months. She is afraid that she will trip on the stairs after dark. She is also concerned about getting attacked. Ada has notified the landlord several times about the problem, but he has not fixed it.

5. Extract a rule from *Green* concerning the standard for breach of a warranty of habitability. *Hint:* The court does not clearly state such a rule.

EXERCISE III-6
Legal Analogies

Find a case that states a rule for a specific factual situation. Next, apply this rule by analogy to as many factual situations as possible. Repeat this exercise until you feel comfortable with applying rules developed for specific factual situations to other factual situations. Again, make sure you consider how similar the analogies are.

II. WRITING ANALOGICAL ARGUMENTS

Once you have become accustomed to making legal analogies, you need to be able to write them in a clear, convincing manner. In Chapter Seven, I will show how analogies fit into the small-scale paradigm (how to write an argument on a single issue or sub-issue). For now, you need to begin practicing how to write just the analogy.

The first step in writing analogies is to present the precedent case (a rule illustration). A writer should present the case to emphasize the reason for using it (the basis of comparison). The writer should leave out anything that doesn't add to the comparison; rule illustrations are not a place for filler.

The case discussion should start with the holding of the case, focusing on the topic of that section or subject (the basis of comparison). The writer should then give the facts that are material to the reasoning of the case on the issue or sub-issue and the basis of comparison. Finally, the writer should give the reasoning of the case, again focusing on the reasoning that supports the basis of comparison.

MODEL: RULE ILLUSTRATION
1. Holding (topic sentence)
2. Facts
3. Reasoning

EXAMPLE

In *Montez*, the court held that there was a cause of action for loss of spousal consortium. In this case, Mr. Montez had been badly injured in a traffic accident that was the defendant's fault. After the accident, Mr. Montez was confined to a wheelchair, and he was unable to have sexual relations with his wife. The court reasoned that Mrs. Montez should be able to recover for loss of consortium because she had suffered a cognizable injury. Her husband was not able to provide her the companionship he had previously, and she was no longer able to have sexual relations with him.

The comparison should begin with a topic sentence that presents the comparison. The writer then should give a detailed comparison of the facts of the two cases, showing how they are similar. There is no need to show similarities between the cases that are not material to the comparison.[5] Next, the writer should include any reasoning from the cases to back up the factual comparison. Finally, the writer should end with a conclusion that demonstrates why the comparison is important to the present case.

MODEL: COMPARISON
1. Opening sentence that presents the comparison
2. Comparison of facts
3. Comparison of reasoning
4. Conclusion and relation to case

EXAMPLE
This court should allow the Jenkins children to recover for the loss of their father's consortium, just like the court allowed recovery for loss of spousal consortium in *Montez*. While in this case there was no loss of sexual relations, as there was in *Montez*, the justification for recovery is even stronger here than it was in *Montez*. Mr. Jenkins's injuries were much more severe than Mr. Montez's. While Mr. Montez was confined to a wheelchair, he was still able to use his arms and converse with his wife. Here, Mr. Jenkins is a quadraplegic, and he suffered a brain injury that prevents him from talking. The reasoning from *Montez* applies here, too. The Jenkins children have suffered a cognizable injury because they have lost the companionship of their father, who was the most important person in their lives. Therefore, this court should allow Joey and Lisa Jenkins to recover for loss of parental consortium.

Pointer: You are writing up an analogy for the benefit of your reader. In all writing, develop the attitude that you will be reader oriented—that you will communicate your ideas to your reader as clearly as possible.

EXERCISE III-7
Writing Analogies

Write out an analogy based on the following sets of facts and the case. Write your analogy in two paragraphs. Your purpose in writing the analogy is to show it to your partner before you incorporate it into an objective memorandum.

1. *Facts of your case:* Maria Koch moved from California to New York two years ago. When she left, she had not sold her house. She hired Tracey Hughes, a licensed real estate broker, to sell her house. She believes that Hughes took a kickback from the buyer to accept a low bid. She has filed a complaint with the California Real Estate Licensing Agency against Hughes.

While she was visiting her sister in California five months ago, Koch was involved in an automobile accident. Larry Wang, a passenger in the other car, was badly injured. He has filed suit in California state court against Koch.

Last week, Koch went to California to testify at a hearing of the California Real Estate Licensing Agency against Hughes. As she was entering the board's headquarters, she was served with a summons and complaint by Wang's attorney. Koch seeks to quash service of the summons and a writ of prohibition to restrain the superior court from proceeding with this action.

Justice v. Hamm (precedent)

In this case, Linda Hamm moved to quash service of a summons on her in a case brought by Laverne Justice. Because Hamm was in California solely to testify in a criminal action, the court granted Hamm's motion.

Linda Hamm witnessed the murder of Lamar Printz on July 25, 2011. She is not a resident of this state; she was in California at the time of Printz's murder to close a business deal. Hal Hedley has sued Hamm in California state court concerning that business deal. Hamm was served in that case on February 12, 2012, when she was in Los Angeles to testify at the murder trial.

It is a rule of general application that during a period reasonably necessary to the giving of testimony in a judicial proceeding, a nonresident witness who enters a state primarily for that purpose is immune from service of summons. (**Cite**) The rule is based on public policy, and even though it is in derogation of the rights of the individual litigant, it is justified by the public interest served by the granting of immunity. (**Cite**) In its common law inception, the privilege was that of the court and was formulated to prevent interruptions and delays in judicial proceedings occasioned by necessary participants being required to defend against other actions. The courts increasingly have emphasized the interest advanced by the voluntary appearance of a nonresident who could not otherwise be made to testify. In such cases, immunity is an inducement to the witness to appear and is said to be his substantive right. (**Cite**)

A recognized exception to the rule of immunity is that it does not apply if the later action, in regard to which immunity from service is claimed, arises out of or involves the same subject matter as the one in which the nonresident has made a voluntary appearance. (**Cite**) The reason for this limitation is that to permit a resident of a foreign state, by means of immunity from service of process, to pick and choose among portions of the subject matter of litigation may result in a hardship to the opposing party.

In this case, Hamm was in California solely to testify at a murder trial, a type of case that soundly implicates the policy behind the rule. This murder case is unconnected to the business case against her. Accordingly, the court granted Hamm's motion.

2. *Facts of your case:* Jimmy Horowitz, fourteen years old, held a party in his parents' basement. Jimmy promised his parents that he would not allow alcohol or drugs at the party; he said that his friends, most of whom his parents did not know, were well behaved. His parents stayed upstairs during the party so that they wouldn't embarrass Jimmy in front of his friends. Billy Fallow brought two bottles of vodka to the party, and he shared them with everyone who wanted a drink. Jimmy saw the bottles of vodka. Jane Trish, who had just gotten her driver's license and who had lived in her car since her parents had died, became drunk from the vodka. Jane didn't have any insurance. While driving home, she lost control of her car and hit Marcus Williams, a pedestrian. The Williams estate would like to sue Mr. and Mrs. Horowitz for negligent supervision of their child.

Parker v. Anderson (precedent)

In this case, the estate of Jonathan Parker sued Thomas and Jill Anderson for the death of Jonathan Parker under a theory of negligent parental supervision of a minor. The lower court found for the plaintiff and awarded the estate $500,000. The court affirmed.

On August 26, 2005, the Andersons' son, Roger, age seventeen, was involved in an accident with Jonathan Parker in which Mr. Parker was killed. The police determined that Roger Anderson was at fault and that he was drunk at the time of the accident. At the time of the accident, Roger was driving his parents' car, which they had given him permission to use. The previous year, the state had suspended Roger's license for two months for drunken driving. The Andersons knew that their son drank at home, and they had recently observed him fall when he was drunk. He often stayed out late with his friends.

The state of Hysteria allows for recovery under a theory of negligent supervision of a minor child under limited circumstances. This cause of action requires that: (1) the parents must have a duty to supervise their minor child; (2) they must have breached this duty; (3) the breach of duty must be a proximate cause of the accident; and (4) the plaintiff must have suffered a significant personal injury. In this case, the only issue is whether the parents had a duty to supervise their minor child. In *Cary*, the court stated that parents can be held liable for failure to supervise their minor child only in limited circumstances. Parents should not be liable for everything their children do because children can be unpredictable. However, when the failure to supervise rises to a high degree of negligence, then parents owe a duty to the public to protect the public from the child. To create a duty of supervision, the minor child's conduct must be dangerous to the personal safety of others, and the parents must be aware of that danger.

In *Cary*, the case that created this cause of action, the parents knew that their child had a loaded gun that he had bought from a classmate. They also knew that he had been violent in the past. Therefore, it was appropriate to hold them liable for damages when their child killed a friend during an argument.

The same rule applies to this case. The Andersons knew that their son was often drunk. Yet they allowed him not only to stay out late with his friends but also to use the family car. Under such circumstances, they should be liable for the death of Jonathan Parker.

Affirmed.

CHAPTER WRAP-UP

Do you feel comfortable dealing with analogies? If not, practice by making up real-world examples and analyzing the analogies in the cases you are reading. Watch for analogical arguments in advertisements. Do you understand what makes a convincing analogy? Can you judge degrees of similarity? Evaluate whether the analogies in the cases you are reading are convincing. Do you think you can find the best case or cases for analogies when you are given a research and writing assignment? Do you understand how to write up a case comparison? Do you understand why I gave you the structure for writing case comparisons? Do you understand each of the components of the case comparison and why they are included? Are you writing in your journal? Does your journal help you better understand your progress in learning legal reasoning? Do not move on to the next chapter until you feel comfortable with analogies and how to write them up.

Preview: Chapter Seven will demonstrate how analogical reasoning fits into the small-scale paradigm (organization of a single argument).

Answers
EXERCISE III-1

1. b. Coffee is brewed in a coffeepot; tea is brewed in a teapot.
2. b. Day is opposite of night; right is opposite of wrong.
3. a. A man is a male human and a woman is a female human; a buck is a male deer and a doe is a female deer.
4. d. Baseball is a summer activity and basketball is a winter activity; swimming is a summer activity and ice-skating is a winter activity.
5. a. The sun generates light; a singer generates a song.
6. c. A boy is a young male human and a man is a mature male human; a colt is a young male horse and a stallion is a mature male horse.
7. d. A head is placed on a pillow; a dish is placed on a table.
8. a. A lemon tastes sour; sugar tastes sweet.
9. d. Gilbert was Sullivan's lyricist; Hammerstein was Rodgers's lyricist.

10. b. Beer is associated with Milwaukee; baseball bats are associated with Louisville.
11. d. Battery is a subject studied in torts; jurisdiction is a subject studied in civil procedure.
12. a. Feline is another name for a cat; equine is another name for a horse.

EXERCISE III-3

1. c. Choice c is the best answer. Both lawn furniture and a pet are personal property, and both were negligently damaged. Choice a applies only to wild animals. Concerning choice b, we cannot be certain whether a trespass is involved here. Concerning choice d, intention is not involved here.

2. c. Fred was mistaken about Marcia's age. This is a mistake of fact. It is reasonable to argue (by analogy) that if a mistake of fact is a defense to murder, it should also be a defense to statutory rape. Choice a is incorrect because John is nineteen. Choice b is incorrect because the definition of statutory rape, unlike rape in general, does not require force and because the rule on consent specifically refers to adults. There are logical reasons not to extend it to minors, because it can be argued that minors are unable to consent. Choice d is incorrect because intention or gross negligence are not mentioned in the rape statutes.

3. a. Mary both wrote and registered her song before Jo. So if the rule from patent law is applicable by analogy to copyright law, Mary would be able to recover for copyright infringement. (This isn't true in real copyright law, but I said to base your answers only on what you were given.) Choice b doesn't help because both parties had registered their songs. Choice c doesn't help because Jo's song became a hit about a year after Mary wrote hers. Choice d is inapplicable because it was stated in the facts that Jo had never heard Mary's song, so there could have been no subconscious copying. Note that I told you that you should answer based only on the information you were given. While choice a may be the most analogous rule based on the premises of this problem, the rule has not been adopted in the real world. The real-world rule is that a person does not infringe upon the song of another, even if the

two songs are identical, as long as the second composer did not copy from the first composer's song.

4.   **d.** Linda consented to having knives thrown at her. If consent is a defense to a battery, it should also be a defense to an attempted battery-assault. The definition of assault does not require a harmful touching, so choice a doesn't help. Concerning choice b, there was no indication in the facts that Linda was unconscious. Choice c is irrelevant to this case.

5.   **b.** Under choice b, a person is liable without fault for conducting dangerous activities—using explosives on his property. Storing toxic chemicals is also a dangerous activity. Choices a and c require some form of fault, and Bob was not at fault. Choice d involves strict liability for personal injury, not property damage, and involves manufacturers.

6.   **d.** Both a re-creation of an accident and photographs of injuries can be prejudicial because the jury might place more importance on them than they merit. Concerning choice a, the photographs would be relevant to the issues in the case. Concerning choice b, no witness testimony is involved. Concerning choice c, there is no issue concerning copies here.

7.   **b.** Since the holocaust memorial also includes secular items in addition to religious symbols, choice b is the best answer. Choice a is not right because it has not been stated that the park has been opened to other groups. Choices c and d present examples of when the Establishment Clause is not violated, but they present factual situations very different from the holocaust memorial problem.

8.   **d.** Choice d is similar to the situation in our case. The out-of-state defendant defamed the plaintiff by an act in another state that harmed the defendant in the forum state. Choices a and b are not similar to the facts of our case. Choice c would be correct if the state considers that tort takes place where the harm occurs. However, you do not know this, and choice d is more specific.

9.   **c.** In both the problem and choice c, the president is using corporate property for her own purposes. The other three answers are not similar to the problem's facts.

10. **a.** In both situations the plaintiff suffered emotional distress that is arguably similar. The plaintiff in choice d also suffered emotional distress, but choice a is the better answer because the distress in choice

d was much more severe than your facts, while the distress in choice a was probably less severe, making the analogy easier to prove. Choice b is wrong because it doesn't involve severe emotional distress. Choice c is wrong because it concerns a negligent tort.

EXERCISE III-4

1. **Yes.** The two key points to unconscionability are a lack of bargaining power and unfair terms. Both the precedent and the parking lot case involve these points, and their material facts are similar. Do you remember what "material" means?

2. **No.** While the contract terms may seem unfair, there is no lack of bargaining power. Your opponent would be able to easily distinguish this case.

3. **Yes.** This is not as strong an analogy as the one in number 1 because a cruise is a more serious transaction than parking in a parking lot and the plaintiffs are sophisticated consumers. However, the facts are similar enough that a competent attorney should be able to argue the analogy.

4. **Probably not.** One of the similarities to the precedent is that Wanda is a poor, uneducated person who lacks bargaining power with a used car dealer. However, the terms of the contract are not unfair. It is very common that a seller can repossess goods if payment is not made.

5. This is probably not a good place to use the precedent. While there is a lack of bargaining power here, one can argue that the clause, no matter how insulting, is not unfair. It is common to buy a used car "as is."

6. As stated in *Williams,* the fact that the terms of the contract became oppressive after the signing of the contract is irrelevant to unconscionability because you look at unconscionability at the time of signing. You may think that this is unfair, but you should not force the doctrine to apply to your facts. Your intuition that the contract is unfair, however, may be correct because there are other doctrines that may help Roger, such as frustration of purpose or bankruptcy.

EXERCISE III-5

1. **Yes.** Both cases involve serious problems with the apartment.

2. **No.** Maybe Manny's problem is a breach of the warranty of habitability, but you can't tell it from *Green*. While no heat would be a serious violation, it lasted for only three days. *Green* involved longer problems, and the landlord didn't make repairs after notice. Accordingly, it is not a good analogy.

3. **No.** The precedent case involved several serious problems. Jorge's case involves only one minor problem, which does not render the apartment uninhabitable.

4. **No.** The precedent involved problems inside an apartment; Ada's problem involves common areas of the building. Ada's problem may be a violation of the warranty of habitability, but you can't tell it from *Green*.

5. A landlord breaches the implied warranty of habitability when serious defects in the leased premises renders the premises uninhabitable and the landlord has not repaired the defects after notice. You have to read the entire case to be able to extract this rule.

EXERCISE III-6

Example: *Case rule:* One who, without justification, scares ducks away so that a hunter cannot shoot at them is liable to the hunter for damages. Other situations that the above rule might be applied to by analogy: 1. A person tries to destroy a barber's business for no justifiable reason. 2. A person spreads a rumor that John has a venereal disease when he doesn't. 3. Mary causes Joan to breach her contract with Bob because she doesn't like Bob. 4. John burns down Bill's house because Bill is black. 5. Marcia and Bill spray-paint Robert's new Porsche, just for kicks.

What all the above factual situations have in common is that a person does an act that causes an injury to another without justification. Because a hunter can recover damages when a person scares his ducks away, it can be reasoned by analogy that the other factual situations also justify an award of damages.

EXERCISE III-7

1. In *Justice*, a court quashed a summons against a defendant who was in the jurisdiction solely to testify at a murder trial because it served

the public policy of protecting defendants who voluntarily appear to testify in judicial proceedings. This case involved a woman who witnessed a murder while she was in California to close a business deal. The woman later sued in that state concerning the business deal. When she appeared to testify at the murder trial, she was served with a summons and complaint in the other case. The court declared that "[i]t is a rule of general application that, during a period reasonably necessary to the giving of testimony in a judicial proceeding, a nonresident witness who enters a state primarily for that purpose is immune from service of summons." (**Cite**) The court noted that the rule was based on public policy, and it serves the public interest by inducing nonresident witnesses to voluntarily appear. (**Cite**) The rule also avoids interruptions and delays in judicial proceedings. (**Cite**) Based on this reasoning, the court quashed the summons.

This court should quash the summons against Marie Koch, just as the court did in *Justice v. Hamm*. While the action in *Justice* was a judicial proceeding and this case involves an administrative hearing, administrative hearings are like judicial proceedings, and the same policy considerations are implicated in each. Administrative proceedings determine legal rights and liabilities, just like judicial proceedings do. Moreover, actions by a real estate licensing board protect the public from unscrupulous brokers. Thus, allowing immunity from process when testifying at such a hearing encourages nonresidents to testify voluntarily, when they might otherwise not appear. This permits the agency to fully adjudicate the case and avoid interruptions and delays. Consequently, the court should grant Koch's motion to quash.

2. In *Parker*, the court permitted recovery for negligent supervision of a minor child because the parents had a duty to supervise their child. In this case, the defendants' seventeen-year-old son was involved in an accident with the decedent, which was the son's fault and in which the decedent was killed. The son was driving his parents' car at the time of the accident, and he had his parents' permission to use the car. The son was drunk at the time of the accident, and his parents knew he had a drinking problem. The court wrote that the state of Hysteria allows for recovery under a theory of negligent supervision of a minor child

under limited circumstances. The elements of this cause of action are that: (1) the parents must have a duty to supervise their minor child; (2) they must have breached this duty; (3) the breach of duty must be a proximate cause of the accident; and (4) the plaintiff must have suffered a significant personal injury. The only issue in *Parker* was whether the parents had a duty to supervise their minor child. The court declared that, while parents should not be liable for everything their children do because children can be unpredictable, when failure to supervise rises to a high degree of negligence, then parents owe a duty to the public to protect the public from the child. In order to create a duty of supervision, the minor child's conduct must be dangerous to the personal safety of others, and the parents must be aware of that danger. Although the Andersons knew that their son was often drunk, they allowed him not only to stay out late with his friends but also to use the family car. The court held that under such circumstances they should be liable for the death of Jonathan Parker.

The parents in this case had a duty to supervise their minor child, just like the parents did in *Parker*. Both cases concerned the death of the decedent in a drunken-driving accident when the parents could have prevented the accident with better supervision of their child. While their son was not the driver of the car that was involved in the accident, the defendants had a duty to supervise their fourteen-year-old child when he was having a party for his friends, just as the parents who knew their son drank did in *Parker*. This is not a case of children being unpredictable; it is a situation where the parents could have prevented the accident if they had supervised their child. Allowing a fourteen-year-old to have an unsupervised party is just as dangerous to the safety of others as allowing a minor to drink and drive, especially when the parents did not know most of those attending the party, and some of the guests were old enough to drive. Consequently, the court should hold the defendants liable for negligent supervision of their child.

NOTES

1. 198 A.2d 914, 916 (1964).

2. 79 U.S. (12 Wall.) 443, 445, 20 L. Ed. 438 (1870).

3. 28 D.C. CODE § 2-302 (Supp. IV, 1965).

4. Based on Green v. Superior Court, 517 P.2d 1168 (1974).

5. First-year students often try to compare cases based on comparison of facts that are not relevant to the basis of comparison. The comparison is not of the whole of the precedent case with your case; it is the differences between the comparison case and your case on a particular issue or sub-issue. That the cases can be distinguished on a separate issue or sub-issue is irrelevant.

CHAPTER FOUR

RULE-BASED REASONING

CHAPTER GOALS

1. To help the reader understand rule-based reasoning.
2. To help the reader understand deductive syllogisms.
3. To help the reader make rule-based arguments.

I. AN INTRODUCTION TO RULE-BASED REASONING

With rule-based reasoning, the writer starts with the rule, shows how the facts fit or don't fit the rule, and concludes. Rule-based reasoning is a variation of the deductive syllogism.

EXAMPLE I

All men are mortal. (major premise)
Aristotle is a man. (minor premise)
Aristotle is mortal. (conclusion)
In other words,
all As are Bs,
all Cs are As;
therefore, all Cs are Bs.

Rule-based reasoning is, of course, very common in legal analysis.

EXAMPLE II

Proof that (a) the defendant's acts were outrageous, (b) the defendant's acts were intentional, and (c) the defendant's acts caused (d) the plaintiff extreme emotional distress establishes intentional infliction of emotional harm. (major premise) The facts prove a, b, c, and d. (minor premise) The plaintiff has established intentional infliction of emotional harm. (conclusion) (Of course, this needs a lot more detail. I am only using it to illustrate the skeletal structure of rule-based reasoning.)

While all five types of legal analysis are important for a convincing legal analysis, of the five, rule-based reasoning is the most important, and it should be the framework for a legal analysis. Reasoning by analogy is weaker than rule-based reasoning because, as noted earlier, reasoning by analogy involves questions of degree.[1] The facts of our case are like the facts of the precedent case, but how close do the facts of our case have to be to the facts of the precedent case to justify applying the rule of the precedent case to our case? There is no clear answer to this question. Therefore, reasoning by analogy should support rule-based reasoning rather than being the principal type of legal argument. (See Chapter Seven on how the types of legal reasoning fit into the small-scale paradigm.) As Professor Garner has noted, "An analogy is a way of defending a premise of a syllogism [rule-based reasoning]; by itself, it is not an argument but merely a small piece of an argument."[2]

On the other hand, syllogisms are powerful because "[w]hen presented with the properly framed major and minor premises of a syllogism, the human mind seems to produce the conclusion without any additional prompting."[3] Professor Gardner has declared, "One who wishes to refute the conclusion of a properly framed syllogism cannot successfully do so by arguing that the conclusion does not flow logically from the premises. The only available strategy is to contest the premises."[4] Therefore, legal writers should be careful to make sure that their arguments are proper syllogisms and that their premises are properly supported (grounded).

II. SYLLOGISMS
A. CONSTRUCTING SYLLOGISMS

The first step in constructing a deductive legal argument is to choose the conclusion of the syllogism.[5] This requires a great deal of preliminary work (forethought stage). Before starting your legal analysis, you must first thoroughly know the facts of your case and the applicable law (do the research). Then, you need to determine your strategy—what arguments you want to make and how you are going to make them. Next, you need to outline the large-scale organization of your argument or discussion. (For more details, see the Chapter Seven Introduction.)

Once you have the large-scale organization, you will use a syllogism for every section you do not subdivide further—every sub-issue or sub-sub-issue. Your conclusion for your syllogism will be the conclusion you want for that section or subsection.

The next step is to develop the major and minor premises. In a legal argument, the major premise is the law, and the minor premise is the application of the law to the facts. The major considerations in developing premises are that: "(1) the premises must yield the desired conclusion; (2) all terms of the syllogism must match; (3) the specification of any two terms specifies the third; (4) the premises must be true; (5) major premises should use the language of tests, steps, or factors; and (6) minor premises should assert brute facts."[6]

EXAMPLE III

A person must pass the bar to be licensed to practice law in Hysteria. (major premise) (law)
John has passed the bar. (minor premise) (facts)
John may be licensed to practice law in Hysteria. (conclusion)

To be convincing, you should present the law in detail in the major premise. It is the job of the advocate to fill in all the details. Don't force your readers to do this; you will lose them. This means that you must explain all the terms.

EXAMPLE IV

Driving a vehicle in a public park violates the statute. (major premise)
Mary drove her car through Lakeland Park. (minor premise)
Mary has violated the statute. (conclusion)

The problem here is that "vehicle" is not defined. To know whether Mary has violated the statute, you need to find a statutory or case definition of "vehicle." A careful reader would also question the term "public park." Is Lakeland Park a public park under a legal definition?

Concerning the minor premise, you need to make sure that your facts fully fit within the law. In Example IV, you not only need to define "public park" for the law section but you also need to show factually that it is a public park. Assume a public park is owned by the government. You would have to prove that Lakeland Park is owned by the government.

The biggest problem I see in students' written analyses is that they often omit the application (the minor premise). I once had a problem that used a seven-part rule to establish whether strict liability was proper in a products liability case. A student spent three pages discussing every detail of the rule. He then stated, "Based on the above rule, our client should recover under a products liability theory." He had left out the application completely!

To state the above another way, major and minor premises should be grounded (contain no gaps in the reasoning). Always test your premises to make sure they are grounded.

To say that a premise is grounded means that the premise is not only true but *self-evidently* true; it requires no further explanation or justification from the advocate. A grounded premise is one that the target audience will accept as true without further elaboration.[7]

A directly grounded premise states a true proposition that either cannot or need not be further explained.[8]

EXAMPLE V

The *Lemon* test requires that a legislative statute have a secular purpose. *Smith v. Jones.* (This example is directly grounded because it is supported by a binding case.)

Barack Obama is president of the United States. (directly grounded because everyone knows it is true)

When you are unable to directly ground a premise, you can indirectly ground it with a "nested" syllogism or set of nested syllogisms.[9] (See Example VI.) The process for this is as follows:

1. Identify the ungrounded premises.
2. Convert the ungrounded premises to the conclusion of a new syllogism.
3. Construct new premises for the new syllogism leading to the required conclusion.
4. Evaluate the new premises to see if they are directly grounded. If they are directly grounded, stop. If not, repeat the process until all premises are directly grounded.[10]

EXAMPLE VI

1. Breaching a duty of care to the plaintiff establishes negligence. *Moyer v. Walters*. (major premise) (This premise is directly grounded because it is supported by binding authority.)
2. When he failed to stop for a red light, the defendant breached a duty of care to the plaintiff. (minor premise) (not directly grounded)
   A. Not stopping for a red light breaches a duty of care. *Greene v. Sebastian*. (major premise) (directly grounded)
   B. The defendant failed to stop for a red light. (minor premise) (directly grounded by evidence)
   C. When he failed to stop for a red light, the defendant breached a duty of care to the plaintiff. (conclusion)
3. The defendant is liable to the plaintiff for negligence. (conclusion)

If possible, you should continue until all the premises are directly grounded. However, you can ground premises with analogies when that isn't possible.

B. CHECKING FOR GAPS
EXERCISE IV-1

Identify the premises in the following that need further grounding (contain gaps). Don't assume that I have written the problems in a proper syllogistic order. You may have to rearrange phrases to see the syllogism.

1. When a person possesses a concealed firearm in New York City, he violates N.Y. Stat. 43.56 (b).

    George carried a starter's pistol while in Corona, Queens. (evidence) Therefore, George violated N.Y. Stat. 43.56 (b).

2. Under Georgia case law, a parent may recover damages for the wrongful death of a minor child. The Pyles' son, Johnny, was killed in a traffic accident, which was the defendant's fault. (evidence) (Assume wrongful death has been proven; it is not at issue.) Consequently, the Pyles can recover damages for the wrongful death of their child from the defendant.

3. Under Kentucky law, an employer is liable for the negligent torts of its employees performed in the course of the employer's business. Martha hired Ted to fix her roof. While doing this, Ted dropped a hammer on the postman, who was delivering the mail. Consequently, Martha is liable to the mailman.

4. Under Ky. Rev. Stat. § 155.58 (d), "a person is guilty of burglary in the third degree if 1. a person knowingly and unlawfully 2. enters or remains in a dwelling, and 3. does so with the intent to commit a crime." The only issue in this case is whether the defendant intended to commit a crime. The facts establish that the defendant broke into the house because he knew it was unoccupied and he wanted a place to sleep for the night. This is criminal trespass under Ky. Rev. Stat. § 155.43 (e). Therefore, the defendant committed a burglary.

5. Under Ky. Rev. Stat. § 155.58 (d), "a person is guilty of burglary in the third degree if 1. a person knowingly and unlawfully 2. enters or remains in a dwelling, and 3. does so with the intent to commit a crime." The only issue is whether the tent that the defendant broke into was a dwelling. *Smith* defines a dwelling as "a permanent structure [assume the usual meaning of "permanent"] in which at least one person regularly

sleeps." The tent in this case had been put up earlier that day, and its owner had intended to take it down the next day. This does not satisfy the usual meaning of "structure." Therefore, the defendant is not guilty of burglary in the third degree.

C. DIAGRAMMING SYLLOGISMS FOR COMPLEX PROBLEMS

Diagramming syllogisms is especially helpful for complex problems. Let's diagram an example based on the law in *Thompson v. Royall* from Chapter Two. **Facts:** Chin wrote a will when he was thirty. Forty years later he decided to revoke that will, because several of the beneficiaries had died and others had ignored him. He had his attorney bring the will to him, and he instructed his attorney to write on each page over the text, including over the signatures on the last page, "This will is revoked, it is null and void." He signed every page of the will. When he died, the beneficiaries under the will tried to get the will probated. You are the attorney for the heirs at law. (Remember to look up terms you don't know.) Was the will revoked?

You want to establish that the will has been revoked under the statute. The statute has two requirements: (1) the doing of one of the acts specified, (2) accompanied by the intent to revoke—the animo revocandi. There is no issue in this case of intent, so you only need to analyze whether one of the specified acts was performed. The statute states, "No will or codicil, or any part thereof, shall be revoked, unless . . . by a subsequent will or codicil, or by some writing declaring an intention to revoke the same, and executed in the manner in which a will is required to be executed, or by the testator, or some person in his presence and by his direction, cutting, tearing, burning, obliterating, canceling, or destroying the same, or the signature thereto, with the intent to revoke." Since our facts clearly do not fit most of the requirements, we only need to analyze canceling. The writing was done in Chin's presence and at his direction, so there is no problem here. Even though cancellation is statutory, this term is ambiguous, so we need to look outside the statute to help define it. *Thompson* goes on to say:

> The above, and other authorities that might be cited, hold that revocation of a will by cancellation within the meaning of the statute contemplates marks or lines across the written parts of the instrument,

or a physical defacement, or some mutilation of the writing itself, with the intent to revoke. If written words are used for the purpose, they must be so placed as to physically affect the written portion of the will, not merely on blank parts of the paper on which the will is written. If the writing intended to be the act of cancelling, does not mutilate, or erase, or deface, or otherwise physically come in contact with any part of written words of the will, it cannot be given any greater weight than a similar writing on a separate sheet of paper, which identifies the will referred to, just as definitely, as does the writing on the back.

Since you are the attorney for the heirs, you want the will to be revoked. Therefore, you start with the proposition "Chin's will was revoked."

1. Cancellation revokes a will.
2. The writing over the text and signatures on each page of his will canceled Chin's will.
3. Therefore, Chin's will was revoked.

This won't work, because there is nothing to show that writing over the text and signatures of a will revokes a will. You have not proved that C = A. Let's try to fill in the missing link with a nested syllogism.

1. Cancellation revokes a will. (grounded in statute)
2. The writing over the text and signatures on each page of his will canceled Chin's will.
    A. Written words placed so as to physically affect the written portion of a will constitute cancellation. (grounded in case)
    B. The writing on each page of Chin's will over the text, including over the signatures on the last page (evidence), physically affected the written portion of his will. (application of law to facts)
    C. Therefore, the writing over the text and signatures on each page of his will canceled Chin's will.
3. Therefore, Chin's will was revoked.

This is much better. The nested syllogism helps define cancellation (A). However, the minor premise of the nested syllogism could be better supported. There are two ways to better support this minor premise. The first way would be to find a case on exactly the same facts. However, you do not have a case exactly on the facts. The other way to support the minor premise is by analogy. This is not as strong as supporting it with grounding in a case or another nested syllogism, but it does support the premise, even if incompletely.

Thompson cites to *Evans's Appeal*. In this case, there were lines drawn through two of the three signatures of the testator appearing in the Evans will, and the paper on which material parts of the will were written was torn in four places. It therefore appeared on the face of the instrument, when offered for probate, that there was a sufficient defacement to bring it within the meaning of both obliteration and cancellation.

You want to argue that Chin's attorney's act of writing on each page over the text, including over the signatures on the last page, "This will is revoked, it is null and void," is like the act in *Evans's Appeal* of drawing lines through two of the three testators' signatures and tearing the paper on material parts of the will in four places. While Chin's attorney did not tear the will, his writing was on every page, including over the signatures; the writing stated specifically "This will is revoked, it is null and void"; and the testator and two witnesses signed on every page. Because both writings appeared on the face of the wills, both the Evans and Chin wills were revoked. (The facts of the precedent case are like our case, so the rule from the precedent case applies to our case.)

Final Version of Syllogism

1. Cancellation revokes a will. (grounded in statute)
2. The writing over the text and signatures on each page of his will cancelled Chin's will.
    A. Written words placed to physically affect the written portion of a will constitute cancellation. (grounded in case)
    B. The writing on each page of Chin's will over the text, including over the signatures on the last page (evidence), physically affected

the written portion of his will. (application of law to facts) (supported by analogy)

   C.   Therefore, the writing over the text and signatures on each page of his will canceled Chin's will.

3.   Therefore, Chin's will was revoked.

Note: Professor James A. Gardner has included two extended examples of using syllogisms in his book *Legal Argument: The Structure and Language of Effective Advocacy* 67–84 (2d ed. 2007).

III. APPLYING RULES TO FACTS
EXERCISE IV-2

Analyze whether Donald is guilty of violating Penal Code 12020 (a) based on the following facts and case. You do not need to use syllogisms here, but you will use rule-based reasoning.

Facts: While Donald Edge was walking home from high school last week, a police officer stopped him for jaywalking. While talking to Donald, the officer noticed the outline of an object in Donald's jacket pocket that appeared to be a knife. The officer asked Donald what the object was, and Donald removed the object from his pocket and gave it to the officer. He recognized the object as a linoleum knife. Donald told the officer that he carried it for protection; he had recently been threatened by a street gang. He had obtained the knife from his father's toolbox. The officer arrested Donald for illegal possession of a dirk or dagger under California Penal Code Section 12020 (a).

The knife is straight and sharpened only on one side. It has a locking blade but lacks a hand guard; it is three inches long and has a dull point.[11]

   California Penal Code § 12020

(a) Any person in this state who does any of the following is punishable by imprisonment in a county jail not exceeding one year or in the state prison: . . .

   (4) Carries concealed upon his or her person any dirk or dagger.

176 Cal. App. 3d 775 (1986)

222 Cal. Rptr. 552

In re CONRAD V., a Person Coming Under the Juvenile Court Law.

WILLIAM FORDEN, as Chief Probation Officer, Plaintiff and Respondent v. CONRAD V., Defendant and Appellant.

OPINION

ABBE, J.

The minor was found to have been unlawfully carrying a concealed dirk or dagger on his person in violation of Penal Code section 12020, subdivision (a). The sole issue we address is whether the knife-like instrument the minor had is a dirk or dagger within the meaning of that section. We conclude it is not and reverse.

The instrument is a metal object three inches in length. The blade is one and one-half inches long, curved on both sides, and beveled and sharpened on the front of one side. The flat side of the blade is smooth and approximately one-eighth inch thick as is the remainder of the instrument. It has no handle and no guard to protect the hand from slipping onto the blade. It appears to be designed to fit between two fingers of the hand with the blade projecting outward. The top portion is smooth and slightly rounded to fit behind two fingers and into the palm of the hand. This knife was the only evidence offered on the issue whether it was a dirk or dagger.

Section 12020 is one of several penal statutes relating to weapons. The statutes fit into five general categories: (1) those which absolutely prohibit possession of certain weapons in the state (e.g., §§ 12020, 653k), (2) those which prohibit possession of weapons in certain places (e.g., §§ 626.10, 12028), (3) those which prohibit possession by certain persons (e.g., §§ 4502, 12021, 12021.1, 12021.5), (4) those which restrict the manner in which weapons can be carried (e.g., §§ 12020, 12025, 12028, 12031), (5) and those which prohibit and punish criminal uses of weapons (e.g., §§ 245, 417, 467, 12022.3, 12022.5 and 12023). The use prohibition statutes are the least specific as to the weapons covered; the absolute prohibitions are described in the most specific terms. Dirks and daggers are expressly mentioned in place (§ 626.10), person (§ 4502), and concealment (§ 12020) prohibition statutes only. They are undoubtedly also included within the general description of dangerous or deadly weapons in some of the use prohibition statutes. (E.g., §§ 245, 4501, and 12022.3.)

Since section 12020, subdivision (a), is a penal statute, it must be strictly construed.[12] Despite the fact the Legislature has often amended section 12020 by adding prohibited weapons and defining others, it has never defined dirk or dagger. The Supreme Court has construed the terms to exclude a folding knife which does not have a blade which locks into place[13] but held as to other knives with different characteristics the determination whether they are dirks or daggers is a question of fact.[14]

It appears, however, that before an instrument can be found to be a dirk or dagger it must possess certain characteristics. CALJIC No. 12.36 (1979 rev.) provides in pertinent part: "The words 'dirk' or 'dagger' are used synonymously and both refer to any straight weapon, designed and fitted primarily for stabbing."

The instruction is an accurate but incomplete definition seemingly derived from *People* v. *Ruiz* (1928),[15] which was cited with apparent approval by the Supreme Court in *Bain* and *Forrest*. *Ruiz* and all the cited standard dictionaries define both dirks and daggers as forms of knives. Subdivision (e) of section 12020 indicates the Legislature so intended, since it provides knives carried in sheaths worn openly suspended from the waist of the wearer are not concealed within the meaning of the section. Since the only concealed weapons which are forbidden by the section are dirks and daggers, each is obviously a form of knife.[16]

The complete definition provided in *Ruiz* is as follows:

> A dagger has been defined as any straight knife to be worn on the person which is capable of inflicting death . . . [t]hey may consist of any weapon fitted primarily for stabbing. . . .[17]

Further requisite characteristics are provided by the Supreme Court's decisions in *Bain* and *Forrest*. The knife must have a locking blade, a hand guard to prevent the hand of the user from slipping onto the blade if the knife is used for stabbing, a handle, and perhaps a blade of certain length.

In *Bain*, the court noted that other legislation regarding weapons indicated there was substantial significance in the length of the blade being less than five inches. This observation was based on the language of section 3024, since repealed. Subsequent penal legislation involving knives indicates any requisite blade length may have changed.

Section 626.10 prohibiting certain weapons on school grounds prohibits dirks, daggers, folding knives with locking blades, and any knife having a blade longer than 3 ½ inches. Section 653k prohibits possession, sale, etc., of any switch blade knife as defined with a blade over two inches. Consequently, the Legislature has evidenced an intent not to regulate possession of knives with a blade length under two inches despite the fact that such knives are capable of causing great bodily injury or of being used as deadly weapons, as are many other objects, such as scissors and letter openers, which are capable of being concealed on the person.

Webster's Third New International Dictionary (1981), page 581, defines "dagger" as "a short knife used for stabbing" and a dirk as "a long straight-bladed dagger."[18] The illustration of a dagger as well as variants thereof, such as an anlace and a stiletto, each picture symmetrical knives with handles and guards between the handle and the blade, with straight-edged blades and sharp points. A historical work on American knives states:

> In pure usage, the dagger, always a weapon, should have a symmetrical tapering blade with two, three or even four edges and a sharp point. It is primarily designed for thrusting or stabbing.[19]

Since this knife (dangerous as it might be if used as a weapon) is sharpened on only one side of the curved blade, has no hand guard, and has only a one and one-half-inch blade, it lacks the minimal characteristics of those knives classified as dirks or daggers by section 12020, subdivision (a).

The judgment is reversed.

I will conclude this chapter with a multipart rule-based example. The example includes other types of reasoning within the details.

EXAMPLE VII

The issue in this case is whether the defendant's calling the plaintiff every hour for five straight days to collect a debt constitutes intentional infliction of emotional harm. A plaintiff must satisfy four elements to recover for intentional infliction of emotional harm: (1) the defendant's conduct was outrageous; (2) the defendant's conduct was intentional; (3) the defendant's conduct caused (4) the plaintiff severe emotional distress.[20]

The defendant's conduct was outrageous. Outrageous conduct is more than a person must endure in everyday life; minor insults, threats, or annoyances do not constitute outrageous conduct.[21] A collection agency that uses normal means to collect a debt is not liable for intentional infliction of emotional harm. *Doe.* However, one court found that a collection agency sending a debtor over one hundred letters in six months was outrageous conduct.[22]

The defendant's conduct was not a normal means of collecting a debt; collection agencies do not call debtors every hour for five straight days. In fact, the conduct in this case is more severe than the bombardment of letters that *Tate* found to be outrageous, because phone calls are more intrusive than letters, and Acme, the defendant company, called the plaintiff several times in the middle of the night.

The defendant's conduct was intentional. Intentional means that the defendant intended to do the act.[23] "Intended" does not require that the defendant intended the act's consequences.[24] Acme intended to call the plaintiff every hour for five days.

The defendant's conduct caused the distress. To establish causation under this tort, the plaintiff must put on expert testimony that the defendant's conduct caused the plaintiff's emotional distress.[25] Dr. Robinson's testimony will help establish this element.

Finally, the plaintiff suffered severe emotional distress. The emotional distress to establish intentional infliction of emotional harm must be more than is suffered in normal life.[26] For example, having difficulty sleeping for a week is not severe emotional distress.[27] In this case, the plaintiff had to consult a psychologist to help her deal with the consequences of the harassment. She had trouble sleeping for several months, had vivid nightmares, and her hands often shook.

In sum, the facts of this case demonstrate that the plaintiff should be able to recover for intentional infliction of emotional harm. First, the defendant's calling the plaintiff every hour for five days was outrageous. Second, the defendant made the calls. Third, expert testimony will establish that the defendant's conduct caused the harm. Finally, the plaintiff suffered severe emotional harm to the extent that she had to consult a psychologist.

Notes to Example

1. Note how well organized the argument is. It starts with an introduction that gives the rule. Then it has one or two paragraphs analyzing each of the rule's four factors. (Some issues require more detail than others.) The final paragraph sums up the argument. Clear organization is important for presenting an argument because it helps the reader follow complex arguments.

2. Note that in addition to stating the factors, there is rule explanation for each of the factors. This fills in the gaps and makes the argument stronger. A real argument would probably include even more rule explanation.

3. While this is mainly an example of rule-based reasoning, other types of reasoning support the rule-based reasoning. For example, the first factor includes reasoning by analogy.

4. The small-scale organization of this example uses the small-scale paradigm I present in Chapter Seven.

5. Notice how each of the factors begins with the conclusion for the factor. I did this for clarity. You should first state your conclusion, and then prove that conclusion in detail.

6. Notice how I put the law first, then the explanation. Readers need to know the law before they can understand your application.

CHAPTER WRAP-UP

How does rule-based reasoning differ from analogical reasoning? What are the advantages of using rule-based reasoning? What are the steps in rule-based reasoning? How is rule-based reasoning deductive reasoning? How do syllogisms relate to rule-based reasoning? What are gaps? Why is it important to avoid gaps in syllogistic reasoning? How do you fill gaps in rule-based reasoning? What is "directly grounded"? What is "indirectly grounded"? Why are definitions so important in the law? How would you apply a multipart rule to a set of facts?

Do not go on to the next chapter until you fully understand syllogisms.

Preview: Chapter Six will discuss an important type of rule—statutes—and show how to apply statutes to facts. Chapter Seven will demonstrate how rule-based reasoning fits into the small-scale paradigm (organization of a single argument).

Answers
EXERCISE IV-1

1. The major premise is grounded in the statute, and the minor premise is grounded in evidence. However, some of the terms and facts might require additional grounding. To analyze this problem, you should look at every term or fact that might be ambiguous. "Person" might be ambiguous in some cases, but it probably is not here. Second, "possesses" might be ambiguous. Does "possess" mean on the person only, or can it include an item in the glove compartment of a car? You should determine whether you need to define "possesses" in relation to your facts. "Concealed" is probably a word you will need to define because the definition differs by jurisdiction. "Firearm" also needs to be defined. In passing the statute, did the legislature intend to ban everything that might conceivably be a firearm? Is a starter's pistol a firearm?

    In addition, how did George carry the starter's pistol? What is a starter's pistol? What is the geographic definition of Corona, Queens? Of course, all of these need to be related to the legal definition.

2. What is the definition of "parent"? What about adoptive parents? What about parents who never supported their children? What is a minor child? Some states define a minor as under eighteen, while other states define a minor as under twenty-one. What is Johnny's age? How is he the child of his parents? The last question is important because of the definition of "parent."

3. What is the definition of an employee? An employee is usually different from an independent contractor. What is a negligent tort? What is "in the course of an employer's business"? Most states have many cases on this last question. What is Martha and Ted's factual relationship? This is important to determine whether Ted is an employee under the legal definition. What are the facts of the dropping of the hammer? Was it

an accident, or did Ted drop it on purpose? There are lots of details in most cases that can change the outcome.

   Habit: Be detailed oriented.

4.   The key element that is missing here is whether criminal trespass is a crime under the statute. Most burglary statutes apply only to certain crimes. Does the statute apply to misdemeanors? If it doesn't apply to misdemeanors, is criminal trespass a felony or a misdemeanor? Does it apply to trespass crimes?

5.   There is no gap in this problem. A case defines what a dwelling is, and the facts are clear that the tent does not satisfy that definition.

EXERCISE IV-2

After having read the facts and case thoroughly, you should have concluded that the issue in this case is whether Donald's knife is a dirk or dagger under the statute. Since the statute does not clearly define dirk or dagger, you must look to the case. The first step in solving this problem is to derive a rule from the case. The case first says, "The words 'dirk' or 'dagger' are used synonymously and both refer to any straight weapon, designed and fitted primarily for stabbing." The case then further defines a dirk or dagger: "A dagger has been defined as any straight knife to be worn on the person which is capable of inflicting death . . . [t]hey may consist of any weapon fitted primarily for stabbing." The court adds, "The knife must have a locking blade, a hand guard to prevent the hand of the user slipping onto the blade if the knife is used for stabbing, a handle, and perhaps a blade of certain length." Also, there is "substantial significance in the length of the blade being less than five inches," but this may have changed. Later: "[T]he Legislature has evidenced an intent not to regulate possession of knives with a blade length under two inches despite the fact such knives are capable of causing great bodily injury or being used as deadly weapons as are many other objects such as scissors and letter openers which are capable of being concealed on the person." Another statutory section shows the legislative intent not to regulate knives less than three and a half inches long. Finally: "In pure usage, the dagger, always a weapon, should have a symmetrical tapering blade with two, three or even four edges and a sharp point. It is primarily designed for thrusting or stabbing." From these definitions, I would derive the following rule: A dirk or dagger is a straight knife, which is (1) worn on the person, (2) primarily fitted for stabbing and capable of inflicting death, and (3) has a locking blade, (4) a hand guard, (5) a blade longer than three and a half inches, and (6) at least two edges and a sharp point.

Pointer: Note that coming up with the above rule is not an exact science, because there is some ambiguity concerning the minimum blade length. I came up with the best rule I could based on this case. This type of ambiguity is very common, and students must accept it as part of the law. Such ambiguity is what creates the opportunity to argue both sides of the law. In other words, embrace the ambiguity.

To determine whether Donald's knife is a dirk or dagger, you need to go through the rule, factor by factor. The knife is a straight knife. First, Donald wore the knife on his person. Second, a linoleum knife is probably not primarily fitted for stabbing. This becomes clearer when you look at the other facts. The knife lacks a hand guard, which would could cause the user to cut his hand when using the knife for stabbing; it is not sharpened on both sides, it has a short blade, and it has a dull point, all of which make the knife a poor knife for stabbing. Third, the knife has a locking blade. Fourth, the knife does not have a hand guard. Fifth, the blade is three inches. Finally, the knife has only one edge and a dull point. In sum, because the knife fails several of the factors for a dirk or dagger, the knife is not a dirk or dagger, and Donald cannot be convicted under section 12020.

Pointer: Note that I compared the definition to Donald's knife in detail. The lawyer who usually wins the case is the careful, thorough lawyer. You need to develop good habits now while you are in law school.

NOTES

1. Wilson Huhn has pointed out that "[w]hile formalism is scientific and grounded in logic, analogical reasoning is an art that is grounded in rhetoric." Wilson Huhn, *The Stages of Legal Reasoning: Formalism, Analogy, and Realism*, 48 VILL. L. REV. 305, 312 (2003).

2. JAMES A. GARDNER, LEGAL ARGUMENT: THE STRUCTURE AND LANGUAGE OF EFFECTIVE ADVOCACY 11 (LexisNexis 2d ed. 2007).

3. *Id.* at 5.

4. *Id.* at 6.

5. *Id.* at 18. A complex argument will consist of several syllogisms, just like it will consist of several sections and subsections.

6. *Id.* at 64.

7. *Id.* at 27.

8. *Id.* at 28.

9. *Id.* at 29.

10. *Id.*

11. This is a variation of a problem we used when I was teaching at Roger Williams University.

12. People v. Bain (1971), 5 Cal. 3d 839, 850 [97 Cal. Rptr. 684, 489 P.2d 564]. I have used the citation format used by the case.

13. People v. Forrest (1967), 67 Cal. 2d 478 [62 Cal. Rptr. 766, 432 P.2d 374].

14. *People v. Bain, supra,* 5 Cal. 3d at p. 851.

15. 88 Cal. App. 502 [263 P. 836].

16. *But see In re* Robert L. (1980), 112 Cal. App. 3d 401 [169 Cal. Rptr. 354].

17. People v. Ruiz, *supra,* 88 Cal. App. at p. 504.

18. Op. cit., p. 642.

19. PETERSON, AMERICAN KNIVES: THE FIRST HISTORY AND COLLECTORS GUIDE (1958), p. 20.

20. Smith.

21. *Id.*

22. Tate.

23. Smith.

24. *Id.*

25. *Id.*

26. Tate.

27. David.

CHAPTER FIVE

SYNTHESIZING CASES: RULE SYNTHESIS

CHAPTER GOALS

1. To help the reader understand synthesis in general.
2. To help the reader understand how case holdings are synthesized into rules.
3. To help the reader develop the ability to synthesize rules.

I. INTRODUCTION TO SYNTHESIZING CASES

Law does not come in a neat package. Rather, it is like a jigsaw puzzle with the pieces scattered around the living room floor. It is the lawyer's job to assemble the pieces of the puzzle (the law) for his case. Yet studies have shown that law students find it difficult to synthesize cases.[1] The purpose of this chapter is to help students develop their ability to synthesize rules.

Synthesizing materials in general helps law students learn better. Two learning psychologists have noted:

> In particular, students may benefit conceptually from learning tasks that promote the construction of a situation model, whereas tasks that can be performed with a more superficial representation of the text, such as using a text base [such as a single treatise], would not lead to better understanding. This distinction is consistent with the idea

that the construction of mental models is the key to students' deeper understanding of subject matter.[2]

These authors distinguish "between *knowledge-telling* and *knowledge-transforming* when students write essays. *Telling* is regarded as a passive transfer of information from text to paper, whereas transformation is regarded as a more active and constructive process in which the writer relates the contents of sources in new ways by making novel connections within source material as well as connections to the reader's knowledge. Knowledge-telling thus likely involves a relatively superficial interaction with the text base, whereas knowledge transforming may involve a more conceptual interaction with the writer's situation model of the text contents."[3]

The results, they concluded, suggest

that in order for students to gain a deeper understanding of the subject matter, writing tasks must require knowledge-transforming and not just knowledge-telling. One way to achieve this, as we have demonstrated, is to give students access to a variety of sources, and a specific argument writing task, that requires them to construct their own take on the information they read.[4]

My discussion of how to read cases in Chapter Two is a synthesis. I used ideas from several existing sources on self-regulated learning and reading cases. I then combined these existing ideas with my ideas to produce an approach to reading cases.

Synthesis in the law involves synthesizing rules in connection with a set of facts. "Rule synthesis is the process of integrating a rule or principle from several cases."[5] This process first requires identification of the task, putting the task in context, coming up with a research strategy, doing legal research to obtain the relevant cases, analyzing the individual cases, and thinking about what you have learned from the case analyses and how you will do the synthesis (the forethought stage). Next, you should synthesize the rule and evaluate how you are doing while performing the synthesis (grouping and blending, the performance stage). Finally, you evaluate your synthesis (the reflection stage). Similarly, one writer has stated, "Lawyers begin this process of synthesis by first identifying the pieces of authority relevant to a legal issue and then fitting these pieces together to determine the overall analytical framework they reasonably support."[6] Most important, "only in making sense of all of the cases will a lawyer be able to formulate a clear picture of the law to determine an appropriate solution to the legal problem at issue."[7]

As mentioned in earlier chapters, the common law develops on a case-by-case basis; law develops over time. One judge decides case A. Another judge uses that case to decide case B, which has similar facts. The next judge then relies on cases A and B to determine case C, which becomes a new precedent. In other words, each new case adds to the story of the rule.

There is not just one formula for synthesizing a rule. How you synthesize a rule depends on the materials being synthesized. Sometimes the materials will produce a single factor; other times the synthesized rule will comprise two or more factors. Often, one case will provide a framework for the rule, with other cases filling in. Other times, you will have to combine cases to produce the rule.

Sometimes a court will synthesize the rule for you. Even in this case you still need to do further work. You must check to see if that synthesis is accurate and that a later case has not modified the rule.

EXERCISE V-1

In the last chapter, we derived the following definition of dirk or dagger from *Conrad V.*

A dirk or dagger is a straight knife, which is (1) worn on the person, (2) primarily fitted for stabbing and capable of inflicting death, and (3) has a locking blade, (4) a handle, (5) a blade longer than three and a half inches, and (6) at least two edges and a sharp point.

1. Does the following case change that definition? Assume it is from the same court as *Conrad V.* Assume you are doing the analysis for a client who has been arrested for possessing a dirk or dagger.

233 Cal. App. 3d 1067 (1991)

285 Cal. Rptr. 147

THE PEOPLE, Plaintiff and Respondent v. CURTIS T. PETTWAY, Defendant and Appellant

OPINION

LOW, P.J.

We hold that a knife with a handle designed to fit in the palm of the hand, with a two- and one-fourth-inch blade protruding between the middle fingers, is a "dirk or dagger" within the meaning of Penal Code section 12020, subdivision (a) (hereafter section 12020(a)). We disagree with *In re Conrad V.*,[8] which held that a similar knife was not a dagger, in part because it did not have a hand guard.

Defendant Curtis T. Pettway appeals from the revocation of probation and the imposition of a three-year state prison sentence. The defendant contends that he did not violate section 12020(a) by wearing a knife with a two- and one-fourth-inch fixed blade concealed in his waistband, and therefore his probation should not have been revoked. We affirm.

In 1989 defendant pled guilty to selling a controlled substance.[9] The court suspended imposition of the sentence and placed the defendant on probation for three years. In October 1990, defendant was detained for urinating in the street. When the officer conducted a pat search, a knife was found on the defendant and he was arrested for carrying a concealed dangerous weapon. On January 23, 1991, the trial court revoked probation for a violation of section 12020(a). This statute makes it a felony for any person to "carr[y] concealed upon his or her person any dirk or dagger." The defendant contends that his knife is not a "dirk or dagger" and he requests that the order revoking probation be reversed.

The test on appeal is whether there is substantial evidence to support the conclusion of the trier of fact. The evidence will be viewed in the light most favorable to the judgment, but the issue will be resolved in light of the whole record.[10] The knife was brought into the probation revocation hearing, where it was examined by the court and found to be a dagger. In order to rule in defendant's favor, it would be necessary to find that the evidence did not support the conclusion as a matter of fact or that as a matter of law the knife was not a dagger.

"Dirk or dagger" is not defined in the code itself. The following definition, however, has been widely followed:

> A dagger has been defined as any straight knife to be worn on the person which is capable of inflicting death except what is commonly known as a "pocket-knife." Dirk and dagger are used synonymously and consist of any straight stabbing weapon, as a dirk, stiletto, etc. (Century Dict.) They may consist of any weapon fitted primarily for stabbing.[11]

"As is the usual practice in interpreting criminal statutes, the term 'dirk or dagger' is to be strictly construed."[12] The test of a dirk or dagger for the purposes of section 12020(a) is whether the instrument is designed primarily for stabbing, and not whether the instrument *can* be used for stabbing or is capable of inflicting death.[13] Depending on its characteristics, an instrument may be a dagger as a matter of law or it may be a dagger as a matter of fact for the trier to find.[14] A pounded bedspring with a pointed tip was held a dirk or dagger as a matter of law because it was designed, and could only be used, to stab.[15] However, a knife that had blades that did not lock into place was not a dagger because its effectiveness as a stabbing weapon was severely limited by this attribute.[16] A knife is not, as a matter of law, a dagger if it has characteristics substantially limiting its stabbing effectiveness.[17]

The weapon in this instance has a wedge-shaped, two- and one-quarter-inch fixed blade. Although one side is sharper than the other, both sides are narrowed to an edge that is thinner than at the center. The blade meets at a tapered point. The handle is on the same plane as the blade and is positioned so that it fits into the palm of the hand, with the blade protruding from between the middle fingers. The handle is covered with a corrugated plastic that helps ensure a secure grip by the wielder. Furthermore, the handle has indentations for the fingers that would hold the knife in place.

Defendant contends that his knife is not a dirk or dagger because there is no hand guard, and the blade is short and is only sharpened on one side. Defendant relies on criteria established in *In re* Conrad V.[18] The court in *Conrad V.* stated that in addition to being a straight weapon designed and fitted primarily for stabbing, a knife must have a locking blade, a hand guard, and perhaps a blade of a certain length. The *Conrad V.* court determined that a weapon similar to that at issue here was not a dirk or dagger, since it did not have a handle or hand guard, had a blade of one and one-half inches, and it was sharpened on only one side; consequently, it lacked the minimal characteristics of knives classified as dirks or daggers.[19] Defendant asserts that his knife is virtually identical to the one pictured in *Conrad V.*, and for the same reasons it is not a dirk or dagger. Although the knives are very much alike, *Conrad V.* is distinguishable. The blade in *Conrad V.* was one and one-half inches long, while the blade in the case at bar is two and one-quarter inches long. The blade in this instance is almost as long as the entire instrument in *Conrad V. Conrad V.* relies on Penal Code section 626.10, prohibiting weapons of a certain length on school grounds, for the proposition that the Legislature chose not to regulate knives with a blade of less than two inches.[20] Because of its length, this knife would not be exempt from regulation even if the *Conrad V.* court was correct that the Legislature intended not to regulate knives less than two inches. A belt buckle knife with a blade of two and one-half to three inches has been found to be a dirk or dagger as a matter of law.[21]

The parties disagree as to whether this is a single-blade or double-blade instrument. While one side of the blade is sharper and longer, the other side is narrowed and meets the longer edge at a tapered point. This enhances its effectiveness as a stabbing weapon.

Finally, the defendant claims that this knife, like that in *Conrad V.*, has no hand guard, and thus the wielder's hand is unprotected. Here we are compelled to disagree with the *Conrad V.* court's analysis. It is true that a knife without a hand guard has limited effectiveness as a stabbing weapon because the wielder's hand could easily slide onto the blade. There is, however, no such danger with the type of knife involved here and in *Conrad V.* The handle rests against the palm of the hand and could not easily slip if the blade met resistance while stabbing.

We disagree with the *Conrad V.* court's statement that such a knife does not have a handle or a hand guard. Both these knives have handles, of a type which actually increases the usefulness and effectiveness as a stabbing weapon and which makes them unsuitable for any other purpose. The design of this knife makes it suitable to be used only in a plunging manner. To use it to cut an apple would leave the wielder's hand at such an odd angle that the wielder would be unable to gain any leverage. The knife could not be used to cut an object placed on a table, because the side of the handle, projecting downward, would keep the blade inches above the table. The handle also makes the knife less suitable for slashing because it would not hold firmly against lateral resistance. Not only is this knife fitted primarily for stabbing, it is fitted for practically no other use. It is a dagger as a matter of law.

Defendant argues that the superior court improperly based its finding on the fact that defendant was carrying the knife for use as a weapon. (Defendant testified he carried it for protection.) There is a division of authority as to the analytical role played by the defendant's reasons for carrying an alleged dagger.[22] There is logic in the position stated by Justice Compton, dissenting in *In re Robert L.*[23] that it is "bootstrapping" to use one element of the crime—the manner in which the instrument is carried—to supply the other element—the instrument's characterization as a dirk or dagger. We need not reach that question here, however, because the physical characteristics of this knife, considered without regard for defendant's intended use, make it, as a matter of law, a dagger.

The judgment is affirmed.

1. Would this case change the result in *Conrad V.*?
2. Does this case change the result in exercise IV-2?

EXERCISE V-2

Synthesize a rule from the following cases. Assume you are going to meet with your partner to discuss this case later in the afternoon.

Case A: Test—To establish intentional infliction of emotional harm, the plaintiff must prove that (1) the defendant's conduct was outrageous, (2) the defendant's conduct was intentional, and (3) the defendant's conduct caused (4) damages to the plaintiff.

Case B: Holding—To establish damages for intentional infliction of emotional harm, the defendant must have suffered severe emotional distress.

II. SYNTHESIZING A SINGLE-FACTOR RULE

Learning case synthesis begins with synthesizing a single-factor rule. First, you must find all the relevant cases on that issue in relation to your facts. This usually means assembling all the mandatory authority from the governing jurisdiction. This is why legal research is so important. If you miss one relevant case, you have misrepresented the law of the jurisdiction. You must also be able to understand what cases belong together (grouping). Once you have determined the relevant group, you should carefully read the relevant cases, making sure you fully understand their reasoning, both explicit and implicit. You need to realize that judges do not always express their ideas well.

Synthesizing a single factor requires that you blend the cases into a coherent whole. In other words, your synthesis must be consistent with all the case holdings and reasoning. To synthesize a single factor, look at the outcome of each case for that factor and how the similarities and differences among the facts and reasoning of those cases affected the outcomes.

EXERCISE V-3

Synthesize the following elements to determine when a plaintiff may recover for negligent infliction of emotional harm when witnessing an accident. Assume you are doing research for a judge.

Case 1: Facts—Plaintiff witnesses her best friend killed by a drunk driver when the driver runs a stop sign and hits the friend in a crosswalk. Outcome: No recovery.

Case 2: Facts—Plaintiff witnesses her sixteen-year-old child killed when a car runs into the passenger side of her car. Outcome: Plaintiff can recover for negligent infliction of emotional harm.

Case 3: Facts—Plaintiff witnesses her husband struck and killed by a drunk driver while he is walking on a sidewalk. Outcome: Plaintiff can recover for negligent infliction of emotional harm.

Case 4: Facts—Plaintiff witnesses her child run down by a motor scooter while the child is playing in the yard. The child loses both of her legs but otherwise recovers. Outcome: No recovery.

EXERCISE V-4

As mentioned above, later cases can change the rule. How do the following cases change the rule you synthesized for cases 1–4?

Case 5: Facts—Plaintiff and her aunt are involved in a small-plane crash for which the defendant is liable. Plaintiff witnesses her aunt's death. Outcome: No recovery.

Case 6: Facts—A father is on the way to pick up his son from baseball practice. While waiting for his father, the son is killed when hit by a car. The defendant is liable for the accident. The father comes upon the accident five minutes after it occurs. His child is lying on the sidewalk. Outcome: No recovery.

Case 7: Facts—A father attends a stock-car race in which his thirty-year-old son is participating. He sees his son die in a fiery crash on the tenth lap. The accident is the fault of the mechanic who failed to properly fix the car's brakes. Outcome: No recovery.

EXERCISE V-5

What would be the outcome of the following situations based on the rule from exercise V-4?

1. An unmarried couple is walking along Lover's Lane. A speeding car kills the woman. Can the man recover?
2. An engaged couple is walking along Lover's Lane. A speeding car kills the woman. Can the man recover?
3. A woman is watching a high-speed chase on television. She sees the car being chased crash into a truck. The driver of the truck is killed. Later, she learns that the driver was her husband. Can the wife recover?
4. While following her son's car, a mother witnesses a fiery accident in which her son is badly injured. He spends several weeks in the burn unit of the hospital and is permanently scarred but survives. Can the mother recover?

III. SYNTHESIZING A MULTIFACTOR RULE

A rule may consist of multiple factors—e.g., duty, breach of duty, causation, damages. Synthesizing multiple-factor rules is similar to synthesizing single-factor rules, except you first must determine what factors the cases require to establish a test (there is a preliminary grouping stage into factors). Separate out the different factors. (A chart might help you do this.) Then look at the outcome of each case for each factor and how the similarities and differences among the facts and reasoning of those cases affected the outcome for that factor.

EXERCISE V-6

Synthesize a rule from the following cases concerning covenants not to compete in an employment relationship. Assume you are doing this to advise a client on this issue.

> Case 1: Holding—A covenant not to compete is in restraint of trade and therefore unenforceable on grounds of public policy unless it is reasonable.
> Case 2: Facts—A covenant not to compete contained a clause restricting competition by the employee for five years after termination of employment. Outcome: Covenant unreasonable.
> Case 3: Facts—A covenant contained a clause restricting competition by the employee for three years and within twenty miles of the company's headquarters. Outcome: Covenant unreasonable.
> Case 4: Facts—A covenant contained a clause restricting competition in the construction business within twenty miles of the company's headquarters for one year. Outcome: Covenant unreasonable.
> Case 5: Facts—A covenant contained a clause restricting competition by the employee for a year and within twenty miles of the company's headquarters. Outcome: Covenant reasonable.
> Case 6: Facts —A covenant contained a clause restricting competition by the employee within thirty miles of the company's headquarters for six months in the sale of weight-loss drugs. Outcome: Covenant reasonable.

EXERCISE V-7

What would be the outcome of the following situations based on the rule from exercise V-6?

1. A covenant contained a clause restricting competition in the retail trade of clothing by the employee for one year within ten miles of the employer's store. Is the covenant reasonable?
2. A covenant contained a clause restricting competition in the retail trade of men's clothing by the employee for six months within ten miles of the employer's store. Is the covenant reasonable?
3. A covenant contained a clause restricting competition in the custom cabinetmaking business for four years within ten miles of the employer's shop. Is the covenant reasonable?
4. A covenant contained a clause restricting competition in the custom oak bed-making business for two years within twenty miles of the employer's shop. Is the covenant reasonable?
5. What type of reasoning are you using with these exercises?

EXERCISE V-8

Synthesize a rule from the following cases concerning when there is a duty to disclose known defects in the sale of commercial real estate. Devise your own purpose for doing this exercise.

Case 1: Rule—A seller generally does not have to disclose known defects when selling commercial real estate.

Case 2: Rule—A seller has to disclose known defects when selling commercial real estate when those defects involve serious safety or health concerns to human beings.

Case 3: Rule—A seller does not have to disclose known defects when selling commercial real estate when those defects could be discovered through due diligence.

Case 4: Rule—A seller must disclose known economic liabilities and potential economic liabilities when selling commercial real estate.

EXERCISE V-9

What would be the outcome of the following situations based on the rule from exercise V-8?

1. The seller of a shopping center knows that the roof leaks during hard rains. Could the seller be liable for nondisclosure?
2. The seller of a commercial property is aware that the property once was a gas station and it had buried gas tanks that leaked and were never cleaned up. Could the seller be liable for nondisclosure?
3. The seller of a commercial property is aware that the IRS has placed a tax lien against the property. Could the seller be liable for nondisclosure?
4. The seller is aware that a large manufacturing plant is going to be built next to the property. This has not been announced publicly. The plant will create traffic tie-ups in the area and lower the value of the property. Could the seller be liable for nondisclosure?
5. The buyer is aware that a large mall is going to be built near the property. This has not been announced publicly. The plant will greatly raise property values in the area. Could the buyer be liable for nondisclosure?
6. The seller hired a leasing agent to lease the stores in a shopping center. The agreement states that the leasing agent will receive commissions if tenants renew their leases. Could the seller be liable for nondisclosure?

EXERCISE V-10

Critique the following analysis. Is it well written? Is it reader oriented? Is it convincing?

In case 1, the court said that a seller "generally does not have to disclose known defects when selling commercial real estate." Case 2 added that a seller "has to disclose known defects when selling commercial real estate when those defects involve serious safety or health concerns to human beings." However, case 3 stated, "A seller does not have to disclose known defects when selling commercial real estate when those defects could be discovered through due diligence." Finally, case 4 declared, "A seller must disclose known economic liabilities and potential economic liabilities when selling commercial real estate."

The facts of our case are that the seller of a commercial property is aware that the property once was a gas station and it had buried gas tanks that leaked and were never cleaned up. Based on the above cases, the buyer probably would be able to recover for nondisclosure.

IV. OTHER CONSIDERATIONS

The final step in a synthesis is to test it. Have you accounted for all the relevant cases in your synthesis? Are the cases relevant to your facts? Is your synthesis convincing? Is there an alternative synthesis? If so, is the original or alternative synthesis better? Has your synthesis produced a clear rule that can be applied to your facts?

Of course, the above assumes that the law in real life is consistent. It isn't. You can't always reconcile all cases on a particular point. Judges sometimes don't blend in a previous case, and sometimes they miss or misunderstand an earlier case.

In an objective analysis (an objective memo), you must do your best to reconcile the earlier cases; this is part of being objective. When two cases are irreconcilably inconsistent, use the case that fits best with the reasoning of the other cases and acknowledge the inconsistency in the text.

In a persuasive analysis (a brief), use the ambiguity to your advantage. However, your synthesis still must be convincing.

I advise you to work more on case synthesis. A good source is Paul Figley, *Teaching Rule Synthesis with Real Cases*.[24] For an advanced example of synthesizing cases, see Jane Kent Gionfriddo, *Thinking Like a Lawyer: The Heuristics of Case Synthesis*.[25]

CHAPTER WRAP-UP

Why is synthesizing cases important? Why do you have to double-check the rule synthesis from a case? What are the steps in synthesizing a single-factor rule? What are the steps in synthesizing a multi-factor rule? Why is it important to test your synthesis? What should you do when the cases can't be reconciled? Why is the answer different for objective versus persuasive documents?

Preview: The remaining chapters of this book will teach you how to use mini-skills in combination. Chapter Six will cover statutory interpretation, which uses rule-based reasoning on the broadest level, with other mini-skills filling in the details. Chapter Seven will demonstrate how mini-skills combine to create the small-scale paradigm—a method for organizing a simple legal analysis. Chapter Eight will show you how mini-skills work in conjunction to create counterarguments. Finally, Chapter Nine will use mini-skills as part of advanced problem solving.

Answers
EXERCISE V-1

1. This case changes the definition of "dirk" or "dagger" in two ways. First, it helps refine the length factor. My conclusion, based on my best reading of *Conrad V.*, was that a dirk or dagger had to have a blade that was at least three and a half inches long. The blade in this case was two and one-quarter inches long. Also, this case cites to another case that found a belt-buckle knife with a two-and-one-half to three-inch blade a dirk or dagger as a matter of law. Thus, we can refine the length factor as requiring a blade longer than two inches. Second, this case refines our understanding of "hand guard." The court writes, "It is true that a knife without a hand guard has limited effectiveness as a stabbing weapon because the wielder's hand could easily slide onto the blade." Here, "the handle rests against the palm of the hand, and could not easily slip if the blade met resistance while stabbing." The court also states that "both these knives have handles, of a type which actually increases the usefulness and effectiveness as a stabbing weapon and makes them unsuitable for any other purpose. The design of the knife makes it suitable to be used only in a plunging manner." In this case, the court has gone from the literalness of *Conrad V.* to an interpretation based on the purpose of the requirement. The knife doesn't literally have to have a hand guard as long as there is something that serves the purpose and prevents the hand from being injured when the knife is used for stabbing.

Pointer: When reading cases, observe whether the court employs the literal definition of a word or looks beyond the literal definition for the purpose.

2. Probably not. While this court disagrees with *Conrad V.* concerning the hand guard, the blade in *Conrad V.* is one and a half inches. The court states, "The blade in this instance is almost as long as the entire instrument in *Conrad V.*" However, the court also writes, "Because of its length, this knife would not be exempt from regulation even if the *Conrad V.* court was correct that the Legislature intended not to regulate knives under two inches." (This is why I said probably not.)

    Pointer: As I have mentioned several times in earlier chapters, cases are often won or lost based on details.

3. While it changes some of the factors, it does not change all of them. The linoleum knife would probably be a poor knife for stabbing because it lacks a hand guard, is not sharpened on both sides, has a short blade, and has a dull point.

EXERCISE V-2

Synthesized rule: Test—To establish intentional infliction of emotional harm, the plaintiff must prove that (1) the defendant's conduct was outrageous, (2) the defendant's conduct was intentional, (3) the defendant's conduct caused emotional distress, and (4) the plaintiff suffered severe emotional distress. This synthesis should have been easy. All you needed to do was to take the rule and combine it with the more specific definition of damages from the second case. Later cases will help you fill out the rule even more and understand the parts. For example, the next case might define severe emotional distress in detail.

EXERCISE V-3

A plaintiff can recover for negligent infliction of emotional harm when witnessing an accident involving the death of a spouse or a child. Another possible way of writing this is a plaintiff may recover for negligent infliction of emotional harm when witnessing an accident involving a family member. The key to synthesizing these cases is to look at how the similarities and differences between the facts affected the outcomes. The cases allowed recovery for death of a spouse or for a minor child, but not for death of a friend or for a serious accident.

EXERCISE V-4

Case 5: A plaintiff can recover for negligent infliction of emotional harm when witnessing an accident involving the death of a spouse or a child. The new case doesn't change the rule, but it clarifies that, for recovery, the death must be a member of the immediate family.

Case 6: A plaintiff can recover for negligent infliction of emotional harm when directly witnessing an accident involving the death of a spouse or a child. The difference here is that the father came upon the scene later.

Case 7: This one is harder because there are two new facts here. The child is an adult, and the child was participating in a dangerous sport. I would think the child's age is the key factor, but I can't argue with someone who contends that the dangerous sport is the key factor. An advocate would argue the interpretation that helped her case. If I were representing a father who witnessed his adult child killed in a typical accident, I would contend that the key factor in this case was the dangerous sport.

EXERCISE V-5

1. There would be no recovery. The woman is not part of his immediate family.
2. No, under the synthesized rule. However, a good attorney would argue for an extension of that rule based on the fact that witnessing the death of a fiancée is just as severe as witnessing the death of a spouse.
3. This situation is not clearly covered by the rule. However, she would probably not recover because she did not know the driver was her husband at the time of the accident.
4. The mother would not recover because her son did not die.

EXERCISE V-6

Under case 1, the key to determining whether a covenant not to compete is enforceable is whether it is reasonable. The other cases establish whether a covenant is reasonable. Next, you must determine how many factors establish reasonableness (how many parts there are to the rule). In this case, there are three factors: duration, geographic area, and type of activity. Then, analyze each factor separately. (Those who are visual thinkers may want to make a chart of the factors and how changes in the factors determine the outcome.)

The first factor is duration. Durations of five years, three years, and one year were a factor in cases where the covenant was found to be unreasonable, while durations of one year and six months were factors in cases where the outcome was found to be reasonable. This is confusing, because there were cases with durations of one year where the covenant was found reasonable and cases where it was found unreasonable. How do we solve this dilemma? Look to see whether the requirements of the rule are conjunctive (all factors required for reasonableness) or disjunctive (only one factor required to satisfy the rule). From looking at the cases, it is obvious that the rule is conjunctive, with all three factors being required to establish reasonableness. Since case 5 found a covenant duration of one year reasonable and the requirements are conjunctive, one year or less must be reasonable.

The second factor is geographic area. Distances of twenty miles were in cases where the covenant was found to be unreasonable, while distances of both thirty miles and twenty miles were found in cases in which the covenant was upheld. Since the rule is conjunctive, the covenant is reasonable for a distance of at least thirty miles.

The final factor is type of activity. Case 4 involved a covenant for the construction business, and the court found the covenant unreasonable. Since we have already established that durations of one year within a distance of twenty miles are reasonable, it must be the type of activity factor that caused the court in this case to rule the covenant unenforceable. Case 6 found a covenant restricting the sale of weight-loss drugs reasonable. Looking at these two cases, it appears that courts will enforce narrow activity restrictions but not broad ones.

Based on the above, we can synthesize the following three-part rule for covenants not to compete in employment contracts: (1) the covenant must be for one year or less; (2) the covenant must be for no more than thirty miles from the company's headquarters; and (3) the type of activity restricted must not be too broad.

Next, you must test the rule to see if it is consistent with all the cases. It is.

A final step is to see whether one can interpret the cases differently than in the above rule. Concerning duration, no case covers a period between one year and three years where the duration was the determining factor. If you were the employer's attorney, you would argue for the longer period. (How would you do this? You would use the reasoning of the cases.) There is no case where a distance of more than thirty miles is determinative of unreasonableness, so the employee's attorney could argue for a larger geographic area. Finally, the cases only generally define type of activity, so there is room for argument by both sides here. From the above, it is obvious that synthesizing rules often provides room for persuasion.

Pointer: The above process may seem complicated. However, it is relatively easy if you synthesize the cases step by step. Remember, providing competent representation is the first rule of legal ethics, and properly synthesizing a rule is part of competent representation.

EXERCISE V-7

1. The covenant is probably not reasonable because the type of activity restricted is too broad. Can you argue for the opposite result?
2. Although this clause is not as broad as the one in the previous problem, it probably is unreasonable because it still restricts a wide range of activity.
3. No. While the restriction on the type of activity is probably not too broad, the clause is for four years.
4. Not under a strict reading of the rule. However, a competent attorney would probably try to have the court extend the rule to his facts because two years isn't that much longer than one year and because the type of activity restricted is narrow.
5. Mainly rule-based reasoning. Applying a rule to the facts.

EXERCISE V-8

A seller does not have to disclose known defects when selling commercial real estate except when those defects involve serious safety or health concerns to human beings, or when a seller knows of economic liabilities or potential economic liabilities against the property. A seller also does not have to disclose known defects when selling commercial real estate when those defects could be discovered through due diligence.

EXERCISE V-9

1. No, unless the roof leak somehow affects the health of tenants or their customers.
2. Yes, gas tanks that have leaked are a potential health hazard and probably a potential economic liability against the property, since the EPA will require that the property be cleaned if it learns of the hazardous condition.
3. While the tax lien is an economic liability against the property, the buyer could discover the lien through due diligence by checking public property records.
4. No. This is not an economic liability or potential economic liability.
5. No. The rule applies to sellers, not buyers.
6. Yes, the commissions are potential economic liabilities against the property. However, the seller does not have to disclose the commissions if the documents are in the records of the property and the buyer has the opportunity to do a due diligence search of those records.

EXERCISE V-10

I hope you concluded that the analysis is worthless. There is no synthesis; the writer just presents the cases one by one. Also, there is no analysis, just a conclusory statement. I will demonstrate how to write up a simple analysis in Chapter Seven.

NOTES

1. DOROTHY H. EVENSEN ET AL., DEVELOPING AN ASSESSMENT OF FIRST-YEAR LAW STUDENTS' CRITICAL CASE REASONING AND REASONING ABILITY: PHASE 2, http://www.lsac.org/lsacresources/Research/GR/GR-08-02.pdf, *4 (Law School Admissions Council 2008).

2. Jennifer Wiley & James F. Voss, *Constructing Arguments from Multiple Sources: Tasks that Promote Understanding and Not Just Memory for Text*, 91 J. EDUC. PSYCH. 301 (1999).

3. *Id.*

4. *Id.* at 309.

5. Paul Figley, *Teaching Rule Synthesis with Real Cases*, 61 J. LEGAL EDUC. 245 (2011).

6. Jane Kent Gionfriddo, *Thinking Like a Lawyer: The Heuristics of Case Synthesis*, 40 TEX. TECH L. REV. 1, 4 (2007).

7. *Id.* at 6.

8. (1986), 176 Cal. App. 3d 775 [222 Cal. Rptr. 552].

9. HEALTH & SAF. CODE § 11352.

10. People v. Johnson (1980), 26 Cal. 3d 557, 578 [162 Cal. Rptr. 431, 606 P.2d 738, 16 A.L.R. 4th 1255].

11. People v. Ruiz (1928), 88 Cal. App. 502, 504 [263 P. 836]; *see, e.g.*, People v. Forrest (1967), 67 Cal. 2d 478, 480, 62 Cal. Rptr. 766, 432 P.2d 374; People v. Villagren (1980), 106 Cal. App. 3d 720, 725 [165 Cal. Rptr. 470].

12. People v. Bain (1971), 5 Cal. 3d 839, 850 [97 Cal. Rptr. 684, 489 P.2d 564].

13. Bills v. Superior Court (1978), 86 Cal. App. 3d 855, 860 [150 Cal. Rptr. 582].

14. *In re* Quintus W. (1981), 120 Cal. App. 3d 640, 644–45 [175 Cal. Rptr. 30].

15. People v. Cabral (1975), 51 Cal. App. 3d 707, 712 [124 Cal. Rptr. 418].

16. People v. Forrest, *supra*, 67 Cal. 2d at 481.

17. *Id.*

18. *Supra*, 176 Cal. App. 3d at 778.

19. *Id.*

20. *In re* Conrad V., *supra*, 176 Cal. App. 3d at 778.

21. People v. McClure (1979), 98 Cal. App. 3d Supp. 31, 32–33 [160 Cal. Rptr. 83].

22. *Compare In re* Robert L. (1980), 112 Cal. App. 3d 401, 405 [169 Cal. Rptr. 354] [ice pick, carried for "protection," is dagger]; *In re* Quintus W., *supra*, 120 Cal.

App. 3d at p. 645 [same as to kitchen knife]; *with* Bills v. Superior Court, *supra*, 86 Cal. App. 3d at 861–62 [intended use of instrument irrelevant under § 12020; barber scissors carried as a defensive weapon held not dagger].

23. *Supra*, at p. 409.

24. 61 J. LEGAL EDUC. 245 (2011), *available at* http://papers.ssrn.com/sol3/papers.cfm?abstract_id=1979601.

25. 40 TEX. TECH L. REV. 1, 18–35 (2007), *available at* http://papers.ssrn.com/sol3/papers.cfm?abstract_id=1012220.

CHAPTER SIX

INTERPRETING STATUTES

CHAPTER GOALS

1. To help the reader understand the basic techniques of statutory interpretation.
2. To help the reader understand the three main approaches to statutory interpretation.
3. To help the reader develop the ability to interpret statutes.
4. To help the reader develop the ability to apply statutes to facts (rule-based reasoning).
5. To help the reader understand how the different types of legal reasoning and corresponding mini-skills fit into statutory interpretation.

I. BASIC TECHNIQUES FOR INTERPRETING STATUTES

While the basis of American law is common law cases, today statutes are just as or more important. Because statutes were intended to control the common law, judges are bound by statutes unless they are unconstitutional. Judges, however, still have a great deal of power in connection with statutes because it is their role to interpret them.

Applying statutes involves rule-based reasoning on the broadest level, with other types of reasoning, particularly reasoning by analogy, filling in the details. When interpreting statutes, you should always begin with the statute's language. Read every word carefully and determine how the parts fit together. Determine whether the parts are conjunctive (all parts required) or disjunctive (only one part needs to be satisfied). If the statute is complex, it is a good idea to diagram it.

EXAMPLE I

Fair Use Statute (copyright)
Notwithstanding the provisions of sections 106 and 106A, the fair use of a copyrighted work, including such use by reproduction in copies or phonorecords or by any other means specified by that section, for purposes such as criticism, comment, news reporting, teaching (including multiple copies for classroom use), scholarship, or research, is not an infringement of copyright. In determining whether the use made of a work in any particular case is a fair use, the factors to be considered shall include

1. the purpose and character of the use, including whether such use is of a commercial nature or is for nonprofit educational purposes;
2. the nature of the copyrighted work;
3. the amount and substantiality of the portion used in relation to the copyrighted work as a whole; and
4. the effect of the use upon the potential market for or value of the copyrighted work.

The fact that a work is unpublished shall not itself bar a finding of fair use if such finding is made upon consideration of all the above factors.

Diagram
Intro

A. Notwithstanding the provisions of sections 106 and 106A [reference]
B. the fair use of a copyrighted work . . . is not an infringement of copyright [main rule]
C. including such use by reproduction in copies or phonorecords or by any other means specified by that section, for purposes such as

criticism, comment, news reporting, teaching (including multiple copies for classroom use) [examples]

Body. In determining whether the use made of a work in any particular case is a fair use, the factors to be considered shall include

    1. the purpose and character of the use, including whether such use

        a. is of a commercial nature or

        b. is for nonprofit educational purposes;

    2. the nature of the copyrighted work;

    3. the amount and substantiality of the portion used in relation to the copyrighted work as a whole; and

        a. the amount

        b. the substantiality

    4. the effect of the use upon the potential market for or value of the copyrighted work.

        a. potential market for the work

        b. value of the work.

Clarification. The fact that a work is unpublished shall not itself bar a finding of fair use if such finding is made upon consideration of all the above factors.

Even simple statutes need additional clarification. (In other words, you will often need nested syllogisms [see Chapter Four] or reasoning by analogy.) "A person shall not drive faster than fifty-five miles per hour on an interstate highway." In this statute, we at least need a definition of "interstate highway." Is it any highway that crosses state lines, or is there a specific definition? For that matter, what is a highway?

Similarly, "A person shall not drive a vehicle in a public park." What is a vehicle? A car? A truck? A moped? A bicycle? What is a public park?

EXERCISE VI–1

1. How do the parts of this statute fit together? Diagram the statute.

      MRPC 1.9(a) A lawyer who has formerly represented a client in a matter shall not thereafter represent another person in the same or a substantially related matter in which that person's interests are materially adverse to the interests of the former client unless the former client gives informed consent, confirmed in writing.

2.   What elements in the above statute are conjunctive? Are any disjunctive?

EXERCISE VI–2

Read the following statute.

MRPC 1.5(b) The scope of the representation and the basis or rate of the fee and expenses for which the client will be responsible shall be communicated to the client, preferably in writing, before or within a reasonable time after commencing the representation, except when the lawyer will charge a regularly represented client on the same basis or rate.

1.   Does the scope of the representation and the basis or rate of the fee and expenses for which the client will be responsible have to be communicated to the client in writing? Why does the rule require disclosure?

2.   When does an attorney not have to disclose the basis or rate of the fee?

EXERCISE VI–3

Apply the fair use statute above to the following problem. **Facts:** Professor Johns has prepared a twenty-page pamphlet on fair use for the students in his copyright class. He used one paragraph from Professor Famous's five-hundred-page copyright treatise verbatim in his pamphlet. Professor Johns had thirty copies of his pamphlet printed, and he gave it (for free) to the thirty students in his class. Professor Famous sued Professor Johns for copyright infringement. Fair use is a defense to copyright infringement. Does Professor Johns have a fair use defense? (Case law would make your answer more complete, but I don't expect you to do any case law research for this problem. However, feel free to look up the terms in an encyclopedia or dictionary.)

Because of problems like the above, courts have developed techniques of statutory interpretation. The first set of statutory interpretation tools is textualist techniques. After having carefully read a statute's language, you should look at other parts of the statute. (Statutes often come in multiple parts.) Is there a title? Is there a definition section? (If you use a statutory definition, does applying that statutory definition to the facts involve rule-based reasoning [nested syllogism] or analogical reasoning?) Is there a preamble or purpose section? For example, if the vehicle in the park statute had a title of "Governance of Motor Vehicles," you would know that bicycles probably aren't covered. Also, you can look at other parts of the statutory code to see if a term is defined. However, be careful in doing this; legislatures often use different definitions in different sections.

You can look at a dictionary to determine the everyday meaning of a word. Courts often stress that statutes should use the everyday meaning of words so that they are understandable by the public. You can look to legal dictionaries for specialized meanings of words. Also, you should not forget cases; one of a judge's major jobs is to define words. If the definition is from a binding case on point, you have to use it. If another state's court has interpreted the same or a similar statute to yours, you can use it, but it is persuasive authority.

Question: If a court uses a case to help it interpret a term in a statute, but the previous case involved somewhat different facts, in using that case, is the court using rule-based reasoning or analogical reasoning? Consider this hypothetical: Jack receives a ticket for driving his moped in the park. The statute says, "A person may not drive a vehicle in a public park." The statute does not define "vehicle," and none of the usual methods of textualist interpretation are helpful. The only other cases held that the statute applied to a car but not to a bicycle. In deciding the case based on these precedents, is the judge using rule-based reasoning or analogical reasoning?

The final textualist technique is "canons of construction"—rules of thumb on how judges should read statutes (interpret language). There are dozens of canons of statutory construction. An example is "interpret general words in a statute in relation to more specific terms." Under this canon, the term "other vehicles" in a statute that stated "Persons shall not operate cars, trucks, and other vehicles in public parks" would be interpreted to include other motorized vehicles, but not bicycles and mopeds.

When a statute is still ambiguous after using the above textualist techniques, some judges will look beyond the statute to legislative history. When a legislature, such as Congress, considers a statute, it often generates a great deal of legislative history. Usually, the most important items are committee reports and statements made by the bill's sponsors during floor debate. Courts often use legislative history to determine the statute's purpose. This allows a court to read a statute more broadly than its language. How would you interpret the vehicle in the park statute if the committee report stated, "The statute is intended to protect pedestrians and bicyclists in parks"?

II. THE THREE APPROACHES TO STATUTORY INTERPRETATION

Judges use the above techniques in different ways, based on their judicial philosophy. There are three main approaches to statutory interpretation: (1) textualism, (2) originalism, and (3) dynamism, with numerous variations on these approaches.[1] Textualism and originalism are the two main approaches used by courts, while dynamism is mainly an approach advocated by scholars.

Textualists attempt to determine what the words mean, rather than trying to establish what the legislature intended.[2] Textualists believe that for legislative intent to become law, it must be contained in a bill that is passed by both houses and signed by the president (or passed over the president's veto).[3] As Justice Scalia has stated, "It is simply incompatible with democratic government, or indeed, even with fair government, to have the meaning of a law determined by what the lawmaker meant, rather than by what the lawmaker promulgated."[4] Moreover, textualists fear that when judges use legislative intent to interpret statutes, they will adopt their values instead of the legislature's.[5] Justice Scalia has declared:

> When you are told to decide, not on the basis of what the legislature said, but on the basis of what it *meant*, and are assured that there is no necessary connection between the two, your best shot at figuring out what the legislature meant is to ask yourself what a wise and intelligent person *should* have meant; and that will surely bring you to

the conclusion that the law means what you think it *ought* to mean—which is precisely how judges decide things under the common law.[6]

Consequently, textualists generally advocate that judges restrict their inquiry to the text in order to avoid undemocratic lawmaking by judges.[7] They also believe that textualism supports policies underlying the rule of law, such as consistency, predictability, and notice.[8]

Justice Scalia has described the textualist approach:

> [F]irst, find the ordinary meaning of the language in its textual context; and second, using established canons of construction, ask whether there is any clear indication that some permissible meaning other than the ordinary one applies. If not—and especially if a good reason for the ordinary meaning appears plain—we apply that ordinary meaning.[9]

Scholars often call Justice Scalia's version of textualism "the new textualism."[10] Professor Eskridge has written:

> The new textualism posits that once the court has ascertained a statute's plain meaning, consideration of legislative history becomes irrelevant. Legislative history should not even be consulted to confirm the apparent meaning of the statutory text. Such confirmation comes, if any is needed, from examination of the structure of the statute, interpretations given similar statutory provisions, and canons of statutory construction.[11]

Originalists believe that the judge's role is to uncover the policy choices the legislature made when it passed a statute.[12] There are two subclasses of originalism—intentionalism and purposivism.[13] Intentionalists try to discern the legislature's *specific intent* when it enacted a statute, usually based on the statute's legislative history.[14] However, when there is no evidence of the legislature's actual intent, "the court may scan the statute's context and history to 'imaginatively reconstruct' what the legislature would have decided if it had actually considered the issue."[15] Judge Posner has declared:

[T]he framers communicate to the judges through legislative texts. . . . If the orders are clear, the judges must obey them. Often, however, because of change of circumstance the orders are unclear and normally the judges cannot query the framers to find out what the order means. . . . It is irresponsible for [judges] to adopt the attitude that if the order is unclear they will refuse to act. . . . Judges should ask themselves . . . what would the framers would have wanted us to do in cases where the enactment is unclear.[16]

Thus, there are two types of intentionalism: archaeological intentionalism, which examines the text and legislative history, and hypothetical intentionalism, which asks what the legislature would have said if it had considered the question.[17]

On the other hand, purposivists objectively interpret a statute *based on its broad purpose*, again relying heavily on legislative history, although they often also study the entire legal landscape.[18] Concerning purposivism, Justice Brewer wrote in 1892:

It is a familiar rule, that a thing may be within the letter of the statute and yet not within the statute, because not within its spirit, nor within the intention of its makers. . . . This is not the substitution of the will of the judge for that of the legislator, for frequently words of general meaning are used in a statute, words broad enough to include an act in question, and yet a consideration of the whole of the legislation, or of the circumstances surrounding its enactment, or of the absurd results which would follow from giving such broad meaning to the words, makes it unreasonable to believe that the legislature intended to include the particular act.[19]

Similarly, Justice Brennan declared:

Looking beyond the naked text for guidance is perfectly proper when the result it apparently decrees is difficult to fathom or where it seems inconsistent with Congress' intention, since the plain-meaning rule is rather "an axiom of experience than a rule of law, and does not preclude consideration of persuasive evidence if it exists."[20]

Judge Hand has described this approach to statutory interpretation:

> We can best reach the meaning here, as always, by recourse to the underlying purpose, and with that as a guide, by trying to project upon the specific occasion how we think persons, actuated by such a purpose, would have dealt with it, if it had been presented to them at that time.[21]

Originalism adopts a structural view of democracy, which mandates that the branches of government act within their fields of competence and democratic authority.[22] This approach "requires that the unelected judiciary act as a good faith agent to implement the elected legislature's policy choices, as embodied in statutes."[23]

Question: When a court uses a statute's broad purpose to help determine how to apply that statute, is the court using rule-based or analogical reasoning?

Dynamism is a consequentialist approach that treats statutes as "tools for responding to society's needs."[24] Such an approach grants judges lawmaking power in the interpretative process, considers societal values, and updates statutes for contemporary needs.[25] In other words, dynamists "use 'practical reasoning' to achieve the best results in changed circumstances,"[26] and they recognize that judges generally adopt an eclectic approach to statutory interpretation, not some grand theory.[27] Two leading advocates of this approach have written:

> Interpretation can be viewed as an honest effort by an "agent" to apply the "principal's" directive to unforeseen circumstances. . . . The dynamic nature of interpretation arises out of the agent's need for practical accommodation of the directive to new circumstances.[28]

Ronald Dworkin has written:

> [A judge] will use much the same techniques of interpretation to read
> statutes that he uses to decide common-law cases. . . . He will treat
> Congress as an author earlier than himself in the chain of law, though
> an author with special powers and responsibilities different than his
> own, and he will see his role as fundamentally the creative one of the
> partner continuing to develop, in what he believes is the best way, the
> statutory scheme Congress began. He will ask himself which reading
> of the act . . . shows the political history including and surrounding
> that statute in the better light.[29]

Dworkin adds that a judge "must rely on his own judgment in answering
these questions, of course, not because he thinks his opinions are automatically right, but because no one can properly answer any question except by
relying at the deepest level on what he himself believes."[30]

Unlike originalists and textualists, dynamists are not concerned that
the "separation of powers" doctrine constrains a judge's power to make
law when interpreting statutes.[31] Rather, they believe that "because dynamism charges courts with a direct responsibility for preserving substantive
democratic values it measures interpretative legitimacy by the 'democratic'
consequences attained, not solely by the 'democratic' processes employed."[32]
Stated from a different viewpoint:

> [D]ynamic statutory interpretation has replaced the democratic com-
> mitment to self-determination with a system of government that vests
> ultimate power making authority in an unelected and unaccountable
> elite, the "guardians," of the common good. And this "common good"
> is apparently to be determined wholly apart from the preferences of
> the members of society.[33]

Question: What is the most important mini-skill in using the dynamic
approach, rule-based reasoning, analogical reasoning, or policy-based
reasoning?

EXERCISE VI-4

Read the following opinions and answer the questions at the end.

Heirs v. Oscar

Majority: Oscar was his rich uncle's favorite nephew, and the uncle left the bulk of his estate to Oscar in his will. Oscar was somewhat of a rake. He liked to party all the time, and his uncle learned of his activities. Oscar's uncle set up an appointment with his lawyer to remove Oscar from his will. Before the appointment, Oscar murdered his uncle. The other heirs challenge Oscar's right to inherit under the will.

The issue in this case is whether a person who murders a testator can inherit from that testator. There are no cases in this jurisdiction on this question. The legislature passed an extensive set of statutes on wills and decedents' estates fifty years ago, and it has amended them several times since. However, no statute encompasses this situation.

The court holds that Oscar should not be able to inherit from his uncle. We believe that the legislature could not have intended that murderers can become enriched by their crimes when it passed the wills statutes.

Dissent: The legislature has passed extensive statutes on wills and decedents' estates. Yet it has not spoken on the issue before us. Since it has enacted such extensive statutes without forbidding inheritance by murderers, this court should not pretend to speak for it.

1. Which opinion is the textualist opinion? Which opinion is the originalist one?
2. Which one do you think comes to the correct result?
3. How did the majority determine legislative intent?
4. Why do you think the dissent favored Oscar, even though he was a criminal?

EXERCISE VI-5

Read the following case thoroughly, then answer the questions at the end.

491 U.S. 440 (1989)

PUBLIC CITIZEN

v.

UNITED STATES DEPARTMENT OF JUSTICE ET AL.

Decided June 21, 1989

JUSTICE BRENNAN delivered the opinion of the Court.

The Department of Justice regularly seeks advice from the American Bar Association's Standing Committee on Federal Judiciary regarding potential nominees for federal judgeships. The question before us is whether the Federal Advisory Committee Act (FACA),[34] applies to these consultations and, if it does, whether its application interferes unconstitutionally with the President's prerogative under Article II to nominate and appoint officers of the United States; violates the doctrine of separation of powers; or unduly infringes the First Amendment right of members of the American Bar Association to freedom of association and expression. We hold that FACA does not apply to this special advisory relationship. We therefore do not reach the constitutional questions presented.

I

A

The Constitution provides that the President "shall nominate, and by and with the Advice and Consent of the Senate, shall appoint" Supreme Court Justices and, as established by Congress, other federal judges.[35] Since 1952 the President, through the Department of Justice, has requested advice from the American Bar Association's Standing Committee on Federal Judiciary (ABA Committee) in making such nominations.

The American Bar Association is a private, voluntary professional association of approximately 343,000 attorneys. It has several working committees, among them the advisory body whose work is at issue here.

Prior to announcing the names of nominees for judgeships on the courts of appeals, the district courts, or the Court of International Trade, the President, acting through the Department of Justice, routinely requests a potential nominee to complete a questionnaire drawn up by the ABA Committee and to submit it to the Assistant Attorney General for the Office of Legal Policy, to the chair of the ABA Committee, and to the committee member (usually the representative of the relevant judicial Circuit) charged with investigating the nominee. The potential nominee's answers and the referral of his or her name to the ABA Committee are kept confidential. The committee member conducting the investigation then reviews the legal writings of the potential nominee, interviews judges, legal scholars, and other attorneys regarding the potential nominee's qualifications, and discusses the matter confidentially with representatives of various professional organizations and other groups. The committee member also interviews the potential nominee, sometimes with other committee members in attendance.

Following the initial investigation, the committee representative prepares for the chair an informal written report describing the potential nominee's background, summarizing all interviews, assessing the candidate's qualifications, and recommending one of four possible ratings: "exceptionally well qualified," "well qualified," "qualified," or "not qualified." The chair then makes a confidential informal report to the Attorney General's Office. The chair's report discloses the substance of the committee representative's report to the chair without revealing the identity of persons who were interviewed, and indicates the evaluation the potential nominee is likely to receive if the Department of Justice requests a formal report.

If the Justice Department does request a formal report, the committee representative prepares a draft and sends copies to other members of the ABA Committee, together with relevant materials. A vote is then taken and a final report approved. The ABA Committee conveys its rating—though not its final report—in confidence to the Department of Justice, accompanied by a statement whether its rating was supported by all committee members or whether it only commanded a majority or substantial majority of the ABA Committee. After considering the rating and other information the President and his advisers have assembled, including a report by the Federal Bureau of Investigation and additional interviews conducted by the President's judicial selection committee, the President then decides whether to nominate the candidate. If the candidate is in fact nominated, the ABA Committee's rating, but not its report, is made public at the request of the Senate Judiciary Committee.

B

FACA was born of a desire to assess the need for the "numerous committees, boards, commissions, councils, and similar groups which have been established to advise officers and agencies in the executive branch of the Federal Government."[36] Its purpose was to ensure that new advisory committees be established only when essential and that their number be minimized; that they be terminated when they have outlived their usefulness; that their creation, operation, and duration be subject to uniform standards and procedures; that Congress and the public remain apprised of their existence, activities, and cost; and that their work be exclusively advisory in nature.[37]

To attain these objectives, FACA directs the director of the Office of Management and Budget and agency heads to establish various administrative guidelines and management controls for advisory committees. It also imposes a number of requirements on advisory groups. For example, FACA requires that each advisory committee file a charter,[38] and keep detailed minutes of its meetings.[39] Those meetings must be chaired or attended by an officer or employee of the federal government who is authorized to adjourn any meeting when he or she deems its adjournment in the public interest.[40] FACA also requires advisory committees to provide advance notice of their meetings and to open them to the public, § 10(a), unless the President or the agency head to which an advisory committee reports determines that it may be closed to the public in accordance with the Government in the Sunshine Act.[41] In addition, FACA stipulates that advisory committee minutes, records, and reports be made available to the public, provided they do not fall within one of the Freedom of Information Act's exemptions[42] and the government does not choose to withhold them.[43] Advisory committees established by legislation or created by the President or other federal officials must also be "fairly balanced in terms of the points of view represented and the functions" they perform.[44] Their existence is limited to two years, unless specifically exempted by the entity establishing them.[45]

C

In October 1986, appellant Washington Legal Foundation (WLF) brought suit against the Department of Justice after the ABA Committee refused WLF's request for the names of potential judicial nominees it was considering and for the ABA Committee's reports and minutes of its meetings. WLF asked the District Court for the District of Columbia to declare the ABA Committee an "advisory committee" as FACA defines that term. WLF further sought an injunction ordering the Justice Department to cease utilizing the ABA Committee as an advisory committee until it complied with FACA. In particular, WLF contended that the ABA Committee must file a charter, afford notice of its meetings, open those meetings to the public, and make its minutes, records, and reports available for public inspection and copying.

See WLF Complaint, App. 5-11. The Justice Department moved to dismiss, arguing that the ABA Committee did not fall within FACA's definition of "advisory committee" and that if it did, FACA would violate the constitutional doctrine of separation of powers.

Appellant Public Citizen then moved successfully to intervene as a party plaintiff. Like WLF, Public Citizen requested a declaration that the Justice Department's utilization of the ABA Committee is covered by FACA and an order enjoining the Justice Department to comply with FACA's requirements.

The district court dismissed the action following oral argument. The court held that the Justice Department's use of the ABA Committee is subject to FACA's strictures, but that "FACA cannot constitutionally be applied to the ABA Committee because to do so would violate the express separation of nomination and consent powers set forth in Article II of the Constitution and because no overriding congressional interest in applying FACA to the ABA Committee has been demonstrated." Congress's role in choosing judges "is limited to the Senate's advice and consent function," the court concluded; "the purposes of FACA are served through the public confirmation process and any need for applying FACA to the ABA Committee is outweighed by the President's interest in preserving confidentiality and freedom of consultation in selecting judicial nominees.". . . We noted probable jurisdiction, and now affirm on statutory grounds, making consideration of the relevant constitutional issues unnecessary. . . .

III

Section 3(2) of FACA, as set forth in 5 U.S.C. App. § 3(2), defines "advisory committee" as follows:

For the purpose of this Act—
(2) The term 'advisory committee' means any committee, board, commission, council, conference, panel, task force, or other similar group, or any subcommittee or other subgroup thereof (hereafter in this paragraph referred to as 'committee'), which is—
(A) established by statute or reorganization plan, or
(B) established or utilized by the President, or
(C) established or utilized by one or more agencies, in the interest of obtaining advice or recommendations for the President or one or more

agencies or officers of the Federal Government, except that such term
excludes (i) the Advisory Commission on Intergovernmental Relations,
(ii) the Commission on Government Procurement, and (iii) any committee which is composed wholly of full-time officers or employees
of the Federal Government.

Appellants agree that the ABA Committee was not "established" by the
President or the Justice Department. Equally plainly, the ABA Committee
is a committee that furnishes "advice or recommendations" to the President via the Justice Department. Whether the ABA Committee constitutes
an "advisory committee" for purposes of FACA therefore depends upon
whether it is "utilized" by the President or the Justice Department as Congress intended that term to be understood.

A

There is no doubt that the Executive makes use of the ABA Committee, and thus "utilizes" it in one common sense of the term. As the district
court recognized, however, "reliance on the plain language of FACA alone
is not entirely satisfactory." "Utilize" is a woolly verb, its contours left
undefined by the statute itself. Read unqualifiedly, it would extend FACA's
requirements to any group of two or more persons, or at least any formal organization, from which the President or an executive agency seeks
advice. We are convinced that Congress did not intend that result. A nod-
ding acquaintance with FACA's purposes, as manifested by its legislative
history and as recited in section 2 of the Act, reveals that it cannot have
been Congress's intention, for example, to require the filing of a charter,
the presence of a controlling federal official, and detailed minutes any time
the President seeks the views of the National Association for the Advancement of Colored People (NAACP) before nominating Commissioners to
the Equal Employment Opportunity Commission, or asks the leaders of an
American Legion Post he is visiting for the organization's opinion on some
aspect of military policy. . . .

FACA was enacted to cure specific ills, above all the wasteful expenditure
of public funds for worthless committee meetings and biased proposals;
although its reach is extensive, we cannot believe that it was intended to
cover every formal and informal consultation between the President or an

executive agency and a group rendering advice. As we said in *Church of the Holy Trinity v. United States*:[46]

> [F]requently words of general meaning are used in a statute, words broad enough to include an act in question, and yet a consideration of the whole legislation, or of the circumstances surrounding its enactment, or of the absurd results which follow from giving such broad meaning to the words, makes it unreasonable to believe that the legislator intended to include the particular act.

Where the literal reading of a statutory term would "compel an odd result," *Green v. Bock Laundry Machine Co.*,[47] we must search for other evidence of congressional intent to lend the term its proper scope.[48] "The circumstances of the enactment of particular legislation," for example, "may persuade a court that Congress did not intend words of common meaning to have their literal effect."[49] Even though, as Judge Learned Hand said, "The words used, even in their literal sense, are the primary, and ordinarily the most reliable, source of interpreting the meaning of any writing," nevertheless "it is one of the surest indexes of a mature and developed jurisprudence not to make a fortress out of the dictionary; but to remember that statutes always have some purpose or object to accomplish, whose sympathetic and imaginative discovery is the surest guide to their meaning."[50] Looking beyond the naked text for guidance is perfectly proper when the result it apparently decrees is difficult to fathom or where it seems inconsistent with Congress's intention, since the plain-meaning rule is "rather an axiom of experience than a rule of law, and does not preclude consideration of persuasive evidence if it exists."[51]

Consideration of FACA's motives in determining whether the term "utilized" was meant to apply to the Justice Department's use of the ABA Committee is particularly appropriate here, given the importance we have consistently attached to interpreting statutes to avoid deciding difficult constitutional questions where the text fairly admits of a less problematic construction. It is therefore imperative that we consider indicators of congressional intent in addition to the statutory language before concluding that FACA was meant to cover the ABA Committee's provision of advice to the Justice Department in connection with judicial nominations.

B

Close attention to FACA's history is helpful, for FACA did not flare on the legislative scene with the suddenness of a meteor. Similar attempts to regulate the federal government's use of advisory committees were common during the 20 years preceding FACA's enactment.[52] An understanding of those efforts is essential to ascertain the intended scope of the term "utilize. . . ."

Although FACA's legislative history evinces an intent to widen the scope of Executive Order No. 11007's definition of "advisory committee" by including "Presidential advisory committees," which lay beyond the reach of Executive Order No. 11007, as well as to augment the restrictions applicable to advisory committees covered by the statute, there is scant reason to believe that Congress desired to bring the ABA Committee within FACA's net. FACA's principal purpose was to enhance the public accountability of advisory committees established by the executive branch and to reduce wasteful expenditures on them.

The House bill that in its amended form became FACA applied exclusively to advisory committees "established" by statute or by the Executive, whether by a federal agency or by the President himself.[53] Although the House Committee Report stated that the class of advisory committees was to include "committees which may have been organized before their advice was sought by the President or any agency, but which are used by the President or any agency in the same way as an advisory committee formed by the President himself or the agency itself," it is questionable whether the Report's authors believed that the Justice Department used the ABA Committee in the same way it used advisory committees. The phrase "used . . . in the same way" is reminiscent of Executive Order No. 11007's reference to advisory committees "utilized . . . in the same manner" as a committee established by the federal government, and the practice of three administrations demonstrates that Executive Order No. 11007 did not encompass the ABA Committee.

Paralleling the initial House bill, the Senate bill that grew into FACA defined "advisory committee" as one "established or organized" by statute, the President, or an Executive agency.[54] Like the House Report, the accompanying Senate Report stated that the phrase "established or organized" was to be understood in its "most liberal sense, so that when an officer brings together a group by formal or informal means, by contract or other arrangement, and whether or not Federal money is expended, to obtain advice and information, such group is covered by the provisions of this bill." While the Report manifested a clear intent not to restrict FACA's coverage to advisory committees funded by the federal government, it did not indicate any desire to bring all private advisory committees within FACA's terms. Indeed, the examples the Senate Report offers—"the Advisory Council on Federal Reports, the National Industrial Pollution Control Council, the National Petroleum Council, advisory councils to the National Institutes of Health, and committees of the national academies where they are utilized and officially recognized as advisory to the President, to an agency, or to a Government official"—are limited to groups organized by, or closely tied to, the federal government, and thus enjoy quasi-public status. Given the prominence of the ABA Committee's role and its familiarity to members of Congress, its omission from the list of groups formed and maintained by private initiative to offer advice with respect to the President's nomination of government officials is telling. If the examples offered by the Senate Committee on Government Operations are representative, as seems fair to surmise, then there is little reason to think that there was any support, at least at the committee stage, for going beyond the terms of Executive Order No. 11007 to comprehensively regulate the workings of the ABA Committee.

It is true that the final version of FACA approved by both Houses employed the phrase "established or utilized," and that this phrase is more capacious than the word "established" or the phrase "established or organized." But its genesis suggests that it was not intended to go much beyond those narrower formulations. The words "or utilized" were added by the Conference Committee to the definition included in the House bill. The Joint Explanatory Statement, however, said simply that the definition contained in the House bill was adopted "with modification." The Conference Report offered no indication that the modification was significant, let alone that it would substantially broaden FACA's application by sweeping within its terms a vast number of private groups, such as the Republican National

Committee, not formed at the behest of the Executive or by quasi-public organizations whose opinions the federal government sometimes solicits. Indeed, it appears that the House bill's initial restricted focus on advisory committees established by the federal government, in an expanded sense of the word "established," was retained rather than enlarged by the Conference Committee. In the section dealing with FACA's range of application, the Conference Report stated: "The Act does not apply to persons or organizations which have contractual relationships with Federal agencies nor to advisory committees not directly established by or for such agencies." The phrase "or utilized" therefore appears to have been added simply to clarify that FACA applies to advisory committees established by the federal government in a generous sense of that term, encompassing groups formed indirectly by such quasi-public organizations as the National Academy of Sciences "for" public agencies as well as "by" such agencies themselves.

In sum, a literal reading of § 3(2) would bring the Justice Department's advisory relationship with the ABA Committee within FACA's terms, particularly given FACA's objective of opening many advisory relationships to public scrutiny except in certain narrowly defined situations. A literal reading, however, would catch far more groups and consulting arrangements than Congress could conceivably have intended. And the careful review that this interpretive difficulty warrants of earlier efforts to regulate federal advisory committees and the circumstances surrounding FACA's adoption strongly suggest that FACA's definition of "advisory committee" was not meant to encompass the ABA Committee's relationship with the Justice Department. That relationship seems not to have been within the contemplation of Executive Order No. 11007. And FACA's legislative history does not display intent to widen the Order's application to encircle it. Weighing the deliberately inclusive statutory language against other evidence of congressional intent, it seems to us a close question whether FACA should be construed to apply to the ABA Committee, although on the whole we are fairly confident it should not. There is, however, one additional consideration which, in our view, tips the balance decisively against FACA's application.

C

"When the validity of an act of the Congress is drawn in question, and even if a serious doubt of constitutionality is raised, it is a cardinal principle that this Court will first ascertain whether a construction of the statute is fairly possible by which the question may be avoided." Crowell v. Benson .[55] It has long been an axiom of statutory interpretation that "where an otherwise acceptable construction of a statute would raise serious constitutional problems, the Court will construe the statute to avoid such problems unless such construction is plainly contrary to the intent of Congress."[56] This approach, we said recently, "not only reflects the prudential concern that constitutional issues not be needlessly confronted, but also recognizes that Congress, like this Court, is bound by and swears an oath to uphold the Constitution."[57] Our reluctance to decide constitutional issues is especially great where, as here, they concern the relative powers of coordinate branches of government.[58] Hence, we are loath to conclude that Congress intended to press ahead into dangerous constitutional thickets in the absence of firm evidence that it courted those perils.

It is undeniable that construing FACA to apply to the Justice Department's consultations with the ABA Committee would present formidable constitutional difficulties.

To be sure, "[w]e cannot press statutory construction 'to the point of disingenuous evasion' even to avoid a constitutional question."[59] But, unlike in *Locke*, where "nothing in the legislative history remotely suggest[ed] a congressional intent contrary to Congress' chosen words,"[60] our review of the regulatory scheme prior to FACA's enactment and the likely origin of the phrase "or utilized" in FACA's definition of "advisory committee" reveals that Congress probably did not intend to subject the ABA Committee to FACA's requirements when the Committee offers confidential advice regarding Presidential appointments to the federal bench. Where the competing arguments based on FACA's text and legislative history, though both plausible, tend to show that Congress did not desire FACA to apply to the Justice Department's confidential solicitation of the ABA Committee's views on prospective judicial nominees, sound sense counsels adherence to our rule of caution. Our unwillingness to resolve important constitutional questions unnecessarily thus solidifies our conviction that FACA is inapplicable.

The judgment of the District Court is Affirmed.

JUSTICE KENNEDY, with whom THE CHIEF JUSTICE and JUSTICE O'CONNOR join, concurring in the judgment.

In a government, where the liberties of the people are to be preserved . . . , the executive, legislative and judicial, should ever be separate and distinct, and consist of parts, mutually forming a check upon each other.[61]

The Framers of our Government knew that the most precious of liberties could remain secure only if they created a structure of Government based on a permanent separation of powers.[62] Indeed, the Framers devoted almost the whole of their attention at the Constitutional Convention to the creation of a secure and enduring structure for the new Government. It remains one of the most vital functions of this Court to police with care the separation of the governing powers. That is so even when, as is the case here, no immediate threat to liberty is apparent. When structure fails, liberty is always in peril. As Justice Frankfurter stated:

The accretion of dangerous power does not come in a day. It does come, however slowly, from the generative force of unchecked disregard of the restrictions that fence in even the most disinterested assertion of authority.[63]

Although one is perhaps more obvious than the other, this suit presents two distinct issues of the separation of powers. The first concerns the rules this Court must follow in interpreting a statute passed by Congress and signed by the President. On this subject, I cannot join the Court's conclusion that the Federal Advisory Committee Act (FACA) does not cover the activities of the American Bar Association's Standing Committee on Federal Judiciary in advising the Department of Justice regarding potential nominees for federal judgeships. The result seems sensible in the abstract; but I cannot accept the method by which the Court arrives at its interpretation of FACA, which does not accord proper respect to the finality and binding effect of legislative enactments. The second question in the case is the extent to which Congress may interfere with the President's constitutional prerogative to nominate federal judges. On this issue, which the Court does not reach because of its conclusion on the statutory question, I think it quite plain that the application of FACA to the government's use of the ABA Committee is unconstitutional.

I

The statutory question in this suit is simple enough to formulate. FACA applies to "any committee" that is "established or utilized" by the President or one or more agencies, and which furnishes "advice or recommendations" to the President or one or more agencies.[64] All concede that the ABA Committee furnishes advice and recommendations to the Department of Justice and through it to the President.[65] The only question we face, therefore, is whether the ABA Committee is "utilized" by the Department of Justice or the President.

There is a ready starting point, which ought to serve also as a sufficient stopping point, for this kind of analysis: the plain language of the statute. Yet the Court is unwilling to rest on this foundation, for several reasons. One is an evident unwillingness to define the application of the statute in terms of the ordinary meaning of its language. We are told that "utilize" is "a woolly verb," and therefore we cannot be content to rely on what is described, with varying levels of animus, as a "literal reading" and "a dictionary reading" of this word. We also are told in no uncertain terms that we cannot rely on (what I happen to regard as a more accurate description) "a straightforward reading of 'utilize.'" Reluctance to working with the basic meaning of words in a normal manner undermines the legal process. These cases demonstrate that reluctance of this sort leads instead to woolly judicial construction that mars the plain face of legislative enactments.

The Court concedes that the executive branch "utilizes" the ABA Committee in the common sense of that word. Indeed, this point cannot be contested. As the Court's own recitation of the facts makes clear, the Department of Justice has, over the last four decades, made regular use of the ABA Committee to investigate the background of potential nominees and to make critical recommendations regarding their qualifications. This should end the matter. The Court nevertheless goes through several more steps to conclude that, although "it seems to us a close question," Congress did not intend that FACA would apply to the ABA Committee.

Although I believe the Court's result is quite sensible, I cannot go along with the unhealthy process of amending the statute by judicial interpretation. Where the language of a statute is clear in its application, the normal rule is that we are bound by it. There is, of course, a legitimate exception to this rule, which the Court invokes, and with which I have no quarrel. Where the plain language of the statute would lead to "patently absurd consequences,"[66] that "Congress could not possibly have intended,"[67] we need not apply the language in such a fashion. When used in a proper manner, this narrow exception to our normal rule of statutory construction does not intrude upon the lawmaking powers of Congress, but rather demonstrates a respect for the coequal legislative branch, which we assume would not act in an absurd way.

This exception remains a legitimate tool of the judiciary, however, only as long as the Court acts with self-discipline by limiting the exception to situations where the result of applying the plain language would be, in a genuine sense, absurd, i. e., where it is quite impossible that Congress could have intended the result, and where the alleged absurdity is so clear as to be obvious to most anyone. A few examples of true absurdity are given in the *Holy Trinity* decision cited by the Court, *ante*, such as where a sheriff was prosecuted for obstructing the mails even though he was executing a warrant to arrest the mail carrier for murder, or where a medieval law against drawing blood in the streets was to be applied against a physician who came to the aid of a man who had fallen down in a fit.[68] In today's opinion, however, the Court disregards the plain language of the statute not because its application would be patently absurd, but rather because, on the basis of its view of the legislative history, the Court is "fairly confident" that "FACA should [not] be construed to apply to the ABA Committee." I believe the Court's loose invocation of the "absurd result" canon of statutory construction creates too great a risk that the Court is exercising its own "*Will* instead of *Judgment*," with the consequence of "substituti[ng] [its own] pleasure to that of the legislative body."[69]

The Court makes only a passing effort to show that it would be absurd to apply the term "utilize" to the ABA Committee according to its common-sense meaning. It offers three examples that we can assume are meant to demonstrate this point: the application of FACA to an American Legion Post should the President visit that organization and happen to ask its opinion on some aspect of military policy; the application of FACA to the meetings of the National Association for the Advancement of Colored People (NAACP) should the President seek its views in nominating Commissioners to the Equal Employment Opportunity Commission; and the application of FACA to the national committee of the President's political party should he consult it for advice and recommendations before picking his Cabinet.

None of these examples demonstrate the kind of absurd consequences that would justify departure from the plain language of the statute. A commonsense interpretation of the term "utilize" would not necessarily reach the kind of ad hoc contact with a private group that is contemplated by the Court's American Legion hypothetical. Such an interpretation would be consistent, moreover, with the regulation of the General Services Administration (GSA) interpreting the word "utilize," which the Court in effect ignores.[70] As for the more regular use contemplated by the Court's examples concerning the NAACP and the national committee of the President's political party, it would not be at all absurd to say that, under the Court's hypothetical, these groups would be "utilized" by the President to obtain "advice or recommendations" on appointments, and therefore would fall within the coverage of the statute. Rather, what is troublesome about these examples is that they raise the very same serious constitutional questions that confront us here (and perhaps others as well). The Court confuses the two points. The fact that a particular application of the clear terms of a statute might be unconstitutional does not, in and of itself, render a straightforward application of the language absurd, so as to allow us to conclude that the statute does not apply.

Unable to show that an application of FACA according the plain meaning of its terms would be absurd, the Court turns instead to the task of demonstrating that a straightforward reading of the statute would be inconsistent with the congressional purposes that lay behind its passage. To the student of statutory construction, this move is a familiar one. It is, as the Court identifies it, the classic *Holy Trinity* argument. "[A] thing may be within the letter of the statute and yet not within the statute, because not within its spirit, nor within the intention of its makers."[71] I cannot embrace this principle. Where it is clear that the unambiguous language of a statute embraces certain conduct, and it would not be patently absurd to apply the statute to such conduct, it does not foster a democratic exegesis for this Court to rummage through unauthoritative materials to consult the spirit of the legislation in order to discover an alternative interpretation of the statute with which the Court is more comfortable. It comes as a surprise to no one that the result of the Court's lengthy journey through the legislative history is the discovery of a congressional intent not to include the activities of the ABA Committee within the coverage of FACA. The problem with spirits is that they tend to reflect less the views of the world from whence they come than the views of those who seek their advice.

Lest anyone think that my objection to the use of the *Holy Trinity* doctrine is a mere point of interpretive purity divorced from more practical considerations, I should pause for a moment to recall the unhappy genesis of that doctrine and its unwelcome potential. In *Holy Trinity*, the Court was faced with the interpretation of a statute that made it unlawful for "any person, company, partnership, or corporation, in any manner whatsoever, to prepay the transportation, or in any way assist or encourage the importation or migration of any alien or aliens, any foreigner or foreigners, into the United States . . . , under contract or agreement . . . made previous to the importation or migration of such alien or aliens, foreigner or foreigners, to perform labor or service of any kind in the United States."[72]

The Church of the Holy Trinity entered into a contract with an alien residing in England to come to the United States to serve as the director and pastor of the church. Notwithstanding the fact that this agreement fell within the plain language of the statute, which was conceded to be the case,[73] the Court overrode the plain language, drawing instead on the background and purposes of the statute to conclude that Congress did not intend its broad prohibition to cover the importation of Christian ministers. The central support for the Court's ultimate conclusion that Congress did not intend the law to cover Christian ministers is its lengthy review of the "mass of organic utterances" establishing that "this is a Christian nation," and which were taken to prove that it could not "be believed that a Congress of the United States intended to make it a misdemeanor for a church of this country to contract for the services of a Christian minister residing in another nation."[74] I should think the potential of this doctrine to allow judges to substitute their personal predilections for the will of the Congress is so self-evident from the case that spawned it as to require no further discussion of its susceptibility to abuse.

Even if I were inclined to disregard the unambiguous language of FACA, I could not join the Court's conclusions with regard to Congress's purposes. I find the Court's treatment of the legislative history one-sided and offer a few observations on the difficulties of perceiving the true contours of a spirit.

Another problem with the Court's approach lies in its narrow preoccupation with the ABA Committee against the background of a bill that was intended to provide comprehensive legislation covering a widespread problem in the organization and operation of the federal government. The Court's discussion takes portentous note of the fact that Congress did not mention or discuss the ABA Committee by name in the materials that preceded the enactment of FACA. But that is hardly a remarkable fact. The legislation was passed at a time when somewhere between 1,800 and 3,200 target committees were thought to be in existence, and the congressional reports mentioned few committees by name. More to the point, its argument reflects an incorrect understanding of the kinds of laws Congress passes: it usually does not legislate by specifying examples, but by identifying broad and general principles that must be applied to particular factual instances. And that is true of FACA.

Finally, though the stated objective of the Court's inquiry into legislative history is the identification of Congress's purposes in passing FACA, the inquiry does not focus on the most obvious place for finding those purposes, which is the section of the Conference Committee Report titled "Findings and Purposes." That section lists six findings and purposes that underlie FACA:

(1) the need for many existing advisory committees has not been adequately reviewed;

(2) new advisory committees should be established only when they are determined to be essential and their number should be kept to the minimum necessary;

(3) advisory committees should be terminated when they are no longer carrying out the purposes for which they were established;

(4) standards and uniform procedures should govern the establishment, operation, administration, and duration of advisory committees;
(5) the Congress and the public should be kept informed with respect to the number, purpose, membership, activities, and cost of advisory committees; and
(6) the function of advisory committees should be advisory only, and that all matters under their consideration should be determined, in accordance with law, by the official, agency, or officer involved.

The most pertinent conclusion to be drawn from this list of purposes is that all of them are implicated by the Justice Department's use of the ABA Committee. In addition, it shows that Congress's stated purposes for addressing the use of advisory committees went well beyond the amount of public funds devoted to their operations, which in any event is not the sole component in the cost of their use; thus the Court errs in focusing on this point.

In sum, it is quite desirable not to apply FACA to the ABA Committee. I cannot, however, reach this conclusion as a matter of fair statutory construction. The plain and ordinary meaning of the language passed by Congress governs, and its application does not lead to any absurd results. An unnecessary recourse to the legislative history only confirms this conclusion. And the reasonable and controlling interpretation of the statute adopted by the agency charged with its implementation is also in accord.

The Court's final step is to summon up the traditional principle that statutes should be construed to avoid constitutional questions. Although I agree that we should "first ascertain whether a construction of the statute is fairly possible by which the [constitutional] question may be avoided,"[75] this principle cannot be stretched beyond the point at which such a construction remains "fairly possible." And it should not be given too broad a scope lest a whole new range of government action be proscribed by interpretive shadows cast by constitutional provisions that might or might not invalidate it. The fact that a particular application of the clear terms of a statute might be unconstitutional does not provide us with a justification for ignoring the plain meaning of the statute. If that were permissible, then the power of judicial review of legislation could be made unnecessary, for whenever the application of a statute would have potential inconsistency with the Constitution, we could merely opine that the statute did not cover the conduct in question because it would be discomforting or even absurd to think that Congress intended to act in an unconstitutional manner. The utter circularity of this approach explains why it has never been our rule.

The Court's ultimate interpretation of FACA is never clearly stated, except for the conclusion that the ABA Committee is not covered. It seems to read the "utilized by" portion of the statute as encompassing only a committee "established by a quasi-public organization in receipt of public funds,"[76] or encompassing "groups formed indirectly by quasi-public organizations such as the National Academy of Sciences."[77] This is not a "fairly possible" construction of the statutory language even to a generous reader. I would find the ABA Committee to be covered by FACA. It is therefore necessary for me to reach and decide the constitutional issue presented.

II

Although I disagree with the Court's conclusion that FACA does not cover the Justice Department's use of the ABA Committee, I concur in the judgment of the Court because, in my view, the application of FACA in this context would be a plain violation of the Appointments Clause of the Constitution.

For these reasons, I concur in the judgment affirming the district court.

1. What approach does the majority use?
2. Why did the majority think that FACA did not apply to the committee?
3. What general principle did the court rely upon?
4. Are you convinced by the majority's discussion of the legislative history?
5. Are you convinced by this argument: "That relationship seems not to have been within the contemplation of Executive Order No. 11007 and FACA's legislative history does not display an intent to widen the Order's application to encircle it"?
6. Are you convinced by the majority's reasoning that FACA does not apply to the ABA Committee because this committee did not specifically mention it in the legislative history?
7. What was really bothering the majority?
8. How can the concurrence reject the majority's reasoning but still reach the same outcome?

9. What approach to statutory analysis does the concurrence employ?
10. Why does the concurrence use this approach?
11. What does Justice Kennedy think the majority has done?
12. According to Justice Kennedy, what are the dangers of the majority approach?
13. Why does Justice Kennedy use the term "unauthoritative"?
14. Are there any canons of statutory construction in the opinions? Identify them and discuss them.
15. Does one opinion seem conservative and the other liberal?

CHAPTER WRAP-UP

Why are judges "bound" when they interpret statutes? Which is superior—a statute passed by Congress or a constitutional provision? Why? How are statutes different from case law? Why do judges interpret statutes rather than Congress? What is the most important thing to do when interpreting a statute? Make a chart of the steps you would take in analyzing a statute. Which steps involve rule-based reasoning and which involve reasoning by analogy? Is policy-based reasoning important in statutory analysis? In interpreting statutes, which is usually better to use, *Black's Law Dictionary* or *Webster's*? Why? Are canons of statutory construction a good technique to interpret statutes? Why do judges look to legislative history? What are the best types of legislative history to use in interpreting statutes? How do judges use legislative history? Which approach do you prefer in analyzing a statute—textualism, originalism, or dynamism? Why? What are the advantages of textualism? What are the advantages of originalism? What are the advantages of dynamism? Why do you think that few judges use dynamism? What approach best satisfies the separation of powers doctrine?

Answers
EXERCISE VI-1

1. A lawyer who has formerly represented a client in a matter shall not thereafter represent another person
   A. in the same or a substantially related matter
   B. in which that person's interests are materially adverse to the interests of the former client

C. unless the former client gives informed consent, confirmed in writing.

2. All the elements are conjunctive except 1(a) and (b).

EXERCISE VI-2

1. No, but a smart attorney will do so anyway.
2. To protect the client to avoid misunderstandings.
3. When there is an ongoing relationship and the basis and rate are the same.

EXERCISE VI-3

This is a rule-based reasoning problem. The key to solving this problem is to break the statute into parts and subparts (as I already did earlier in the chapter) and apply each part and subpart to the facts. You also need to determine how the parts fit together.

The main part of the statute is the four fair-use factors. The introduction gives a cross-reference, a general rule, and some examples of fair use. Next, the body gives the four fair-use factors. Finally, there is a clarification at the end of the statute.

Did you look at the cross-reference? (You could have easily done this on the Internet. An engaged learner would have.) If you had looked at the cross-reference, you would have discovered it doesn't affect your analysis here, but other times it might. Next, look at the main rule so that you understand the problem. There is also a list of fair-use examples. The examples help you because the use might be teaching or scholarship and it might also be commentary.

Turning to the four-factor test, are the four factors conjunctive or disjunctive? It says "the factors to be considered," so this is probably a weighing test. Factor one looks at the purpose and character of the use, including whether such use is of a commercial nature or is for nonprofit educational purposes. It is further defined as concerning whether the use is of a commercial nature or is for nonprofit educational purposes. Because our client gave the pamphlet out for free, the use is noncommercial, and it is noncommercial educational use. Accordingly, factor one weighs in our client's favor.

Factor two is the nature of the copyrighted work. The copyrighted work is nonfictional. I know from case law that a nonfictional work receives less copyright protection than a fictional one. (As I said in the problem, I did not expect you to do case law research for this problem. You might have figured out what "nature of the use" meant from a legal encyclopedia or treatise.) Therefore, this factor favors our client's use.

Factor three is the amount and substantiality of the portion used in relation to the copyrighted work as a whole. Amount means raw percentage (from encyclopedia or treatise). Our client used only a paragraph out of a five-hundred-page treatise, which is less than 1 percent. Substantiality refers to the quality of the use—whether the user has taken the essence or heart of the work (encyclopedia or treatise). Although our client's use was verbatim, it is unlikely that a single paragraph from a five-hundred-page book would be the essence or the heart of the original. Accordingly, our client probably wins on this factor.

The final factor is the effect of the use upon the potential market for or value of the copyrighted work. It is unlikely that our client's use will fail either part of this factor. Taking only one paragraph is unlikely to cause potential readers not to buy a five-hundred-page book.

The clarification tells us not to look just at factor one but to weigh all the factors.

All four factors favor our client, so our client probably has a fair-use defense.

EXERCISE VI-4

1. The majority is originalist, while the dissent is textualist.
2. You probably thought that the majority opinion was the correct one because a murderer shouldn't be able to inherit from a person he murdered. However, the correct moral outcome is not always the one dictated by the law. Do you understand why?
3. Although the legislature hadn't spoken on the issue, the court hypothesized that a reasonable legislature could not have intended that a murderer inherit. A little confusing, isn't it?

4. As you can see from my discussion earlier in this chapter, courts and commentators differ as to the role of judges in interpreting statutes. The dissent adopted a narrow view of the judge's role. On the other hand, the majority hypothesized the legislative intent, even though they had nothing to base it on except their own opinions. In this case, they reached what almost everyone would think is the right result, but can you see any problems with doing this in general?

EXERCISE VI-5

1. It adopts an originalist approach. The opinion looks at the purpose behind the statute to help understand whether the ABA Committee is covered by the statute.
2. Congress could not have intended such an absurd result.
3. "[F]requently words of general meaning are used in a statute, words broad enough to include an act in question, and yet a consideration of the whole legislation, or of the circumstances surrounding its enactment, or of the absurd results which follow from giving such broad meaning to the words, makes it unreasonable to believe that the legislator intended to include the particular act." This is stated several different ways throughout the case.
4. Your opinion, but think carefully about this question.
5. Again, this is your opinion, but I am not convinced. Just because an earlier Executive Order meant one thing does not necessarily mean that a later statute must follow that interpretation, especially when convincing evidence is lacking.
6. I'm not. Statutes are usually intended to have broad applicability. The legislative history generally does not mention every possible application of a statute.
7. The fact that if FACA applied to the committee it would require significant procedural requirements for the committee and destroy the confidentiality of the committee's proceedings. Obviously, committee members would be reluctant to give their true opinions of judicial candidates if those opinions could become public.

8. The majority reaches its outcome based on statutory analysis. The concurrence based its opinion on the Constitution—the separation of powers.

9. A textualist approach.

10. Kennedy doesn't consider FACA applying to the ABA Committee to be an absurd result under statutory analysis principles. (He states, "When used in a proper manner, this narrow exception to our normal rule of statutory construction does not intrude upon the lawmaking powers of Congress, but rather demonstrates a respect for the co-equal legislative branch, which we assume would not act in an absurd way.") To preserve the separation of powers built into the Constitution. ("Where it is clear that the unambiguous language of a statute embraces certain conduct, and it would not be patently absurd to apply the statute to such conduct, it does not foster a democratic exegesis for this Court to rummage through unauthoritative materials to consult the spirit of the legislation in order to discover an alternative interpretation of the statute with which the Court is more comfortable.") "Reluctance to working with the basic meaning of words in a normal manner undermines the legal process."

11. Kennedy thinks the majority has amended the statute by "judicial interpretation."

12. "I believe the Court's loose invocation of the 'absurd result' canon of statutory construction creates too great a risk that the Court is exercising its own 'Will instead of Judgment,' with the consequence of 'substituti[ng] [its own] pleasure to that of the legislative body.'" "I should think the potential of this doctrine to allow judges to substitute their personal predilections for the will of the Congress is so self-evident from the case which spawned it as to require no further discussion of its susceptibility to abuse." "The problem with spirits is that they tend to reflect less the views of the world from whence they come than the views of those who seek their advice."

13. Because he considers the legislative history used by the majority to be weak. In addition, he does not view legislative history as law (authority). It was not enacted by Congress or signed by the presidents as statutes are. Like most textualist judges, Justice Kennedy is generally suspicious of using legislative history.

14. Yes, there are several. Majority: "A court should construe a statute so as not to raise a constitutional question." "When the result of the application of a statute is absurd, the court can look beyond the plain meaning of the statute." Concurrence: "Where the language of a statute is clear in its application, the normal rule is that we are bound by it."

    The first canon is questionable because Congress does pass unconstitutional statutes. This is why the power of judicial review exists. As Justice Kennedy declared:

    > The fact that a particular application of the clear terms of a statute might be unconstitutional does not provide us with a justification for ignoring the plain meaning of the statute. If that were permissible, then the power of judicial review of legislation could be made unnecessary, for whenever the application of a statute would have potential inconsistency with the Constitution, we could merely opine that the statute did not cover the conduct in question because it would be discomforting or even absurd to think that Congress intended to act in an unconstitutional manner.

    Regarding the second and third canons, notice that they say the same thing from different viewpoints. In addition, in general, there are so many canons that some are contradictory. In sum, be careful when using canons.

    Habit: Did you read the case with a purpose? As I mentioned in Chapter Two, readers tend to retain more when they read with a purpose.

15. First, you should be careful in using these terms because their meaning has changed over time. Nevertheless, the majority is a liberal opinion because the originalist approach allows courts to interpret statutes broadly. This permits courts to "do justice." Kennedy's opinion is a conservative one because it doesn't allow courts much leeway to broaden statutes. Textualists argue that their approach is better because it allows the public to better understand the law and because it gives stability and certainty to the law. They also believe that it better respects the legislative function (separation of powers).

NOTES

1. Karen M. Gebbia-Pinetti, *Statutory Interpretation: Democratic Legitimacy and Legal System Values*, 21 SEATON HALL LEGIS. J. 233, 267 (1997); Carlos E. Gonzàlez, *Reinterpreting Statutory Interpretation*, 74 N.C. L. REV. 585, 594 (1996). *See generally* R. Randall Kelsom, *Statutory Interpretation Doctrine on the Modern Supreme Court and Four-Doctrinal Approaches to Judicial Decision-making*, 25 PEPPERDINE L. REV. 37 (2012); Nancy Staudt, Lee Epstein, Peter Wiedenbeck & Rene Lindstadt, *Judging Statutes: Interpretive Regimes*, 38 LOY. L. Rev. 1909 (2005). Many American textualists, including Justice Scalia, also examine related provisions of the same text and look for unity in the legal world. *See* Green v. Bock Laundry Machine Co., 490 U.S. 504, 528 (1989) (Scalia, J., concurring); United Savings Ass'n v. Timbers of Inwood Forest, 484 U.S. 365, 371 (1988); *see also* William N. Eskridge, Jr., *The New Textualism*, 37 UCLA L. REV. 621, 660–63 (1990) [hereinafter Eskridge, *The New Textualism*]. For a more detailed discussion of the three approaches to statutory interpretation, see my article *Pragmatic Textualism and the Limits of Statutory Interpretation*, 35 WAKE FOREST L. REV. 973 (2000).

2. Gebbia-Pinetti, *supra* note 1, at 272.

3. ANTONIN SCALIA, A MATTER OF INTERPRETATION: FEDERAL COURTS AND THE LAW 25 (Princeton Univ. Pr. 1997); *see also* U.S. CONST. art I, §§ 1, 7.

4. SCALIA, *supra* note 3, at 17. He believes that "[g]overnment by unexpressed intent . . . is tyrannical." *Id.*

5. *Id.* at 17–18; Public Citizen v. U.S. Dep't of Justice, 491 U.S. 440, 471–73 (1989) (Kennedy, J., concurring) ("The problem with spirits is that they tend to reflect less the views of the world from whence they come than the views of those who seek their advice." *Id.* at 473).

6. SCALIA, *supra* note 3, at 18.

7. Gebbia-Pinetti, *supra* note 1, at 279; *see also* Martin H. Redish & Theodore T. Chung, *Democratic Theory and the Legislative Process*, 68 TUL. L. REV. 803, 821–22 (1994).

8. Antonin Scalia, *The Rule of Law as a Law of Rules*, 56 U. CHI. L. REV. 1125 (1989); Redish & Chung, *supra* note 7, at 822.

9. Chisom v. Roemer, 501 U.S. 380, 404 (1991) (Scalia, J., dissenting).

10. Eskridge, *The New Textualism*, *supra* note 1, at 623.

11. *Id.* at 623–24.

12. Gebbia-Pinetti, *supra* note 1, at 280; *see also* HENRY M. HART, JR. & ALBERT M. SACKS, THE LEGAL PROCESS: BASIC PROBLEMS IN THE MAKING AND APPLICATION OF LAW xiii (William N. Eskridge, Jr. & Philip P. Frickey eds., 1994).

13. Gebbia-Pinetti, *supra* note 1, at 281; *see also* Redish & Chung, *supra* note 7, at 812–17.

14. Gebbia-Pinetti, *supra* note 1, at 281–82; *see also* Edward O. Correia, *A Legislative Conception of Legislative Supremacy*, 42 CASE W. RES. L. REV. 1129 (1992); Earl M. Maltz, *Statutory Interpretation and Legislative Power: The Case for a Modified Intentionalist Approach*, 63 TUL. L. REV. 1 (1988) (modified version of intentionalism); JAMES WILLIARD HURST, DEALING WITH STATUTES 32 (1982).

15. Gebbia-Pinetti, *supra* note 1, at 282.

16. Richard A. Posner, *Legal Formalism, Legal Realism, and the Interpretation of Statutes and the Constitution*, 37 CASE W. RES. L. REV. 179, 190 (1986–87).

17. Redish & Chung, *supra* note 7, at 813–14. Judge Posner calls the hypothetical approach "imaginative reconstruction." Richard A. Posner, *Statutory Interpretation—in the Classroom and in the Courtroom*, 50 U. CHI. L. REV. 800, 817 (1983).

18. Gebbia-Pinetti, *supra* note 1, at 283; *see also* Redish & Chung, *supra* note 7, at 815–16; HART & SACHS, *supra* note 12, at 1374–80.

19. Rector of Holy Trinity Church v. United States, 143 U.S. 457, 459 (1892).

20. *Public Citizen*, 491 U.S. at 455 (citations omitted).

21. Borella v. Borden Co., 145 F.2d 63, 64–65 (2d Cir. 1944), *aff'd*, 325 U.S. 679 (1945). Obviously, there is a strong similarity between purposivism and hypothetical originalism.

22. Gebbia-Pinetti, *supra* note 1, at 288.

23. *Id.* at 289.

24. *Id.* at 291. On dynamism, *see generally* WILLIAM N. ESKRIDGE, JR., DYNAMIC STATUTORY INTERPRETATION (Harvard Univ. Pr. 1996); GUIDO CALABRESI, A COMMON LAW FOR THE AGE OF STATUTES (Law Book Exchange Ltd. 1982); and the works by Professors Eskridge, Frickey, Dworkin, and Aleinikoff cited *infra*.

25. Gebbia-Pinetti, *supra* note 1, at 291–302; *see also* William N. Eskridge & Philip P. Frickey, *Statutory Interpretation as Practical Reasoning*, 42 STAN. L. REV. 321, 345 (1990) ("Statutory interpretation includes creative policy making by judges ...") [hereinafter Eskridge & Frickey, *Practical Reasoning*]; T. Alexander Aleinikoff, *Updating Statutory Interpretation*, 87 MICH. L. REV. 20, 21 (1988).

26. Gebbia-Pinetti, *supra* note 1, at 297; *see also* Eskridge & Frickey, *Practical Reasoning*, *supra* note 25, at 321.

27. Eskridge & Frickey, *Practical Reasoning*, *supra* note 25, at 321–22.

28. WILLIAM N. ESKRIDGE, JR. & PHILIP P. FRICKEY, CASES AND MATERIALS ON LEGISLATION: STATUTES AND THE CREATION OF PUBLIC POLICY 604 (2d ed. 1995).

29. RONALD DWORKIN, LAW'S EMPIRE 313 (Belknap 1986).

30. *Id.* at 313–14.

31. Gebbia-Pinetti, *supra* note 1, at 303.

32. *Id.*; *see also* Jane S. Schacter, *Metademocracy: The Changing Structure of Legitimacy in Statutory Interpretation*, 108 HARV. L. REV. 593 (1995) ("[T]he metademocratic axis arranges interpretative rules based not on demonstrated fealty to legislative design, but instead on the ability to resolve statutory ambiguity and, at the same time, to advance a long-term project of democratic structure." *Id.* at 596).

33. Redish & Chung, *supra* note 7, at 841.

34. 86 Stat. 770, *as amended*, 5 U.S.C. App. § 1 et seq. (1982 ed. and Supp. V).

35. Art. II, § 2, cl. 2.

36. § 2(a), as set forth in 5 U.S.C. App. § 2(a).

37. § 2(b).

38. § 9(c),

39. § 10(c).

40. § 10(e).

41. 5 U.S.C. § 552b(c). § 10(d).

42. *See* 5 U.S.C. § 552.

43. § 10(b).

44. §§ 5(b)(2), (c)

45. § 14(a)(1).

46. 143 U.S. 457, 459 (1892).

47. 490 U.S. 504, 509 (1989).

48. *See also, e.g.,* Church of the Holy Trinity, *supra*, at 472; FDIC v. Philadelphia Gear Corp., 476 U.S. 426, 432 (1986).

49. Watt v. Alaska, 451 U.S. 259, 266 (1981).

50. Cabell v. Markham, 148 F.2d 737, 739 (CA2), *aff'd*, 326 U.S. 404 (1945).

51. Boston Sand & Gravel Co. v. United States, 278 U.S. 41, 48 (1928) (Holmes, J.). *See also* United States v. American Trucking Ass'ns, Inc., 310 U.S. 534, 543–44 (1940) ("When aid to construction of the meaning of words, as used in the statute,

is available, there certainly can be no 'rule of law' which forbids its use, however clear the words may appear on 'superficial examination.'").

52. *See* Note, *The Federal Advisory Committee Act*, 10 HARV. J. LEGIS. 217, 219–21 (1973).

53. H.R. 4383, 92d Cong., 2d Sess. § 3(2) (1972).

54. S.B. 3529, 92d Cong., 2d Sess. §§ 3(1), (2) (1972).

55. 285 U.S. 22, 62 (1932).

56. Edward J. DeBartolo Corp. v. Fla. Gulf Coast Bldg. & Constr. Trades Council, 485 U.S. 568, 575 (1988).

57. Edward J. DeBartolo Corp., *supra*, at 575.

58. *See* Am. Foreign Serv. Ass'n v. Garfinkel, 490 U.S. 153, 161 (1989) (per curiam).

59. United States v. Locke, 471 U.S. 84, 96 (1985), *quoting* Moore Ice Cream Co. v. Rose, 289 U.S. 373, 379 (1933).

60. 471 U.S. at 96.

61. C. Pinckney, Observations on the Plan of Government Submitted to the Federal Convention of May 28, 1787.

62. *See, e.g.*, THE FEDERALIST Nos. 47–51 (J. Madison).

63. Youngstown Sheet & Tube Co. v. Sawyer, 343 U.S. 579, 594 (1952) (concurring opinion).

64. 5 U.S.C. App. § 3(2).

65. *Ante*, at 452.

66. United States v. Brown, 333 U.S. 18, 27 (1948).

67. FBI v. Abramson, 456 U.S. 615, 640 (1982) (O'Connor, J., dissenting) (emphasis added).

68. *See* 143 U.S. at 460–61.

69. THE FEDERALIST No. 78, p. 469 (C. Rossiter ed., 1961) (A. Hamilton).

70. *See infra*, at 477.

71. *Holy Trinity, supra*, at 459.

72. 143 U.S. at 458.

73. *See id.*

74. *Id.* at 471.

75. Crowell v. Benson, 285 U.S. 22, 62 (1932).

76. *Ante*, at 460.

77. *Ante*, at 462.

CHAPTER SEVEN

WRITING A SIMPLE ANALYSIS: THE SMALL-SCALE PARADIGM

CHAPTER GOALS

1. To help the reader understand how to organize a simple analysis (the small-scale paradigm).
2. To show the reader how the legal reasoning mini-skills (rule-based reasoning, analogical reasoning, distinguishing cases, and synthesis) apply to the small-scale paradigm.
3. To help the reader spot gaps in legal arguments.

The five types of legal reasoning I have been discussing throughout this book come together when you write your analysis. Legal reasoning and legal writing are inseparable.[1] Legal writing is not just a translation of a legal analysis, but the analysis itself. This chapter will discuss the small-scale paradigm and demonstrate how the different types of legal reasoning work within that paradigm.

By small-scale organizational paradigm, I mean the basic unit of organization for argument and discussion sections. First, however, you need to create the large- and medium-scale organization of your argument or discussion section. In doing this, you first organize by issue and then usually organize each issue by the law. You should break the law (the rule) into parts, then organize sub-issues and sub-sub-issues by the parts.

EXAMPLE

Assume you are outlining an argument section concerning intentional infliction of emotional harm. The four parts of this tort are (a) the defendant's acts were outrageous, (b) the defendant's acts were intentional, and (c) the defendant's acts caused (d) the plaintiff extreme emotional distress. These four parts serve as the main headings. Then subdivide further based on subdivisions in the law.

I.   The defendant's conduct was outrageous.
II. The defendant's conduct was intentional.
III. The defendant's conduct caused—
    A. Cause in fact
    B. Proximate cause
IV. Severe emotional distress
    A. Duration
    B. Intensity

Next, modify the outline based on what is actually at issue based on your facts. You will remove some headings and subheadings, and you may add some.

I.   The defendant's conduct was outrageous.
    A. Factual ground A
    B. Factual ground B
II. The defendant's conduct caused—
III. Severe emotional distress
    A. Duration
    B. Intensity

I deleted "The defendant's conduct was intentional" because it was not at issue in my hypothetical. I eliminated the subdivisions under causation because proximate cause is not at issue.

I. THE SMALL-SCALE PARADIGM

When the rule cannot be broken down further, the writer should use the small-scale paradigm to organize the sections and subsections. My small-scale paradigm is as follows:[2]

1. Conclusion
2. Law
   A. Rule
   B. Rule Explanation
   C. Rule Illustration(s)
3. Application:
   A. Apply the Principles (Rule Application)
   B. Case Comparison(s)

I begin with a one-sentence conclusion for clarity. The reader needs to know at the beginning what the conclusion of the argument is. For example, a conclusion might be "the defendant established minimum contacts with Alabama because it was foreseeable that he would be sued in Alabama, since he caused injury to an Alabama resident in Alabama." The rest of the small-scale paradigm then backs up that conclusion using the five types of legal reasoning.

The law section should begin with a clear statement of the rule (usually one sentence). This is important for clarity. In addition, since, as discussed in earlier chapters, rule-based reasoning is the most important type of legal reasoning, the law section should start with the rule. As mentioned in Chapter Five, the writer must synthesize (inductive reasoning) the rule from all the relevant cases and other legal material, unless a case has already done the synthesis. Even if a case has already done the synthesis, the writer must ascertain that later cases have not changed the rule.

The rule explanation explains the rule, expands on the rule, and gives the policy behind the rule. It usually proceeds from the general to the specific, going from a general explanation of the rule to a specific explanation of the law as it applies to the facts of the writer's case. This is a very important section because the meaning of the rule will usually not be clear from just the statement of the rule. For example, assume the rule for this subsection is that "to establish minimum contacts with a state, it must be foreseeable that the defendant will be sued in that state." What does "foreseeable" mean? The writer must help the reader understand the rule by taking material from a variety of cases. In other words, the rule explanation is an important part of the synthesis; there is more to case synthesis than just synthesizing the rule. The rule explanation is also important because it can discuss the policy behind the rule.

A rule illustration uses one or more cases to show how the rule works in a factual context, and it helps set up the case comparison(s) in the application. The case or cases for the rule illustration should usually be as close as possible to the facts of the main case. In the first sentence of the rule illustration, the writer should tell the reader why the case is being cited. In other words, the writer should start with the holding, focusing on the sub-topic of the section. Then the writer should give the facts and reasoning of the case, again focusing on the topic of the subsection, and leaving out anything that is irrelevant. Whether the writer uses one rule illustration or two or three depends on the complexity of the sub-issue and how good the cases are. However, having at least two rule illustrations allows for both reasoning by analogy and distinguishing cases.

After having fully presented the law, the writer should apply the law to the facts *in detail*. In other words, the writer should show how the facts fit into the above law. The writer should start by applying the principles and save the case comparisons for last. The purpose of case comparisons is to strengthen the analysis, not substitute for the analysis.

Pointer: When you write, mark the sections of the small-scale paradigm with different colored marking pens.

The above small-scale paradigm uses all five types of legal reasoning. The framework for the paradigm is rule-based reasoning. It presents the rule and explains the rule, then applies the rule in detail in the first half of the application section. (See Chapter Four.) The rule illustration section and the case comparison portion of the application section supply reasoning by analogy and distinguishing cases. (See Chapters Three and Eight.) The rule illustration section and the case comparison section come after the rule and rule explanation and the application of principles because their purpose is to reinforce the rule-based reasoning. Policy can be placed in the rule explanation and/or the rule illustrations, and then applied in the application of principles and the case comparison parts of the application section. It also reinforces the rule-based reasoning arguments.

As noted above, the small-scale paradigm provides a true synthesis of the law. The rule is synthesized from all relevant cases. The rule explanation is also a synthesis of all relevant cases. The first part of the application then applies the synthesized law to the facts. Thus, the paradigm does more than compare cases (it gives more than pieces of the law); it provides all the law, with the case comparisons providing the most relevant highlights.

In conclusion, a well-designed small-scale paradigm can help students and lawyers employ all five types of legal reasoning. While this author's small-scale paradigm is not the only way to do this, it incorporates all five types of legal reasoning: rule-based reasoning, reasoning by analogy, distinguishing cases, policy-based reasoning, and inductive reasoning, while emphasizing the most important type of legal reasoning—rule-based reasoning.

Pointer: You have two purposes when you write a legal document: to educate and convince. Always keep these purposes in mind when you are writing. Teach your reader your analysis or argument; convince your reader that your analysis or argument is correct.

EXAMPLE OF SMALL-SCALE PARADIGM
Introduction
One of the factors that the Supreme Court looks at when evaluating the use under fair use is whether its purpose and character are transformative. I will evaluate this sub-factor using the small-scale paradigm based on the following facts: Mary loves the television show *Bold*. In fact, she loves the show so much that she put up a website about the show on the Internet. The show's copyright holder sued her for copyright infringement. She wants to use a fair-use defense. Mary's website contains her drawings of the show, discussions of the characters, discussions of the show's themes, and biographies of the show's stars.

EXAMPLE
Mary's website is transformative of the show *Bold* because it presents the show's material in a new form. [←conclusion] [rule→] A use

is transformative if it adds something new to the original with a further purpose or different character, altering the original with new expression, meaning, or message.[3] [←rule] [rule explanation→] In other words, the new work should not merely supersede the objects of the original.[4] As one court has stated, "Rather than making some contribution of new intellectual value and thereby fostering the advancement of the arts and sciences, an untransformed copy is likely to be used simply for the same intrinsic purpose as the original, thereby providing limited justification for a finding of fair use."[5] Transformative works lie at "the heart of the fair use doctrine's guarantee of breathing space within the confines of copyright" because they further the goal of copyright—to promote science and the arts.[6] On the other hand, an untransformed use usually has the same intrinsic purpose as the original, limiting any justification for fair use.[7] [←rule explanation]

[first rule illustration→] In *Warner Bros. Entertainment, Inc. v. RDR Books*,[8] a court held a Harry Potter lexicon to be transformative because it served as a reference work.[9] The author's purpose in writing the book was "to create an encyclopedia that collected and organized information from the Harry Potter books in one central source for fans to use for reference."[10] In analyzing the lexicon, the court stated, "Presumably, Rowling created the Harry Potter series for the express purpose of telling an entertaining and thought-provoking story centered on the character Harry Potter and set in a magical world. The Lexicon, on the other hand, uses material from the series for the practical purpose of making information about the intricate world of Harry Potter readily accessible to readers in a reference guide."[11] The court concluded, "Because it serves these reference purposes, rather than the entertainment or aesthetic purposes of the original works, the Lexicon's use is transformative and does not supplant the objects of the Harry Potter works."[12]

[second rule illustration→] In contrast, in *American Geophysical*,[13] the court held that photocopying articles for laboratory use was not transformative. In this case, Texaco had photocopied magazine articles from journals it had subscribed to so they would be in a more usable format for the laboratory. The court noted that when, as in this case, the secondary use is merely an untransformed duplication, the value generated by this use is little more than the value of the original.[14] Thus, "Texaco's photocopying merely transforms the material object embodying the intangible article that is the copyrighted original work."[15]

[application, applying the rule➜] Mary's website is transformative because it adds something new to the original in that it includes her drawings of the show, discussions of the characters, a discussion of the show's themes, and biographies of the show's stars, all of which alter the original with new expression and meaning. It has a different purpose than the original. *Bold*'s purpose is entertainment, while Mary's website is informative. The website does not supersede the original; rather, it helps explain the show. Because it adds to the original, the website satisfies the purpose of copyright in advancing the arts and the sciences.

[first case comparison➜] Mary's website is transformative because it serves as a reference work, like the Harry Potter lexicon in *Warner Bros.* Its purpose is to make information about *Bold* available to the public. It contains Mary's drawings, her discussion of the characters, her discussion of the show's themes, and her biographies of the actors, similar to the material in the lexicon. Also like the lexicon, the website lacks the entertainment or aesthetic value of the original. Consequently, Mary's website is transformative, just like the Harry Potter lexicon.

[second case comparison➜] In contrast, Mary's website is not like the copying in *American Geophysical* because it is much more than the photocopying in that case. Unlike the use of untransformed copying in *American Geophysical*, Mary's website adds value to the original with its own original material. Because of the original material, it does much more than embody the original intangible article, which was found not to be transformed in *American Geophysical*.

Comments

1. Notice how I began the paradigm with a clear statement of the conclusion. Isn't it clearer if the writer starts the analysis with the conclusion, rather than the issue or the law?
2. Notice that I gave a clear presentation of the rule as the second sentence. An analysis is easier to understand if you start with the rule, then explain what it means.

3. Do you see how having both a rule explanation and a rule illustration helps the reader understand the law better?
4. Do you see how having two rule illustrations helps your reader understand the law better and how the law applies to your case?
5. Can you label the parts of the rule illustrations and case comparisons? (If you are having problems doing this, look again at Chapter Three.)
6. Look at the topic sentences of the paragraphs. Do they fulfill their functions as topic sentences?
7. Look to see if each paragraph is well organized.

COMMON PROBLEMS WITH THE SMALL-SCALE PARADIGM

- The conclusion is not clearly stated at the beginning.
- The writer starts to apply the facts before discussing the law. After the one-sentence conclusion, you should start the rule section.
- The rule section does not begin with a clear rule.
- The rule explanation is too general. Part of the rule explanation should explain the rule as it specifically applies to the facts.
- The writer has not fully explained the rule. Use syllogistic reasoning and make sure there are no gaps.
- The rule explanation does not synthesize the reasoning from the relevant cases.
- The cases used in the rule illustration are not close to the facts in your case.
- The rule illustration includes irrelevant material (not on issue).
- The rule illustration does not start with the case holding.
- The case holding does not emphasize the topic of the section.
- The rule illustration does not follow the model given in Chapter Three (holding—facts—reasoning).
- The rule application does not apply the law from the rule and rule explanation. Apply the law to the facts in detail.
- The case comparisons do not follow the model given in Chapter Three (sentence that presents the comparison—comparison of facts/comparison of reasoning—conclusion and relation to case).
- The case comparisons are not in detail.

- The case comparisons include comparisons that are not relevant to the issue.

II. LOOKING FOR GAPS IN THE SMALL-SCALE PARADIGM

In Chapter Four, I discussed checking for gaps in your logical reasoning. You also need to make sure there are no gaps in the sections or subsections of your small-scale paradigm. Gaps in your arguments create an opening for your opponent.

EXERCISE VII-1

Are there any gaps in the following arguments?

1. The plaintiff, a citizen of Ohio, has established personal jurisdiction over the defendant in Ohio, based on the defendant's act in Indiana that created harm in Ohio. A state has personal jurisdiction over an out-of-state defendant when that defendant establishes minimum contacts with the forum.[16] In *Dudley v. Helmut,* the court held that when a person shoots a bullet in one state at a person in another state and that other person is harmed, the state where the harm occurred has personal jurisdiction over the defendant. In that case, a wrongful death action, the defendant, who had never been in Kentucky, shot a bullet from Tennessee at the plaintiff's decedent. The court reasoned that causing harm in a state satisfied the requirement of minimum contacts because the shooting affected a person in the forum.[17] The court declared, "A defendant should not be able to avoid this court's jurisdiction when a citizen of this state is harmed by an act that partially occurred in a different state."[18] This is like a contract that was substantially performed in two states; both states would have jurisdiction over the defendant.[19]

   The Ohio court has personal jurisdiction over the Indiana defendant in this case because the defendant's act of posting defamatory information on the Internet from her Indiana home was intended to harm the plaintiff in Ohio. Although the defendant has never visited Ohio, she admits that her defamation was intentional. She has stated, "That guy will not make a fool out of me. I will ruin his life. He can run, but he can't hide." Consequently, the defendant has established minimum contacts with Ohio.

This case is like *Dudley*. In *Dudley*, the defendant shot a bullet from one state to another, harming the plaintiff; in this case, the defendant shot a defamation from Indiana to Ohio, injuring the plaintiff. Just like in *Dudley*, harm occurred to a citizen of the forum. Since the tort was performed in two states, both states should have jurisdiction over the defendant, just like *Dudley* and the case it relied upon.

2.   The plaintiff, a citizen of Ohio, has established personal jurisdiction over the defendant in Ohio, based on the defendant's act in Indiana that created harm in Ohio. A state has personal jurisdiction over an out-of-state defendant when that defendant establishes minimum contacts with the forum.[20] An act in one state that causes harm in the forum establishes minimum contacts.[21] In *Dudley v. Helmut*, the court held that when a person shoots a bullet in one state at a person in another state and that other person is harmed, the state where the harm occurred has personal jurisdiction over the defendant. In that case, the defendant, who had never been in Kentucky, shot a bullet from Tennessee at the plaintiff's decedent in a wrongful death action. The court reasoned that causing harm in a state satisfied the requirement of minimum contacts because the shooting affected a person in the forum.[22] The court declared, "A defendant should not be able to avoid this court's jurisdiction when a citizen of this state is harmed by an act that partially occurred in a different state."[23] This is like a contract that was substantially performed in two states; both states would have jurisdiction over the defendant.[24]

The Ohio court has personal jurisdiction over the Indiana defendant in this case because the defendant's act of posting defamatory information on the Internet from her Indiana home was intended to harm the plaintiff in Ohio. Although the defendant has never visited Ohio, she admits that her defamation was intentional. She has stated, "That guy will not make a fool out of me. I will ruin his life. He can run, but he can't hide." Consequently, the defendant has established minimum contacts with Ohio.

3.   Mary's website is transformative of the show *Bold* because it presents the show's material in a new form. A use is transformative if it

adds something new to the original with a further purpose or different character, altering the original with new expression, meaning, or message.[25] In other words, the new work should not merely supersede the objects of the original.[26] As one court has stated, "Rather than making some contribution of new intellectual value and thereby fostering the advancement of the arts and sciences, an untransformed copy is likely to be used simply for the same intrinsic purpose as the original, thereby providing limited justification for a finding of fair use."[27] Transformative works lie at "the heart of the fair use doctrine's guarantee of breathing space within the confines of copyright" because they further the goal of copyright—to promote science and the arts.[28] On the other hand, an untransformed use usually has the same intrinsic purpose as the original, limiting any justification for fair use.[29]

In *Warner Bros. Entertainment, Inc. v. RDR Books*,[30] a court held a Harry Potter lexicon to be transformative because it served as a reference work. The author's purpose in writing the book was "to create an encyclopedia that collected and organized information from the Harry Potter books in one central source for fans to use for reference."[31] In analyzing the lexicon, the court stated, "Presumably, Rowling created the Harry Potter series for the express purpose of telling an entertaining and thought-provoking story centered on the character Harry Potter and set in a magical world. The Lexicon, on the other hand, uses material from the series for the practical purpose of making information about the intricate world of Harry Potter readily accessible to readers in a reference guide."[32] The court concluded, "Because it serves these reference purposes, rather than the entertainment or aesthetic purposes of the original works, the lexicon's use is transformative and does not supplant the objects of the Harry Potter works."[33]

In contrast, in *American Geophysical*,[34] the court held that photocopying articles for laboratory use was not transformative. In this case, Texaco had photocopied magazine articles from journals it had subscribed to so they would be in a more usable format for the laboratory. The court noted that when, as in this case, the secondary use is merely an untransformed duplication, the value generated by this use is little more than the value of the original.[35] Thus, "Texaco's photocopying merely transforms the material object embodying the intangible article that is the copyrighted original work."[36]

Mary's website is transformative because it adds something new to the original—drawings of the show, discussions of the characters, a discussion of the show's themes, and biographies of the show's stars, all of which alter the original with new expression and meaning. It has a different purpose than the original. *Bold*'s purpose is entertainment, while Mary's website is informative. It does not supersede the original; rather, it helps explains the show. Because it adds to the original, the website satisfies the purpose of copyright in advancing the arts and sciences.

Mary's website is transformative because it serves as a reference work, like the Harry Potter lexicon in *Warner Bros*. Its purpose is to make information about the show available to the public. It contains Mary's drawings, her discussion of the characters, her discussion of the show's themes, and her biographies of the actors, similar to the material in the lexicon. Also like the lexicon, the website lacks the entertainment or aesthetic value of the original. Consequently, Mary's website is transformative, just like the Harry Potter lexicon.

4. The plaintiff, a citizen of Ohio, has established personal jurisdiction over the defendant in Ohio, based on the defendant's act in Indiana that created harm in Ohio. A state has personal jurisdiction over an out-of-state defendant when that defendant establishes minimum contacts with the forum.[37] An act in one state that causes harm in the forum establishes minimum contacts.[38] This is because a tort can consist of several steps that have connections with more than one state.[39] For example, a fraudulent act may occur in one state but cause damages in another.[40]

In *Dudley v. Helmut*, the court held that when a person shoots a bullet in one state at a person in another state and that other person is harmed, the state where the harm occurred has personal jurisdiction over the defendant. In that case, the defendant, who had never been in Kentucky, shot a bullet from Tennessee at the plaintiff's decedent in a wrongful death action. The court reasoned that causing harm in a state satisfied the requirement of minimum contacts because the shooting affected a person in the forum.[41] The court declared, "A defendant should not be able to avoid this court's jurisdiction when a citizen of this state is harmed by an act that partially occurred in a different state."[42] This is like a contract that was substantially performed in two states; both states would have jurisdiction over the defendant.[43]

The Ohio court has personal jurisdiction over the Indiana defendant in this case because the defendant's act of posting defamatory information on the Internet from her Indiana home was intended to harm, and it did harm, a plaintiff in Ohio. Although the defendant has never visited Ohio, she admits that her defamation was intentional. She has stated, "That guy will not make a fool out of me. I will ruin his life. He can run, but he can't hide." Defamation is a multipart tort that can occur in more than one state. This is like a fraudulent act that occurs in one state but causes damages in another . Consequently, the defendant has established minimum contacts with Ohio.

This case is like *Dudley*. In *Dudley*, the defendant shot a bullet from one state to another, harming the plaintiff; in this case, the defendant shot a defamation from Indiana to Ohio, injuring the plaintiff. Just like in *Dudley*, harm occurred to a citizen of the forum. Since the tort was performed in two states, both states should have jurisdiction over the defendant, just like *Dudley* and the case it relied upon.

5. The plaintiff, a citizen of Ohio, has established personal jurisdiction over the defendant in Ohio, based on the defendant's act in Indiana that created harm in Ohio. A state has personal jurisdiction over an out-of-state defendant when that defendant establishes minimum contacts with the forum.[44] An act in one state that causes harm in the forum establishes minimum contacts.[45] This is because a tort can consist of several steps that have connections with more than one state.[46] For example, a fraudulent act may occur in one state but cause damages in another.[47]

In *Dudley v. Helmut*, the court held that when a person shoots a bullet in one state at a person in another state and that other person is harmed, the state where the harm occurred has personal jurisdiction over the defendant. In this case, the defendant, who had never been in Kentucky, shot a bullet from Tennessee at the plaintiff's decedent in a wrongful death action. The court reasoned that causing harm in a state satisfied the requirement of minimum contacts because the shooting affected a person in the forum.[48] The court declared, "A defendant should not be able to avoid this court's jurisdiction when a citizen of this state is harmed by an act that partially occurred in a different state."[49] This is like a contract that was substantially performed in two states; both states would have jurisdiction over the defendant.[50]

The Ohio court has personal jurisdiction over the Indiana defendant in this case because the defendant's act of posting defamatory information on the Internet from her Indiana home was intended to harm, and it did harm, a plaintiff in Ohio. Also, the fact that the defendant vacationed in Ohio two summers ago helps establish jurisdiction over her. Why should she be able to enjoy the benefits of Ohio state parks but not be subject to its jurisdiction? Finally, both her kids go to Ohio State. It would be crazy to allow her kids to enjoy the benefits of attending an Ohio public school but not subject her to Ohio's jurisdiction. Consequently, Ohio has personal jurisdiction over the defendant.

This case is like *Dudley*. In *Dudley*, the defendant shot a bullet from one state to another, harming the plaintiff; in this case, the defendant shot a defamation from Indiana to Ohio, injuring the plaintiff. Just like in *Dudley*, harm occurred to a citizen of the forum. Since the tort was performed in two states, both states should have jurisdiction over the defendant, just like *Dudley* and the case it relied upon.

CHAPTER WRAP-UP

Labeling the sections of the small-scale paradigm, like I did in the example earlier in this chapter, in your writing will help you determine whether you are using the sections correctly. Organization is important on all levels, from the large-scale level down to the sentence level. **Habit:** Make sure your writing is organized to help your reader understand it. Why is it important to use a small-scale paradigm similar to the one in this chapter? Why is it important to present the law before the application? Why is it important to present the rule application before the case comparisons? Why is it important to mine cases (see Chapter Two)? Develop the habit of checking your arguments for gaps in the reasoning!

Answers
EXERCISE VII-1

1. There is no rule explanation. Having a rule illustration is not enough. As mentioned earlier, reasoning by analogy alone can be weak because it is based on similarities of degree. A rule explanation and a rule illustration with corresponding rule application and case comparison makes for a much stronger argument. Moreover, your reader will probably not understand the law without a rule explanation. Finally, using only a rule illustration or two makes it look like you are selectively citing the law.

2. There are two problems here. The easy one is that there is no case comparison. The harder one is that the rule explanation is only one sentence. "Minimum contacts" requires much more explanation than one sentence. Similarly, it is difficult to apply the law to the facts in detail when you have so little law.

    Habit: You should always fully educate your reader in the law that applies to your facts.

3. The writer left out the second case comparison. This is no need for a rule illustration that is not compared to your facts.

4. The rule explanation here is much better than in 2. However, the writer has relied on only one case for the rule and the rule explanation, which looks bad. While it is possible that one case will supply everything you need for the law section, this occurs only in rare instances.

5. The problem here is with the rule application. Except for the first sentence, the rule application does not correspond to the law in the law section. This is a problem I see a great deal in student papers, although usually not this egregiously. Not only do the extra facts serve as mere filler, it seems like the writer is making up the law. If vacationing in a state establishes jurisdiction over a person on an unrelated matter, then the law should be included in the law section. The same is true about the defendant's kids going to Ohio State.

NOTES

1. As Professors Rideout and Ramsfield have stated, "The act of writing is intimately involved with the act of construing the law—describing and synthesizing the applicable law, applying legal rules, drawing analogies and distinguishing facts, and developing legal arguments." J. Christopher Rideout & Jill J. Ramsfield, *Legal Writing: A Revised View*, 69 WASH. L. REV. 35, 55 (1994). Likewise, BEST PRACTICES has stated, "After all, it does no good to teach a student to think like a lawyer if the student cannot convey that thinking in writing." ROY STUCKEY ET AL., BEST PRACTICES IN LEGAL EDUCATION 149 (Clinical Legal Educ. Ass'n 2007).

2. I have synthesized this paradigm from a number of sources, including RICHARD K. NEUMANN, JR., LEGAL REASONING AND LEGAL WRITING: STRUCTURE, STRATEGY, AND STYLE 97–143 (Aspen Pub., 5th ed. 2005); HELENE S. SHAPO, MARILYN R. WALTER & ELIZABETH FAJANS, WRITING AND ANALYSIS IN THE LAW 113–29 (Foundation Pr. Rev. 4th ed. 2003); and LINDA EDWARDS, LEGAL WRITING AND ANALYSIS 89–108 (Little, Brown & Co. 2003).

3. Campbell v. Acuff-Rose, 510 U.S. 569, 579 (1994); *see also* Blanch v. Koons, 467 F.3d 244, 251–52 (2d Cir. 2006) (Does the secondary use add value to the original?); Am. Geophysical Union v. Texaco, Inc., 60 F.3d 913, 923 (2d Cir. 1994) ("The 'transformative use' concept is pertinent to a court's investigation under the first factor because it assesses the value generated by the secondary use and the means by which such value is generated.").

4. *Campbell*, 510 U.S. at 579.

5. *Am. Geophysical*, 60 F.3d at 923.

6. *Campbell*, 510 U.S. at 579.

7. *Am. Geophysical*, 60 F.3d at 923.

8. 575 F. Supp. 2d 513 (S.D.N.Y. 2008).

9. I have simplified the facts of this case to make it easier to understand.

10. *Warner Bros.*, 575 F. Supp. 2d 513. {{AU: Correct? Id. not correct here.}}

11. *Id.*

12. *Id.*

13. 60 F.3d at 913.

14. *Id.* at 923.

15. *Id.*

16. Casey v. Lamp.

17. *Id.*

18. *Id.*

19. *Id.*

20. *Casey.*

21. *Id.*

22. *Id.*

23. *Id.*

24. *Id.*

25. Campbell v. Acuff-Rose, 510 U.S. 569, 579 (1994); *see also* Blanch v. Koons, 467 F.3d 244, 251–52 (2d Cir. 2006) (Does the secondary use add value to the original?); Am. Geophysical Union v. Texaco, Inc., 60 F.3d 913, 923 (2d Cir. 1994) ("The 'transformative use' concept is pertinent to a court's investigation under the first factor because it assesses the value generated by the secondary use and the means by which such value is generated.").

26. *Campbell, supra* note XX, at 579.

27. *Am. Geophysical*, 510 U.S. at 923.

28. *Campbell, supra* note , at 579.

29. *Am. Geophysical*, 510 U.S. at 923.

30. 575 F. Supp. 2d 513 (S.D.N.Y. 2008).

31. *Id.*

32. *Id.*

33. *Id.*

34. 510 U.S. at 913.

35. *Id.* at 923.

36. *Id.*

37. Casey v. Lamp.

38. *Id.*

39. *Id.*

40. *Id.*

41. *Id.*

42. *Id.*

43. *Id.*

44. Casey v. Lamp; Garner v. Williams.

45. Casey v Lamp.

46. Morris v. Rogers.

47. Garner v. Williams.

48. *Id.*

49. *Id.*

50. *Id.*

CHAPTER EIGHT

RESPONDING TO OPPOSING ARGUMENTS AND DISTINGUISHING CASES

CHAPTER GOALS

1. To help the reader understand when and where to respond to opposing arguments.
2. To help the reader understand how to respond to opposing arguments.
3. To help the reader understand how to distinguish unfavorable cases.
4. To help the reader understand how the different types of legal reasoning help create counterarguments.
5. To help the reader develop the ability to apply these skills.
6. To help the reader develop the ability to be persuasive in counterarguments.

In this chapter, I will discuss how to respond to the other side's arguments and how to distinguish cases. Part I of this chapter will examine when and where to respond to opposing arguments. It will explain when in the litigation to make counterarguments and where in the brief. Part II will present ways to counter opposing arguments and unfavorable cases. This part will cover general ways to respond to opposing arguments, how to distinguish cases, and how to use rule-based reasoning. The final part will discuss persuasiveness in counterarguments.

I. WHEN AND WHERE TO RESPOND TO OPPOSING ARGUMENTS

A writer cannot respond to all arguments made by the opposition. Most courts have page limits for briefs, and the human mind has a limited attention span. Moreover, it is preferable to argue two things completely than ten things poorly. Consequently, the writer should carefully choose which arguments he or she wishes to respond to.[1]

You should generally respond to those arguments that you think have a significant chance of convincing a judge to rule in your opponent's favor on an issue or sub-issue. In other words, it is a question of strategy. A writer should also choose counterarguments in relation to his or her theory of the case.

Determining when to respond in the litigation depends on how the court wants the case briefed and argued. A typical appellate case is structured in the following order: petitioner's brief, respondent's brief, petitioner's reply brief, oral argument (petitioner, respondent, petitioner's rebuttal). A common question concerning this structure is whether a petitioner should include counterarguments in the original brief (anticipate the other side's arguments). A petitioner should generally include a counterargument in the first brief if the argument is one a competent attorney would usually raise.[2] This allows the petitioner to attack the argument before the respondent has a chance to raise it. However, if it is an unusual or creative argument, the petitioner should wait for the reply brief so as to not give the respondent a good argument he or she might not have considered.

The respondent should raise all relevant counterarguments in the respondent's brief. While the respondent may have the opportunity to do this in oral argument, waiting is unwise. Most judges will have thoroughly read the briefs before oral argument, and their minds could already be made up.

The petitioner's reply brief is intended solely for responding to what the respondent raises in the response brief. It is not intended for raising new arguments that the petitioner forgot in the original brief. Again, it is best to respond to respondent's arguments here rather than waiting for oral argument.

Concerning oral argument, a petitioner should include all important counterarguments in the main part of the argument. The petitioner should save the rebuttal time, which is usually short, for responding to the respondent or issues raised by the judge during the respondent's argument. The petitioner should focus on just one or two major points during rebuttal. There will not be enough time to respond to everything the respondent said. Finally, it is a good practice to always reserve rebuttal time because it is always preferable to get in the last word.[3]

The next step is to determine where to respond in a brief. There are three places for counterargument: (1) as a separate section, (2) after the small-scale paradigm for each issue or sub-issue, or (3) as part of the small-scale paradigm.

In a few cases, a counterargument may be so important that it merits its own section or subsection.[4] A writer will generally want to present his or her arguments first, followed by counterargument. This allows the reader to see the positive arguments first, which creates a psychological advantage. You should only put counterargument early in a brief if it is so important that it needs to be there. In that case, do the best you can to make it look like positive argument by using the techniques in Part III below. In organizing a counterargument that has its own section or subsection, you should use a small-scale paradigm like the one in Chapter Seven, which incorporates the different types of legal reasoning.

A writer will often put a counterargument after the small-scale paradigm for each section or subsection. The best way to organize a brief is to use a small-scale paradigm for each issue or sub-issue. In other words, a brief will consist of several paradigms (mini-analyses) (see Chapter Seven). In this instance, a good place to put a counterargument is after the small-scale paradigm (example I).

EXAMPLE I
Small-Scale Paradigm
Counterargument

This is often the best location for counterargument because it puts the argument and counterargument together rather than separating them, which allows the reader to forget the details of the positive argument. It also gives the writer a psychological advantage because the reader sees the positive argument first, which weakens the other side's argument even before the reader has reached it. This placement also permits the writer to fully develop the counterargument.

Another place to put counterargument is within the small-scale paradigm, which I discussed in Chapter Seven. This works well for shorter counterarguments.

EXAMPLE II
Conclusion
Law
   Rule
   Rule Explanation
   Rule Illustration
Application
   Apply Rule
   Compare Cases

A writer can place counterargument in either the rule application section or case comparison section of the application. (If the writer puts it in the rule-based reasoning parts, then rule-based reasoning is involved. If the writer puts it in the comparison parts, distinguishing cases [reverse analogical reasoning] is involved.) A rule application usually shows how a rule or part of a rule applies to the facts of the brief. On the other hand, the writer might want to show that the rule doesn't apply to the facts of the brief. This fits well in the rule application of the paradigm.

A writer may want to distinguish a case—show that the facts of the precedent case are not like the facts of the present case so the court should not apply the precedent case rule to the present case. A writer can do this with the rule illustration and case comparison sections of the paradigm. The writer would illustrate a case in the rule illustration section, then distinguish that case in the case comparison section. A particularly effective way to use this structure is to have two cases in the rule illustration section, then show in the case comparison section how case 1 is like the present case and how case 2 is not like the present case (example III).

EXAMPLE III

Conclusion
Law
    Rule
    Rule Explanation
    Rule Illustration
        Case A
        Case B
Application
    Apply Rule
    Compare Cases
        Case A (show similarity)
        Case B (distinguish)

II. HOW TO RESPOND TO OPPOSING ARGUMENTS AND UNFAVORABLE CASES

A. GENERAL WAYS OF RESPONDING TO YOUR OPPONENT'S ARGUMENTS

The first part of responding to your opponent's case is to make your case as strong as possible. Go through your brief and think how your opponent might counterargue. Then go back to your brief and revise it to make it as secure as possible from your opponent's attacks. You can never make your arguments completely invincible because if they were, there would probably not be an appeal. However, you can vastly improve your arguments by stepping into your opponent's shoes.

Next, you should look through your opponent's arguments to determine what arguments are necessary and unnecessary for the outcome. Writers should ask which of the opponent's arguments will hurt them most. Also, look for arguments that, even if true, will not cause the judge to rule for the other side, and mention them only briefly, if at all. Likewise, since you will have limited space in your brief, you may not want to respond to opposing arguments that are very strong. Save the space for arguments you can win. Similarly, when your opponent has the burden of proof on more than one element, you do not have to respond to all elements (example IV).[5] Affirmative defenses are other examples.

EXAMPLE IV

Even if the defendant did run the red light, she is not liable for plaintiff's injuries because her acts did not cause the accident and plaintiff's injuries.

You need to be able to recognize how your opponent has been persuasive and how to overcome that persuasiveness. You should also look at how the opposing side has framed the issues and sub-issues. Whenever possible, reframe the issues and sub-issues from your client's point of view. Of course, this reframing must be reasonable, and you will need to show in detail why your version is correct.

Similarly, you should try to define terms "in a way that stacks an argument in your favor."[6] "Don't automatically accept the meaning your opponent attaches to a word."[7] There are several techniques for working with words.

1. *Term changing:* Don't accept the terms your opponent uses. Insert your own.
2. *Redefinition:* Accept your opponent's terms while changing their connotation.
3. *Definition jujitsu:* If your opponent's terms actually favor you, use them to attack.
4. *Definition judo:* Use terms that contrast with your opponent's, creating a context that makes him or her look bad.[8]

Here is a striking example of how working with words can make a strong counterargument.[9] A driver returns a rental car with scrapes down both sides. The rental company wants him to pay for the damage because it was his fault (operator error). The driver, however, redefines the issue as one of the rental company providing the wrong equipment. "What did the company mean by renting me a car too big for the Riviera's narrow, walled streets?"[10]

Next, you should look carefully at the details of your opponent's arguments. What are the assumptions behind them? Has your opponent stated the law correctly? Has your opponent stated the facts correctly? Are your opponent's arguments well-supported with reasoning? Is that reasoning convincing? Has the other side satisfied all elements of a conjunctive test? Has your opponent confused causation with correlation?[11] How has your opponent defined important terms? Where has the other side gotten those definitions? Has your opponent used the same definition for a term throughout the brief? Is the dispute about a fact or about a definition? Is your opponent trying to confuse the two?

The next step is to look through the cases the other side has cited. Make sure you analyze each of your opponent's cases carefully. Don't assume the other side has stated the case correctly. Also, your opponent may have left out something that is favorable to your case. Shepardize all of your opponent's cases! Next, decide which cases you need to respond to and which ones you can ignore. You won't have room to respond to all of your opponent's cases, so just respond to the more damaging ones.

Often, you can respond to an unfavorable case by citing another case on the same issue that says the opposite. You should usually choose the case that is closest to your facts and that has the fewest holes in it. Make sure you know the precedential value of the case you want to attack. You can't use a lower court case from a jurisdiction outside the forum to counter a recent case from the highest court of the forum. If all the cases are persuasive authority, you should consider citing several cases to show that your cases are not isolated. Also, show that the reasoning of the favorable cases is better than the reasoning of the unfavorable ones. The other way to counter the other side's cases is to distinguish them, which is the topic of the next subsection.

You can also try to argue that a binding case should be overturned. A writer does this by attacking the reasoning of the case and by presenting policy arguments demonstrating that a case was wrongly decided or that conditions have changed (policy-based reasoning). However, courts rarely overrule precedent, so it is generally preferable to try to distinguish the precedent from your facts.

You should also look through your opponent's brief to see where and how he has been persuasive.[12] (Mark places in your opponent's brief where he is trying to be persuasive. Also, label which type of persuasive device, such as word choice, he is using.) Good writers will counterattack their opponent's persuasiveness (example V). Emotion is a strong motivator; don't allow the other side to get away with emotional language. When you attack briefs that rely too much on persuasive language, you help show that the brief's underlying reasoning is weak.

EXAMPLE V

The police viciously attacked the protesters with tear gas. (Petitioner)

The police lawfully subdued the protesters when they ignored an order to leave the parking lot. (Respondent)

Finally, consider the policy and reasoning behind your opponent's arguments. Whenever possible, show the consequences that ruling for your opponent will have, on both the individuals in your case and the public at large. In talking about what effect policy will have, use the future tense; it is "the language of choices and decisions."[13]

B. DISTINGUISHING CASES

The most important technique for counterargument is distinguishing cases. When your opponent has cited a case that seems to hurt your side, you need to show how that case is not applicable to the situation. You can distinguish a case based on the facts or based on the reasoning/policy (or preferably both).

Distinguishing cases based on the facts is the opposite of reasoning by analogy. With reasoning by analogy, the writer shows that the facts of case A (the precedent case) are substantially similar to the facts of case B (the writer's case), so the rule of case A applies to case B. In distinguishing cases, the writer demonstrates that the facts of case A (the precedent case) are not substantially similar to the facts of case B (the writer's case), so the rule from case A does not apply to case B. Both analogies and distinguishing cases involve similarities or distinctions of degree, so the writer must make the analogy or dissimilarity convincing.

As with analogies, the first step in distinguishing cases is to present the precedent case. This can be done in the rule illustration of the small-scale paradigm (example III) or in the first part of a separate section, subsection, or paragraph that is just counterargument (example I). A writer should present the rule illustration so as to emphasize the reason for discussing the case (the basis of comparison). The writer should leave out anything that doesn't add to the comparison; rule illustrations are not a place for filler.

Also, as with analogies, the rule illustration should start with the case holding, focusing on the topic of that section or subject (the basis of comparison). The writer should then give the facts that are material to the reasoning of the case on the issue or sub-issue and the basis of comparison. Finally, the writer should give the reasoning of the case, again focusing on the reasoning that supports the basis of comparison (example VI).

EXAMPLE VI
Rule Illustration
Holding
Facts
Reasoning

In *Smith*, the court held that Alabama had personal jurisdiction over the out-of-state defendant because the defendant had signed the relevant contract in Alabama. (**Cite**) While the parties had negotiated the contract in North Carolina and the contract was to be performed in Georgia, the parties had signed the contract at the plaintiff's corporate headquarters in Birmingham, Alabama. The court declared that a forum has personal jurisdiction over a defendant who has signed a contract in the forum because the defendant has invoked the benefits and burdens of forum law by signing the contract there. (**Cite**) While a plaintiff does not carry the benefits and burdens of state law anywhere the plaintiff goes, if the defendant has performed an act in the forum, such as negotiating a contract there, signing a contract there, or providing for performance of a contract there, the forum has jurisdiction over that defendant under the due process clause. (**Cite**)

The comparison will come as the last part of the application of the small-scale paradigm (example III) or immediately after the presentation of the case if you are using a self-contained counterargument (example I). The key to distinguishing cases is to make the comparison of facts as detailed as possible. One must base the comparisons on material facts (example VII).

EXAMPLE VII

Our case is not like *Smith,* because *Smith* involves a brown cow and our case involved a black cow. (bad) (This assumes that there are no material differences between brown cows and black cows other than color.)

Our case is distinguishable from *Smith* because in *Smith* the contract was signed in the forum, while in our case the contract was signed outside the forum. (good) (This assumes that where the contract is signed is material to the outcome.)

The comparison should begin with a sentence that presents the comparison, as in example VII above. The writer then should give a detailed comparison of the facts of the two cases, showing how they are different. There is no need to show differences between the cases that are not material to the comparison.[14] Next, the writer should include any reasoning from the cases to back up the factual comparison. Finally, the writer should end with a conclusion that demonstrates why the comparison is important to the case.

EXAMPLE VIII

Our case is distinguishable from *Smith* because in *Smith* the contract was signed in the forum state, while in our case the contract was signed outside the forum. In *Smith*, the parties signed the contract in Alabama, the forum state, while in our case the contract was signed in New York, with Alabama being the forum. In *Smith,* the court reasoned that the fact that a contract was signed in the forum created significant connections with Alabama, so the parties invoked the benefits and burdens of Alabama law. Even though both *Smith* and our case involve plaintiffs that were domiciled in the forum, *Smith* did not mention this as a factor that might allow personal jurisdiction. The other factors mentioned by *Smith* that might create personal jurisdiction, such as partly negotiating the contract in the forum state or partially performing the contract in the forum, are not present in our case. While such factors do invoke the benefits and burdens of forum law because, as *Smith* stated, a state generally has jurisdiction over acts performed within its boundaries, the plaintiff being a domiciliary in the forum, with nothing more, does not create jurisdiction because, as *Smith* also noted, a plaintiff does carry the benefits and burdens of its home state law everywhere it goes. In sum, because in our case, unlike *Smith*, the contract was signed outside the forum, Alabama does not have personal jurisdiction over the defendant because the defendant has not invoked the benefits and burdens of Alabama law.

Distinguishing cases, like analogical reasoning, involves differences of degree (example IX). You have to convince the court that the cases your opponent cites are dissimilar enough from your case that the rules from those cases should not apply to your facts. Your opponent will try to argue that they are similar enough for the rules to apply. Judge Aldisert has developed the following criteria to test analogies:

- The acceptability of the analogy varies proportionally with the number of correlates that have been identified.
- The acceptability of the analogy depends on the number of positive resemblances (similarities) and negative resemblances (dissimilarities).
- The acceptability of the analogy is influenced by the relevance of the purported analogies. An argument based on a single relevant analogy with a single instance will be more cogent than one that points out a dozen irrelevant resemblances.[15]

This test can be modified to apply to distinguishing cases: In making an attempt to distinguish a case convincingly, find as many relevant distinguishing features as possible and compare the relevant differences with the relevant similarities.

EXAMPLE IX

Hypothetical: The question before the court is whether an owner of a pit bull that escapes and bites someone is strictly liable for the personal injury caused by the pit bull. In case A, a man kept a tiger on his property that escaped and bit a neighbor, causing him personal injury. The court held that although the owner was not liable for negligence, as he had taken all reasonable precautions to prevent the tiger from escaping, he was strictly liable for the injuries caused by the tiger because a tiger is a dangerous animal. In case B, a woman owned a toy poodle that bit a neighbor when a loud explosion occurred nearby. The court held that the poodle's owner was not strictly liable because a toy poodle is not a dangerous animal and its owner would not expect that it might bite someone.

Analysis: In this scenario, the plaintiff will try to show that the facts of the current case are like case A and distinguishable from case B; the defendant will try to do the opposite. Both sides will have good-faith arguments because the current case is somewhat different from both the precedent cases. In other words, the comparisons are a matter of degree. The plaintiff will probably win because a pit bull is more like a tiger than a toy poodle, since both pit bulls and tigers are dangerous animals. While the defendant can argue in good faith that both pit bulls and poodles are often pets, the plaintiff probably has the best argument.

One can also distinguish cases based on the reasoning or policy of the cases. Case A (the precedent case) is distinguishable from case B because the policy (or the reasoning) behind case A is different from the policy (or the reasoning) of case B, so the rule from case A does not apply to case B (example X).

EXAMPLE X

Allowing greater restrictions on free speech for high school students than for the public in general, as we saw in *Tarrytown School District*, does not apply to college students because college students are not as likely to get into fights as less mature high school students are. In *Tarrytown*, the court said that sending high school students home for having politically charged messages on T-shirts did not violate the First Amendment because the school had an interest in preventing violence that might be caused by those messages. In our case, the policy of preventing violence does not outweigh the First Amendment because college students are more mature than high school students and therefore much less likely to get into fights over provocative messages on clothing.

EXERCISE VIII-1

Distinguish the following cases from your facts.

1. *Max v. Caspar.* **Facts:** In this case, Max and Caspar are disputing who owns a fox. Max is a fox trapper, and he laid several fox traps in Jefferson Woods. A fox became caught in Max's trap, but on seeing Max approach, the fox escaped. The fox ran into Caspar's house. Caspar shut all the doors and windows so the fox could not escape. Later, Caspar and a friend were able to lure the fox into an escape-proof cage. Fox pelts are valuable where Max and Caspar live. **Holding:** Caspar owns the fox because he was able to secure the fox. Although Max first captured the fox, the fox escaped.

    Your case 1: Your client's dog, Great Dane, is a dog-show champion. Your client has registered him with the National Kennel Club, which allows your client to enter him in dog shows. One day, Great Dane escaped and came on to a neighbor's property. The neighbor put a collar and leash on Great Dane, and she now claims him as her own.

    Your case 2: Your client is a trapper who sells fox pelts for a living. One day, he was approaching one of his traps, and he saw Melissa Scott take a fox from his trap. Your client wants to sue Melissa for the value of the fox.

2. *Bailey v. Knowles Driving School.* John Brown is an instructor for Knowles Driving School. While John was giving a lesson to Martha Leslie, the car Martha and John were in was involved in an accident with Jackie Bailey, who was seriously injured. Jackie sued Knowles and

Brown. The court found that Brown was negligent in supervising Leslie. The court also held that Bailey could recover from Knowles Driving Schools under respondeat superior because Brown was acting in the scope of his employment at the time of the accident.

Your case 1: Your client owns a driving school that employs the codefendant, David Isaacs, as a driving instructor. David agrees to give Larry Koch's teenage son a free driving lesson on Saturday afternoon. Larry's son causes an accident due to David's negligent supervision, and Nanette Avery is badly injured. Nanette sues David and your client's school.

Your case 2: Your client owns a driving school that employs Martha Jenkins as a secretary. One day Martha goes crazy, steals one of the school's cars, and is involved in an accident, which is her fault. The injured person sues Martha and your client's school.

3. *Mann v. State.* Jack Mann and Lavon Terry robbed the Second National Bank of Wisconsin. During the robbery, Terry shot and killed the bank guard. The state convicted Jack Mann for felony murder. Under the felony-murder doctrine, the state can hold a defendant liable for murder committed by another defendant when a person is killed while the defendants are committing a felony. This doctrine is intended to deter felonies that involve inherently dangerous situations. Because an armed robbery fits this description, this court affirms.

Your case 1: Mary and Peggy embezzle from their employer by routing money to their offshore bank account. After having just made the transfer, and on the way to the airport to meet Peggy, Mary is pursued by the police. Trying to escape, Mary hits a pedestrian, who is killed. The state indicts Peggy for felony murder.

Your case 2: Roy and Benny steal a car. They drive the car to Benny's home and discover computer equipment in the trunk. They decide that Roy will get the computer equipment and Benny will keep the car. Later that evening, the police chase Benny, and he hits and kills a pedestrian. The state indicts Roy for felony murder.

Your case 3: Rob and John walk into a bank wearing only skimpy bathing suits. While Rob watches for the police, John gives a note to the teller asking her to put $10,000 in a bag. The teller, who has a weak heart, has a heart attack and dies. The state indicts Rob for felony murder.

Your case 4: Susan and Pam commit an armed robbery of a jewelry store. During the robbery, a store guard kills Pam. The state indicts Susan for felony murder.

4. *Gonzales v. Wong.* The issue in this motion to dismiss is whether Mr. Wong is a citizen of Ohio for diversity jurisdiction. The general rule is that a person is a citizen of the last state where he resided and intended to stay. Evidence of intent can be provided by voter registration, driver's license, property ownership, etc. In this case, Mr. Wong moved to Ohio two weeks before the matter being litigated. He bought a house in Ohio, registered to vote there, and applied for an Ohio driver's license. This court concludes that Mr. Wong is a citizen of Ohio.

Your case 1: Pat goes to school at Ohio State, where she lives in a dorm. Her parents live in Kentucky, and she spends her summers there, as well as visiting most weekends. She has a Kentucky driver's license, but she is not registered to vote anywhere. Is Pat a citizen of Ohio?

Your case 2: Manuel goes to Minnesota State. His parents live in Oregon, and he has an Oregon driver's license. Manuel has accepted a job in St. Paul, Minnesota, when he graduates. Distinguish this case from case 1.

5. *Friendly v. Richards Department Store.* Harriet Friendly was shopping at Richards Department Store. When she checked out, the cashier forgot to deactivate one of the theft tags. The theft tag went off as she was leaving the store. A security guard stopped Harriet, and he asked her to come to his office. After they got to his office, the security guard asked Harriet to remain there while he got the store manager. He locked the office door. Harriet tried to open the door, but she found it was locked. The guard returned to his office with the manager. When the manager discovered that Harriet had actually paid for the item, the manager said she could go. Harriet sued the store for false imprisonment.

A plaintiff must prove three things to establish false imprisonment: (1) the defendant must have intended to confine the plaintiff within boundaries fixed by the defendant; (2) the defendant's act must have directly or indirectly confined the plaintiff; and (3) the defendant must be conscious of the confinement. A defendant may confine a plaintiff by physical barriers, physical force, or threat of physical force. Here, the first requirement is satisfied by the security guard locking Harriet in his office. Because the door was locked, Harriet was actually confined by the security guard. Finally, Harriet was conscious of her confinement because she tried the door.

Your case 1: Patel is shopping at his usual grocery store. One of the grocery store employees thinks he sees Patel slip a box of cookies into his backpack. The employee stops Patel when he tries to leave the store without paying for the cookies. He tells Patel to wait while he gets the manager. Patel hands his backpack to the manager to allow her to search it. The manager does not find any cookies, and she tells Patel he can leave. Patel sues the store for false imprisonment.

Your case 2: Debbie was shopping at Nerdstrom's Department Store. A security guard thought he saw her shoplift a blouse. He took Debbie to his office, and he told her to stay or he would call the police. When he returned with the manager, the manager could not find that Debbie had shoplifted anything. He told her she could go. Debbie sued the store for false imprisonment.

Your case 3: Joan was shopping at Richards Department Store. She put a blouse into her purse, and she left the store without paying for it. A security guard observed her take the blouse on a security camera, and he stopped her in the parking lot. The guard asked her to come to his office. After they got to his office, the guard asked her to remain there while he got the store manager. He locked the office door. Joan tried to open the door, but she found it was locked. The guard returned to his office with the manager, who discovered the stolen blouse and called the police. Can you distinguish this case from *Friendly v. Richards*?

Your case 4: Jackson was shopping at Richards Department Store. When he checked out, the cashier forgot to deactivate one of the theft tags. The theft tag went off as he was leaving the store. A security guard stopped Jackson and asked him to come to his office. After they got to his office, the security guard asked Jackson to remain there while he got the store manager. He locked the office door. The guard returned to his office with the manager. When the manager discovered that Jackson had actually paid for the item, the manager said he could go. Jackson sued the store for false imprisonment.

EXERCISE VIII-2

Return to *Justice v. Hamm* in Chapter Three (exercise III-7, number 1). Distinguish the following situations from that case.

1. Laura Adderly, a resident of New York, witnessed a traffic accident in California. Before leaving the state, she too had an automobile accident. The driver of the other car sued Adderly in California state court. Her testimony at the trial in which she was a witness lasted two weeks, and she was so exhausted at the end of it that she spent a week in Palm Springs recovering. The driver's attorney served Adderly at the airport as she was leaving California for New York.
2. Pat moved from Los Angeles, California, to Albany, New York. Mica Landry, a real estate agent who sold Pat's house when she moved to New York, sued Pat in a California state court to recover commissions she claimed Pat owed her from the sale. Pat filed a complaint against Landry with the California real estate board, claiming breach of fiduciary duty. Landry's attorney served Pat with a summons and complaint in the commission case when she came to California to testify before the real estate board.
3. Donna Edwards, a resident of Kansas, was involved in a business transaction with Acme Limited. When the business transaction went bad, Donna sued Acme for damages in a California state court for breach of contract and breach of fiduciary duty. She also was involved in a separate business deal with Buzz Corp. Buzz Corp. sued Donna in California state court for breach of contract and breach of fiduciary duty concerning that transaction. Buzz Corp.'s attorney served her with a summons and complaint when she came to California to testify in the Acme case.
4. Distinguish your answer in *Koch* (exercise III-7, number 1) from your answer in 3 directly above.
5. Synthesize a rule for immunity from service of process based on *Justice* and 1–3 above.

C. USING RULE-BASED REASONING IN COUNTERARGUMENTS

Another method that writers use in responding to the other side's case is rule-based reasoning. As discussed in detail in Chapter Four, with rule-based reasoning, the writer starts with the rule, shows how the facts fit or don't fit the rule, and concludes. Rule-based reasoning is another variation of the deductive syllogism.

EXAMPLE XI

> All men are mortal. (major premise)
> Aristotle is a man. (minor premise)
> Aristotle is mortal. (conclusion)

While the above structure is most often used to satisfy a test, you can also employ it to show that the test has not been satisfied, to rebut the plaintiff's presentation of the test (example XII). An advantage for the defendant is that with a conjunctive test the defendant only needs to prove that one factor fails.

EXAMPLE XII

The defendant, however, is incorrect that there is a secular purpose behind the 1954 act because adding the words "under God" to the Pledge of Allegiance has no secular purpose, and thus the act violates the Establishment Clause. [←conclusion] [major premise→] The *Lemon* test requires that a legislative act have a secular legislative purpose to satisfy the Establishment Clause. (**Cite**) In applying this purpose prong, the appropriate question is whether a government's actual purpose is to endorse or disapprove of religion. (**Cite**) To determine this, courts often scrutinize the legislative record to ascertain the government's purpose for enacting the statute. The proposed secular purpose cannot be a sham. (**Cite**) [←major premise]

[minor premise→] In the present case, the legislative history of the 1954 act reveals that the main purpose for adding the words "under God" to the Pledge of Allegiance was motivated by religion. The legislative history states:

> At this moment of our history the principles underlying our American Government and the American way of life are under attack by a

system whose philosophy is at direct odds with our own. Our American Government is founded on the concept of the individuality and the dignity of the human being. Underlying this concept is the belief that the human person is important because he was created by God and endowed by Him with certain inalienable rights which no civil authority may usurp. The inclusion of God in our pledge therefore would further acknowledge the dependence of our people and our Government upon the moral directs of the Creator. At the same time it would serve to deny the atheistic and materialistic concepts of communism with attendant subservience of the individual. (**Cite**)

There could not be a clearer example of a religious purpose. While the legislative history suggests that the addition of the words "under God" may have been meant to quell the threat of communism, this alleged purpose is a sham. The 1954 act attacked communism by advancing religion. The legislative history reveals that the act's stated purpose was to "acknowledge the dependence of our people and our Government upon the moral directs of the Creator." The act established the existence of God by differentiating the United States from communist nations by recognizing a supreme being. Congress could have employed other words to fight communism without adding the words "under God" to the pledge. The pledge is already patriotic without those words. [←minor premise]

In addition to using syllogisms to structure counterarguments, one can attack an opponent's syllogisms. The three main ways of attacking a syllogism are (1) attack the major premise, (2) attack the minor premise, and (3) show that the syllogism is improperly constructed.[16] Since the major premise in a legal argument is the law, attacking the major premise involves criticizing your opponent's presentation of the law. You will want to show that your opponent's statement of the law as it applies to your case is incorrect. Sometimes the other side will have incorrectly stated the law, but more commonly your opponent will have incompletely stated the law or omitted an exception (example XIII).

EXAMPLE XIII

The secular purpose prong of the *Lemon* test does not require that *all* purposes behind a statute be secular, just that the statute's *predominant* purpose is secular. (response to example XII)

Because briefs are persuasive, a writer can argue his or her interpretation of the law as counterargument to the other side's presentation of the law. In other words, you should demonstrate that your interpretation of the law is correct; you are redefining the law in your favor. If you can convince the judge that your version of the law is correct, then you have destroyed your opponent's major premise and his or her syllogism. Your version, of course, needs to be reasonable or it will not convince the court. The first step is careful research. You need to find the cases and other materials that support your version of the law. Next, you need to test your version to make sure that it doesn't contain any gaps. Finally, you need to write it persuasively. The two most important elements of persuasive writing are good legal analysis and detail.

Another way to attack a syllogism is to attack the minor premise. A writer can show that the other side misstated or mischaracterized the facts. Is the minor premise supported by the record? Read the record carefully several times and mark important facts. Do not assume that your opponent has presented the facts accurately or has not missed anything. Again, you will want to write up the facts from your viewpoint. However, be careful to give an accurate presentation of the facts.

To be convincing, major and minor premises should be grounded (contain no gaps in the reasoning). Always test your opponent's premises to see if they are grounded (fully supported), either directly or indirectly.

Finally, a writer can attack the other side's rule-based reasoning by showing that the syllogism is improperly constructed—the conclusion does not follow from the premises.[17] While Gardner says this type of error is rare,[18] those of us who teach legal writing see it frequently. Diagramming the syllogism helps one discern logical errors; a writer can hide a lot of faulty reasoning in a thick page of prose. As Professor Thouless has written, "We should get out of the habit of judging the soundness of an argument by considering whether we agree with its conclusion, and concentrate instead on examining its form."[19]

EXAMPLE XIV

A corporation is domiciled in a state for purposes of subject matter jurisdiction when it is incorporated in that state or it has its principal place of business there. (major premise).

The Gigantic Corporation has a large plant in Kentucky. (minor premise)

The Gigantic Corporation is domiciled in Kentucky. (conclusion)

All As are Bs.

C is ? (not established)

Therefore, C is A.

Here, the conclusion doesn't follow from the premise. The minor premise doesn't correspond with the major premise because the minor premise doesn't show that Gigantic Corporation is domiciled in Kentucky or has its principal place of business in Kentucky. Having a large plant in Kentucky (without more) doesn't satisfy the requirements of the major premise.

Another example of faulty reasoning is the fallacy of the undistributed middle. "It has this name because the term common to both premises, the middle term B, does not cover the whole class . . . in either of the premises. That is, in both premises the word omitted before B is 'some,' not 'all.'"[20]

EXAMPLE XV

All men are mortal.

Aristotle is mortal.

Therefore, Aristotle is a man.

All intentional torts are torts.

Negligence is a tort.

Therefore, negligence is an intentional tort.

All As are Bs.

C is a B.

Therefore, C is an A.

Other logical fallacies to look for in your opponent's arguments include the following:

1. Tautologies—Repeating the same thing as if it proved something ("If you die without a will, you'll die intestate.")
2. False dilemma—"You're given two choices when you actually have many choices."
3. Complex cause—"Only one cause gets the blame (or credit) for something that has many causes."
4. Red herring—A distraction from the real argument
5. Slippery slope—Allowing this will lead to dire consequences. ("If we allow same-sex marriage, it will lead to the legalization of polygamy.")
6. False comparison—"Two things are similar so they must be the same." ("Made with all natural ingredients." Arsenic is all natural.)[21]

III. MAKING IT PERSUASIVE

Once you have created your counterarguments, you need to make them persuasive. The best way to do this is to make your counterarguments look like positive arguments. A writer should never sound defensive. In writing up the law, structure and phrase to stress the law that helps you. Do not word things in a way that presents or summarizes the other side's argument. (For example, avoid "The plaintiff has argued . . .")

EXAMPLE XVI

In this situation, you want the exception to govern because it supports your case.

Poor: The usual rule is that the court should choose the law of the place of the accident. However, that rule does not apply when the law of the place of the accident is against the public policy of the forum.

Better: A court should choose the law of the forum when the law of the place of the accident is against the public policy of the forum.

As stated above, you should also present the facts from your point of view.

A writer should use all persuasive techniques that he or she would use elsewhere in the brief in counterargument. This includes word choice, strategic placement of positive and negative law or facts within the section or the paragraph, etc. For example, a writer can place unfavorable facts in the middle of the paragraph where the reader is less likely to notice and remember them. Also, a writer should generally give more space to arguments that support his or her side and less space to arguments that do not. Finally, a writer should use persuasive techniques to paint a picture in readers' minds. The more vivid the picture, the more likely the win.

Very important in making counterarguments persuasive is backing up your arguments with authority and choosing the cases and other materials that best support your side. It is worth the extra time researching to find the one or two cases that are closest to your facts and the outcome you want. In choosing cases, you should be very careful to read the entire case to make sure there is nothing in that case that hurts your side.

When you are finished making your counterarguments persuasive, read them several times to ascertain what kind of effect they will have on your reader. It is the writer's job to communicate to the reader; a writer should be reader oriented. Have you expressed your ideas in the clearest manner possible? Have you been persuasive without overdoing it? Read every word you have written to make sure that you convey the intended meaning and emotional connotation.

EXERCISE VIII-3

Distinguish the following facts in depth from *Williams* in Chapter Three, using the format set forth in this chapter.

Your facts: Donald Marks, a managing partner at a large law firm, purchased a custom-made sports car from Satan Motors, a small custom car manufacturing company, for $1 million. He signed a form contract, which included a clause in small print that stated, "Buyer must make all payments by the first of each month. There is no grace period in making payments. If the buyer does not make payment by the first of each month, the seller may repossess the automobile, sue for all payments due under this contract, and obtain possession of buyer's immortal soul." When Marks made the final payment one day late, Satan Motors filed suit for possession of the car and Marks's soul.

CONCLUSION

Counterargument and distinguishing cases are vital parts of persuasive briefs. The above has shown the details of when and where to use counterargument, how to make counterarguments including distinguishing cases, how to use syllogisms and criticize them, and how to make counterarguments persuasive. However, the key to counterargument, like the key to all persuasive writing, is developing a critical approach to evaluating arguments and counterarguments. This requires careful reading of opposing briefs, careful analysis, the ability to read your arguments critically, an attention to detail, and, most important, a careful evaluation of whether your counterarguments are convincing.

CHAPTER WRAP-UP

Why is counterargument important? Should you reply to all your opponent's arguments? When is the best time to use counterargument before a trial court? When is the best time to use counterargument before an appellate court? Where is the best place to put counterargument in a brief? What is the relationship between strategy and counterargument? Make a diagram of counterargument techniques. Which of these techniques are most effective? What is the key to distinguishing a case? How is distinguishing cases like reasoning by analogy? How is it different? How can you distinguish a case based on policy or reasoning? How can you use rule-based reasoning to formulate a counterargument? How can you attack syllogisms? Make a diagram of persuasive techniques.

Answers
EXERCISE VIII-1

1. Case 1: The distinguishing point is that a fox is a wild animal that has no owner, while a show dog has an owner. Ownership of a lost domesticated animal is not generally obtained by a finder.

   Case 2: In *Max v. Caspar*, the fox escaped through its own efforts. Here, Melissa stole the fox from the trap. To award the fox to Melissa would encourage theft.

2. Case 1: David was not acting within the scope of his employment when he gave Larry's son the lesson, so respondeat superior does not apply, and your client is not liable.

   Case 2: Martha was not acting within the scope of her employment when she stole the car and got into the accident.

3. Case 1: Embezzlement is not an inherently dangerous crime, so the felony-murder rule should not apply.

   Case 2: *Mann* involved a murder that was committed during a felony. Here, the felony is over, and the criminals have divided the loot.

   Case 3: Here, I would argue that unarmed robbery is not an inherently dangerous crime. In addition, it is unlikely that Rob would foresee that the teller had a bad heart.

   Case 4: You would argue that the law was intended to protect innocent bystanders, not those who commit the crime. Some jurisdictions accept this argument; some don't.

4. Case 1: No. You would argue that Pat does not intend to remain in Ohio. Despite the fact that she currently resides in Ohio, all the incidences of citizenship are with Kentucky.

   Case 2: You would argue that Manuel's acceptance of a job in Minnesota demonstrates his intent to remain in Minnesota, despite some evidence to the contrary.

5. Case 1: It is doubtful that Patel was directly or indirectly confined. There were no physical barriers, and the security guard did not confine Patel by force or threat of physical force.

   Case 2: It is doubtful that Debbie was confined. Threatening to call the police does not constitute conduct that directly or indirectly confines the plaintiff.

   Case 3: No, you can't. The material facts are all the same. The added fact that she actually stole the blouse is irrelevant because there is nothing in the law that you were given that makes this fact relevant. This may seem wrong to you, but you must use the law you are given.

   Case 4: This case is exactly the same as *Friendly v. Richards*, except that Jackson didn't try to leave. Therefore, you can argue that he was not conscious of his confinement. You may want to do more research on what constitutes confinement and consciousness of confinement.

EXERCISE VIII-2

1. Since *Justice* stated that the immunity applies to "a period reasonably necessary to the giving of testimony in a judicial proceeding," one can infer that Hamm was in California only long enough to testify at the murder trial. Adderly's week-long vacation does not implicate the public policy of encouraging nonresidents to appear.

2. *Justice* states that a "recognized exception to the rule of immunity is that it does not apply if the later action, in regard to which immunity from service is claimed, arises out of or involves the same subject matter as the one in which the nonresident has made a voluntary appearance." (**Cite**) The reason for this limitation is that "to permit a resident of a foreign state, by means of an immunity from service of process, to pick and choose among portions of the subject matter of litigation may result in a hardship to the opposing party." In this case, the commission's action and the real estate board complaint involve the same subject matter—the sale of the house.

3. You could argue that Donna didn't need an incentive to appear in her own lawsuit, so the immunity rule was unnecessary.

4. I hope in *Koch* you said that there was immunity and in 3 you argued that there wasn't. However, both cases are similar. *Koch* involved a complaint brought by Koch in an action before an agency that alleged wrongdoing by a real estate agent in a transaction involving Koch, and she was served in a separate lawsuit when she appeared to testify at that agency hearing. In 3, the plaintiff appeared in her lawsuit to assert her right for damages, and she was served in a separate lawsuit. The distinction, which some courts might not accept, is that Koch was testifying before the agency to protect the public interest, not her own interest, while in 3, the plaintiff was protecting her interest. This is a small but significant difference. I drafted this example to illustrate the small distinctions involved in arguing analogies and distinguishing cases.

5. During a period reasonably necessary to the giving of testimony in a judicial or similar proceeding, a nonresident witness who enters a state primarily for that purpose is immune from service of summons in a case, unless the later action arises out of or involves the same subject matter as the one in which the nonresident has made a voluntary

appearance or the person served is the plaintiff in the later action. I hope you synthesized this rule by putting the "pieces of the puzzle" in the right places. As with a jigsaw puzzle, don't force any of the pieces.

EXERCISE VIII-3

In *Williams*, a court held a form contract between a poor consumer and a retail furniture store unconscionable. From 1957 to 1962, Williams purchased several household items from Walker-Thomas on an installment plan. The terms of each purchase were contained in a printed form contract, which set forth the value of the purchased item and purported to lease the item to the buyer for a monthly rental payment. The contract provided that title would remain in Walker-Thomas until the total of all the monthly payments made equaled the stated value of the item, at which time the buyer could take title. In the event of a default in the payment of any monthly installment, Walker-Thomas could repossess the item. In addition, the contract provided that "the amount of each periodical installment payment to be made by [purchaser] to the Company under this present lease shall be inclusive of and not in addition to the amount of each installment payment to be made by [purchaser] under such prior leases, bills or accounts; and all payments now and hereafter made by [purchaser] shall be credited pro rata on all outstanding leases, bills and accounts due the Company by [purchaser] at the time each such payment is made." This provision kept a balance due on every item purchased until the balance due on all items, whenever purchased, was liquidated. As a result, the debt incurred at the time of purchase of each item was secured by the right to repossess all the items previously purchased by the same purchaser, and each new item purchased became subject to a security interest arising out of the previous dealings. In April 1962, Williams bought a stereo set for $514.95. When she defaulted shortly thereafter, Walker-Thomas sought to replevy all the items purchased since December 1957. The lower court granted judgment for Walker-Thomas, and the District of Columbia Court of Appeals affirmed.

In reversing the lower courts, the court of appeals declared that unconscionable contracts are unenforceable as a matter of law. The court stated:

Unconscionability has generally been recognized to include an absence
of meaningful choice on the part of one of the parties together with
contract terms which are unreasonably favorable to the other party.
Whether a meaningful choice is present in a particular case can only
be determined by consideration of all the circumstances surrounding the transaction. In many cases the meaningfulness of the choice
is negated by a gross inequality of bargaining power. The manner in
which the contract was entered is also relevant to this consideration.
Did each party to the contract, considering his obvious education or
lack of it, have a reasonable opportunity to understand the terms of
the contract, or were the important terms hidden in a maze of fine
print and minimized by deceptive sales practices? . . . [W]hen a party
of little bargaining power, and hence little real choice, signs a commercially unreasonable contract with little or no knowledge of its terms,
it is hardly likely that his consent, or even an objective manifestation
of his consent, was ever given to all the terms. In such a case . . . the
court should consider whether the terms of the contract are so unfair
that enforcement should be withheld.

The test of reasonableness is whether the terms are "so extreme as to appear
unconscionable according to the mores and business practices of the time
and place." The court of appeals remanded because the trial court had made
no factual findings on the issue of unconscionability.

Our case is distinguishable from *Williams* because there is not a lack of
bargaining power here. While the terms of the contract may seem somewhat oppressive, Marks was a sophisticated buyer. In contrast to Williams,
who was a poor, uneducated consumer, Marks is a highly educated managing partner at a large law firm who can afford a million-dollar car. Unlike
Williams, he did not lack meaningful choice; a person can buy many kinds
of cars for a million dollars. Moreover, as an attorney, he had more than a
reasonable opportunity to understand the terms of the contract. While the
clause may have been in a form contract in small print, an attorney knows
to read the entire contract, especially when making such an expensive purchase. Because Marks was a sophisticated attorney, the policy of protecting

uneducated, poor consumers is not implicated here, and the court should rule in the plaintiff's favor.

Note: I had to use two paragraphs for the rule illustration because *Williams* is so complicated. I used bad facts in the comparison because the bad facts didn't hurt my argument, since they concerned the other facet of the test. It is usually best to reveal bad facts to the court rather than having your opponent present them in counterargument to your argument.

NOTES

1. Professor James Gardner has declared, "It is worth bearing in mind that lawyers can be competitive, and they sometimes find it easy to get into a slugfest with their opponents in which each and every point made by the other side prompts a massive counterattack. The goal of advocacy, however, is simply to win your case, not to gratify your ego by crushing your opponent." JAMES A. GARDNER, LEGAL ARGUMENT: THE STRUCTURE AND LANGUAGE OF EFFECTIVE ADVOCACY 134 (Lexis-Nexis 2d ed. 2007). Stated differently, you are trying to win over a panel of judges, not destroy your opponent.

2. Of course, state rules of professional responsibility generally require that attorneys cite to adverse authority that is binding and on point. Even without this rule, this author believes that it is very poor strategy to ignore adverse binding authority. It is better to raise and distinguish it before the other side can.

3. A litigator should avoid a practice that sometimes occurs in moot court competitions—reserving time for rebuttal, then waiving that time at the end to make it appear that the other side has not raised any arguments that need response. The judges will know what you are doing. More important, it is rare that a petitioner cannot find something to respond to, and an attorney should never waste time that could be used to make a valid argument.

4. You should not put all counterarguments together in a section at the end of the brief, as many legal writing students like to do.

5. However, if you have strong counterarguments to your opponent's arguments on more than one part of the test, you can include them if there is space.

6. Jay Heinrichs, Thank You for Arguing: What Aristotle, Lincoln, and Homer Simpson Can Tell Us About the Art of Persuasion 108 (Three Rivers 2007).

7. *Id.* at 110.

8. *Id.* at 119.

9. *Id.* at 116.

10. *Id.*

11. Jay Heinrichs mentions the Chanticleer fallacy, which is named after a rooster who thought his crowing caused the sunrise. *Id.* at 11.

12. If you can write persuasively, you should also be able to recognize when the other side is using persuasion.

13. Heinrichs, *supra* note 6, at 3.

14. First-year students often try to distinguish cases by comparing facts that are not relevant to the basis of comparison. The comparison is not of the whole of the precedent case with your case; it is the differences between the comparison case and your case on a particular issue or sub-issue. That the cases can be distinguished on a separate issue or sub-issue is irrelevant.

15. Ruggero J. Aldisert, Winning on Appeal: Better Briefs and Oral Argument 280 (Nat'l Inst. Trial Advoc. 1996).

16. *See* Gardner, *supra* note 1, at 131–32.

17. *Id.* at 132.

18. *Id.*

19. Robert H. Thouless, Straight and Crooked Thinking 61 (Pan Books Ltd. 3d ed., 1974).

20. *Id.* at 60.

21. Heinrichs, *supra* note 6, at 137–54.

CHAPTER NINE

ADVANCED PROBLEM SOLVING AND CREATIVITY

The principal goal of education is to create men who are capable of doing new things, not simply of repeating what other generations have done— men who are creative, inventive, and discoverers.

JEAN PIAGET[1]

CHAPTER GOALS

1. To help the reader understand problem solving.
2. To help the reader understand creativity.
3. To help the reader understand domain transfer (applying existing problem-solving skills to different types of problems).
4. To help the reader develop the ability to solve complex problems.

I. A MODEL FOR LEGAL PROBLEM SOLVING

In earlier chapters, I gave you several exercises that required you to use problem-solving skills. In doing those exercises, you probably employed different problem-solving approaches, depending on the nature of the problem (different mini-skills or a different combination of mini-skills). Before moving on, I would like to give you a model for solving legal problems. Other approaches may work better for certain problems, but this model gives you an example of the kinds of steps you need to take when solving legal problems. Any model of legal problem solving needs to follow the outline for self-regulated learning—forethought, performance, reflection.

Problem solving is "the ability to combine previously learned principles, procedures, declarative knowledge, and cognitive strategies in a unique way within a domain of content to solve previously unencountered problems."[2] For law, problem solving often "involves identifying and evaluating the analytical arguments reasonable lawyers would make with respect to the particular set of legal issues presented by a fact pattern and then predicting how a court would assess those arguments and resolve each issue."[3] In other words, legal problem solving does not usually lead to a single correct answer, but rather to a prediction.[4]

A general model for problem solving might be: (1) identify the problem, (2) define the problem, (3) form a strategy, (4) organize information, (5) solve the problem (including monitoring your progress), and (6) evaluate the solution.[5] Can you determine which of these steps are forethought, which are performance, and which are reflection?

For purposes of this explanation, I have created a fact situation that needs solving. A franchisee of a nationwide auto parts chain has come to you with a problem. He has just received a franchise, and he is looking for a space in which to put his store. The owner of a shopping center, Jackson & Pollock, has offered your client an ideal space at a good price. However, the previous tenant signed a lease for the property for ten years, nine of which still remain. Jackson & Pollock claims that the tenant abandoned the premises and thus terminated the lease. Your client wants to know if it is safe to lease the premises.

The first step in the forethought stage is identifying the problem. The most important aspect of this step is to gather the facts. You would use the normal methods for gathering the facts—talking to your client, discovery, investigation—and then evaluate the facts to see which ones are material. (From your fact investigation, you would establish that the problem to be solved is whether your client can safely lease the premises on the ground that the previous tenant's lease was terminated by abandonment and nonpayment of rent.) You should also identify the domain of the problem (property law, landlord tenant law) and your purpose in solving the problem. The second step is to define the problem—develop an issue that clearly states the problem and combines the facts and the law. (There will often be overlap between the first two steps.) Part of this step is to relate the problem to your previous knowledge. If your previous knowledge allows you to fully define the problem, you can move on to the next step. If not, do background reading in a source such as a treatise or encyclopedia to help you define the problem. (You might state your client's issue as: Does a tenant abandoning premises and not paying rent after abandonment terminate a lease?)

The next step is to develop a strategy. For a legal problem solver, this involves two stages—developing a research strategy and developing a legal problem-solving strategy. Research is an essential part of the forethought stage in legal problem solving. You need to effectively and efficiently find the statutes, cases, and other materials that will provide the law for solving your problem. Again, if your prior knowledge does not allow you to do this, you should do some background reading. (At this point, imagine how you might approach researching your client's lease termination problem. Did you first identify the governing law for a lease termination? Is it federal or state law? Which jurisdiction, state, or federal circuit is involved? Is it case law, statutory law, or administrative law? Did you decide how you will research the problem? Are you planning to use an online data base, a digest, a treatise, etc.? Did you update your research? Did you look at the pocket part and use Shepard's?, etc.) At this point in legal problem solving, instead of moving on to create a problem-solving strategy, you should probably organize the materials your research uncovered. For example, if your problem involves only cases, you should read and analyze each case (Chapter Two) and synthesize your case analyses to produce the law that governs your facts (Chapter Five). If your problem involves a complicated rule, you should diagram the rule using syllogisms, making sure that all premises are grounded as well as possible, even if this requires the use of several nested syllogisms (Chapter Four) or analogies (Chapter Three). If your problem involves statutory analysis, you should use techniques of statutory interpretation (Chapter Six).

Now that you know the governing law, you should organize the problem and develop a problem-solving strategy. How will you approach your problem? What mini-skills are involved? Have you considered alternative strategies? Have you considered how you have solved similar problems in the past? Do you have the tools needed to solve the problem? Are you interested in solving the problem?

What is the desired outcome? What are the steps in reaching this outcome? (For more complex problems, you might want to diagram your problem-solving strategy.) Always consider repeating earlier steps if you are having problems.

In the performance stage, you use your strategy to solve the problem and come to a conclusion. In this case, you apply the law of lease termination in the relevant jurisdiction to your client's problem to come to a solution. During this stage, you should make sure you are fully focusing your attention on the problem and not letting distractions make you a lazy reader. You will probably be applying the law to the facts in this stage. You should also be self-monitoring to make sure that your problem-solving strategy is working (use your inner voice). If you are having trouble, you may need to reconsider your strategy. Question every step as you go through the problem-solving process. If you are writing up your solution, you should use the small-scale paradigm in Chapter Seven. (Of course, for our problem, you will probably be writing a client letter. In that case, you need to consider your audience, especially if your client is not an attorney.) As noted above, the performance stage in legal problem solving might require you to come up with all reasonable alternatives and then decide which alternative is best or which one a court would adopt.

In the reflection stage, you need to evaluate your solution. Did you reach the desired outcome? If not, why? Is your solution convincing? (In our case, the client wants an answer he can rely on. He wants to avoid litigation.) Did you leave any unanswered questions? What about alternatives? Did you consider all approaches to legal reasoning? Put yourself in the shoes of a judge; would your solution be convincing to a judge? Put yourself in the shoes of someone who might attack your solution; what would the argument be? Could you counter the argument? Could you make your solution stronger based on the argument? Put yourself in the shoes of your client; will your client be satisfied? Was your client fully satisfied? If not, what can you do better next time? If you wrote up your solution, does the writing effectively communicate the solution to your intended reader?

You should also reflect on what you learned. Did you employ an effective problem-solving process? Was it efficient? What will you do differently next time? How was your research strategy? How did you feel after you read the cases?

A note on purpose: Having a purpose when problem solving is very important because it focuses and motivates you. Now that you are at an advanced stage of problem solving, your purpose should be as detailed as possible. You should view your purpose in context, such as a litigation lawyer, an estate planner, or a deal lawyer. Within those areas, you should focus on the specific step of the litigation or transaction. For example, Tina Stark writes, "Deal lawyers start from the business deal. The terms of the business deal are the deal lawyer's facts. The lawyer must then find the contract concepts that best reflect the business deal and use those concepts as the basis of drafting the contract provisions."[6] These three sentences tell me more about how to draft a contract than two semesters of contracts in law school. Can you come up with similar statements for litigation lawyers or estate-planning attorneys?

Stark continues: "Translating the business deal into contract concepts is only one aspect of thinking like a deal lawyer. The better deal lawyers are able to look at a transaction from the client's perspective and add value to the deal. Looking at a contract from the client's perspective means understanding what the client wants to achieve and the risks it wants to avoid. 'Adding value to the deal' is a euphemism for 'finding and resolving business issues.' These skills are problem-solving skills and are an integral component of a deal lawyer's professional expertise. They require a sophisticated understanding not only of substantive law, but also of business, the client's business, and the transaction at hand."[7]

Decide for yourself: Will a student solve problems better using the above or using an approach that does not focus on context and purpose? Which approach will the problem solver find more interesting and motivating?

OUTLINE OF BASIC PROBLEM-SOLVING MODEL

Gather facts, frame issues, research, brief cases, synthesize, develop problem-solving strategy, apply law to facts, form conclusions, write up, evaluate.

II. CREATIVITY: THINKING OUTSIDE THE BOX

Being a good lawyer involves thinking outside the box—coming up with new solutions to problems and making new connections (thinking in ways other than logical or linear).[8] New solutions and new connections advance the law.

Sometimes the creative thinker is the one who sees things no one else does. For example, Monk's (the television detective) first case involved a woman who had died of an overdose of horse tranquilizers. Everyone, including the coroner, thought it was a suicide. Monk, however, thought it was a murder. He was the only one who noticed that there was no water in the room the woman had died in. How had she taken the horse tranquilizers?

A. DEALING WITH AMBIGUITY

The first step in creativity is being able to deal with ambiguity and use it to your advantage. Ambiguity is part of the law. Rules are usually open to multiple interpretations. Ambiguity might be the most important part of the law because it is the basis of our adversarial system (it allows for each side to make opposing arguments) and it allows change in the law.

There are many reasons for ambiguity in cases. First, judges are not always great writers. Second, ambiguity is built into language. Words can mean different things in different contexts. Third, law is ambiguous because it develops on a case-by-case basis; it doesn't consider yet-to-be-litigated factual situations. Fourth, an appellate judge may have to make part of a case ambiguous to get a majority. Finally, ambiguity allows for flexibility in the law.

Rather than being upset by ambiguity, law students should embrace it. Using ambiguity is what being a successful lawyer is about. A successful lawyer takes an ambiguous case and convinces the court that it supports his or her argument. A good example of using ambiguity to help your case is arguing that a narrow case holding creates a broad standard, as we saw in *J'Aire* in Chapter Two. You can also make reasonable inferences from cases.

An example of using ambiguity in your favor involves writing up a rule from your client's point of view.

EXAMPLE I

Defendant's viewpoint: An agreement not to compete is a restraint of trade and therefore unenforceable on grounds of public policy unless it is reasonable.

Plaintiff's viewpoint: An agreement not to compete is enforceable if it is reasonable, particularly when it involves the company's proprietary secrets.

EXERCISE IX-1

For the following words, think up at least two meanings:

(a) chair
(b) place
(c) opus
(d) dryer
(e) book
(f) suit
(g) party
(h) bug
(i) romantic
(j) pants
(k) steep
(l) bag
(m) era
(n) paper
(o) ball
(p) game
(q) rock
(r) glass
(s) card
(t) window
(u) table
(v) check
(w) piston

(x) hit

(y) drive

(z) clip

B. DEVELOPING THE ABILITY TO SEE OUTSIDE ONE'S PREJUDICES AND PRECONCEIVED NOTIONS

The next step in thinking outside the box is developing the ability to see outside your prejudices and preconceived notions. Lawyers need to be able to put themselves in their opponents' shoes. Not only does this help an attorney make his case stronger, it allows him to make arguments for his client that he might not otherwise make.

EXERCISE IX-2

What language is the following statement in?

Har

dwo

rkan

dha

rdpla

yle

adtohap

pin

ess.

EXERCISE IX-3

Think of an opinion that you hold strongly. Now look at the situation from the viewpoint of a member of the opposite sex. Has your opinion changed? Now look at the situation from the viewpoint of a member of a different race or religion or someone of a different age. Repeat this exercise until you are comfortable with all points of view.

EXERCISE IX-4

1. Find a case in a casebook or reporter. Write a decision that comes to exactly the opposite conclusion from the case (the dissent). Repeat this exercise until you are comfortable with both sides of an argument.

2. Find a case in a casebook or reporter. Write a decision that comes to the same conclusion as the case but uses different reasoning (a concurrence). Repeat this exercise until you are comfortable with making an argument based on different reasons.

EXERCISE IX-5

1. Find a story in a newspaper. Rewrite it in terms that a child can understand.

2. Think of your favorite sport. Explain it so that someone who has never seen it or heard of it can understand it.

3. Think of a difficult topic, such as racial discrimination or divorce, and explain it in terms that a child would understand. Repeat this exercise until you are able to explain any topic in the simplest terms possible.

4. Think of a historical event that occurred during your life that you remember well. Now try to write up the event in the way that a historian would one hundred years after the event.

5. Look at some of your favorite cases. Rewrite them as if you were a reporter for a newspaper.

6. Look at some of your favorite cases. Assume you are the counsel for the winning side. Write a letter to your client explaining the case and what it means for him or her. Then assume you are the losing counsel and do the same.

EXERCISE IX-6

Use the synthesized rule from exercise IV-2 [A dirk or dagger is a straight knife, which is (1) worn on the person, (2) primarily fitted for stabbing and capable of inflicting death, and (3) has a locking blade, (4) a hand guard, (5) a blade longer than three and a half inches, and (6) at least two edges and a sharp point] to answer the following question. Ronald, sixteen, has a straight-edged knife that he wears on his person. Ronald is stopped by a police officer for not having reflectors on his bike. Noticing the hand guard of Ronald's knife, the officer arrests him under section 12020. Can Ronald be convicted? Choose the best answer.

A. Ronald cannot be convicted because he is a minor.
B. Ronald can be convicted because the knife has a hand guard, a locking blade, a five-inch blade, two sharp edges, and a very sharp point. He carries the knife for protection.
C. Ronald cannot be convicted because the police officer discovered the knife during an illegal stop.
D. Ronald can be convicted because the knife is primarily fitted for stabbing and capable of inflicting death.

C. BEING CREATIVE

Successful lawyers produce creative answers to legal problems. Creative answers are those that have not been thought of before or have not been used frequently before. These creative answers advance the law. For example, in products liability law, it is often hard to prove negligence against a manufacturer because of lack of evidence. Someone had to be the first to propose that plaintiffs should be able to use strict liability to establish a products liability claim.

It does not require genius to come up with creative answers. The most important thing is to be willing to look beyond the established answers for something new. The following exercises involve creative thinking.

EXERCISE IX-7

A boy and his father are in a traffic accident. The father is killed, and the boy is rushed to the hospital for emergency surgery. The surgeon walks in and exclaims, "I cannot operate. This boy is my son." Explain.

EXERCISE IX-8

A young boy walks into a restaurant. A beautiful woman stands up and says, "That's my boy." Another beautiful woman stands up and says, "That's my boy." Both women are correct. The boy has never been adopted, neither of the women have been a surrogate, and neither of the women is a step-parent. Explain.

EXERCISE IX-9

1. A bus gets caught in a tunnel because the bus is slightly taller than the tunnel opening. The bus driver tries to back out, but she is unsuccessful; the forward momentum of the bus has caused it to become stuck. A tow truck also cannot get the bus out. There is a way to get the bus unstuck. What is the solution?

2. Marjorie Victim was murdered in her home in Pasadena, California at exactly 1:30 a.m. on November 4, 2012. The D.A. believes that Marjorie's boyfriend, Jack Ripper, committed the crime. Two reliable witnesses identified Jack as the man they saw leave the crime scene at about 1:30 a.m. However, Jack has an alibi. He was stopped by a policeman at 1:20 a.m. that night for having a burned-out taillight. The officer is certain it was Jack, and, in fact, Jack can be clearly seen on the patrol car's video camera. The place the officer stopped Jack is approximately thirty miles from Marjorie's house. Jack had no other means to get to Marjorie's house other than his car. The only road he could have taken to Marjorie's house had a 45-mph speed limit, and it had several speed traps that night. Despite Jack's seemingly solid alibi, the D.A. is convinced Jack is the killer. Suddenly the D.A. comes up with the answer. What did the D.A come up with? (Jack does not have any siblings.)

Creativity has two parts: thinking up a unique solution, then criticizing it to make sure it works. The first part is called "brainstorming," which means to come up with as many ideas as possible without being critical. (Let yourself loose in this stage.) Being critical is the second part.

EXERCISE IX-10

Think up at least ten uses for this book. Brainstorm; don't be critical.

EXERCISE IX-11

Think up at least ten uses for a pencil. Brainstorm; don't be critical.

EXERCISE IX-12

List at least ten defenses to civil battery. Brainstorm; don't be critical.

III. APPLYING EXISTING PROBLEM-SOLVING SKILLS TO DIFFERENT TYPES OF PROBLEMS

As mentioned in the chapter introduction, an important problem-solving skill is being able to recognize which problem-solving skill or skills apply to a particular problem (thinking across domains, or domain transfer). Professor Halpern has written, "When critical-thinking skills are taught so that they transfer appropriately and spontaneously, students learn to actively focus on the structure of problems or arguments so the underlying characteristics become salient, instead of the domain-specific surface characteristics."[9] The key to this process is deep learning. Students must have "a robust understanding of underlying principles and deep structure"; they must understand not only what to do but also why.[10] This hinges upon how the skill was originally learned, how the information is stored in long term-memory, and how it was used.[11]

One can effectively organize material in long-term memory by developing "interconnected knowledge structures" (schemas)—relating concepts to other concepts.[12] "Information that is associated with material being learned can function as an effective retrieval cue when the learning is completed."[13] For example, as I noted in Chapter Two, when you are reading, think about how what you are reading relates to other concepts, question the text, and think of alternatives. Similarly, think about how a case relates to other relevant cases. Likewise, charting or diagramming an organization helps you remember it. Finally, Halpern encourages using authentic materials, which are similar to real-world situations, to aid transfer.[14]

Halpern uses "sunk costs"—"the general idea . . . that prior investments are not relevant to decisions about future costs"—as an example.[15] She writes, "The goal of transferable thinking skills would be achieved if students recognize sunk-costs arguments when they are being made in totally different settings and can apply what has been learned about these arguments in the new settings." Her first example of a sunk cost is a friend who is investing $500 to repair a beat-up old car, which he has already "sunk" a lot of money into. Under the sunk-cost theory, the previous investment is irrelevant. A creative thinker would then be able to transfer sunk-cost concepts to dissimilar situations, such as Congress spending additional money on a missile system that it has already spent millions on, or a man marrying a girlfriend because they have already spent so much time together.

Examples of domain transfer in the law would be transferring concepts of fairness from tort law to contracts law or transferring concepts of federalism to choice of law. The transfer could also be transferring a method of solving a property problem to a contracts problem. Likewise, applying principles from statutes and cases to drafting contracts is transfer.[16]

The most innovative example of domain transfer I have seen is in the *J'Aire* case, which you analyzed in Chapter Two. The judge took a method for analyzing wills cases and applied it to a negligent interference with economic advantage case. You should review this case. What type of legal reasoning did the judge use at this point? Note that, while the facts are very different, the relationships among the parties are exactly the same between the precedent cases and the *J'Aire* facts.

Thus, having skills exercises in all courses is vital to being able to transfer skills from one domain to another because learners need to practice skills in a variety of contexts.[17] Equally important, using authentic materials and real-world situations helps transfer, so law schools need more skills courses, simulation courses, and clinical courses than they currently have. Finally, Professor Schwartz suggests that students "develop their own examples and problems, develop analogies between the prior learning and the new learning, and . . . paraphrase their learning."[18] In other words, self-regulated learners are good at domain transference.[19]

IV. ADVANCED PROBLEM-SOLVING EXERCISES
A. GENERAL PROBLEM-SOLVING EXERCISES

EXERCISE IX-13

These exercises may be difficult for a beginner. However, even first-year law students will gain something from reading the thinking processes in the solutions.

1. Slow Joe Jones, a wide receiver, was the last pick in the 2008 NFL draft. ABZ Football Cards, the leading maker of football cards, tries to sign all rookies to exclusive contracts to allow ABZ to use their likenesses on football cards in exchange for $50 and ten free footballs. Joe, thinking he will probably be cut at training camp, signs the contract, and takes the $50 and ten free footballs. The last day before the first cut, Joe tries a new brand of shoelaces and runs the fastest fifty-yard dash in NFL history. He goes on to be the rookie of the year and most valuable player in the Super Bowl. After the Super Bowl, BCZ Football Cards wants to sign Joe to an exclusive contract to allow BCZ to use Joe's likeness on football cards in exchange for $10 million. ABZ has threatened to file a lawsuit against Joe should he breach its contract by signing one with BCZ. Can Joe do anything to invalidate his contract with ABZ? Assume that the ABZ contract satisfies the usual requisites of contract law.

2. Jo and Mary walk into your office and say they want to start a partnership. They say that they each are going to put up 50 percent of the money necessary to start up the business, and they are going to hire one employee, Marge, to run it. They don't want to be double-taxed like they would be with a corporation. Both have considerable savings, and they want to make sure that these savings can't be reached by the partnership creditors. You suggest that they set up a limited partnership. However, neither Jo nor Mary is willing to be the general partner whose assets would be reachable, and they can find no one who is willing to take the risk of being the general partner. Is there another solution?

3. **Facts:** Polly Trueheart became engaged to William Philanderer last year. They were to be wed in a large church in West Hempstead, Hysteria, their hometown. William gave Polly a $5,000 engagement ring. Last

week, William broke off the engagement because he didn't like Polly's new haircut. William also demanded return of the engagement ring. You represent Polly. Can she keep the ring?

Law: Most states have a common-law rule that the woman must return the ring to her former fiancé because it was a conditional gift given in contemplation of marriage. Hysteria has a rule that the woman need not return the ring if she is not at fault in breaking the engagement. Finally, West Hysteria and North Hysteria have statutes that state the woman does not have to return the ring because it is an unconditional gift.

B. THINK-ALOUD EXERCISES

Think-aloud exercises will help you develop your advanced problem-solving skills and your inner voice. They will help you apply your legal skills in situations different from those in which they were learned (domain transfer). As mentioned earlier, recognizing the proper skill or skills to use to solve a problem is an important part of problem solving. In a think-aloud exercise, the student "talks through" a problem (hypothetical) with a teacher or another person.[20] "A 'think aloud' is an effort by an expert in the field to articulate all of the thoughts, ideas, and hypotheses the expert has as he reads though and analyzes a problem (including all the thoughts, ideas, and hypotheses the expert rejected)."[21] In other words, a think aloud forces the speaker to verbalize all the steps in the problem-solving process. Students should ask themselves questions during the think-aloud process.[22] "The more actively the student questions his or her understanding of the material, the better he or she is likely to grasp the legal concepts."[23] It helps students to develop "the ability to reason through problems effectively in practice."[24]

Actually, thinking aloud is a way that lawyers discuss cases. When I was in practice, I would often sit down with another lawyer, and we would "talk through" the case. This forced both of us to slow down and abandon our prejudices and preconceived notions. In other words, talking through a case helped us avoid jumping to a conclusion.

It is best to do think-aloud exercises with a professor or another lawyer. (However, two students can work together, with one student being the teacher and the other the student.) The professor can ask questions during the think aloud to help focus the student's cognitive development. Of course, the think aloud can be recorded so the student can listen to his or her thought processes.

THINK-ALOUD EXAMPLE

I will use the fair-use example from Chapter Six as a think-aloud example. Although I am familiar with copyright law, I will go through all the problem-solving steps. I am adding to the problem that you have your client's book.

The first thing I will do is read through the facts to try to identify the problem. It looks like a copyright problem. Our client has used a paragraph from someone else's treatise, and he's been sued. He wants to know if he can use a fair-use defense. So the issue is probably whether our client has a fair-use defense to copyright infringement.

The next thing is to identify what law applies. We already know it is copyright and fair use. Is it federal or state law? We discussed copyright and fair use a little in property a couple of years ago. I seem to remember that there is a federal copyright statute. Here it is, in title 17 of the U.S. Code. I wonder if there is a fair-use section. Would it be better to look in the index or the table of contents? I'll look in the table of contents, because that will let me look at the structure of the statute. Here it is, section 107. It comes right after 106 on exclusive rights in copyrighted works; 106b is irrelevant because it's on visual works. After 107 are additional limitations on exclusive rights. None of the other sections seem to apply.

The next thing to do is to break down the statute [see the breakdown in Chapter Six]. How do the parts fit together? The main part of the statute is the four fair-use factors. The introduction gives a cross-reference, a general rule, and some examples of fair use. Next, the body gives the four fair-use factors. Finally, there is a clarification at the end of the statute.

How should I approach this? I've already looked at 106 and 106b, and they are irrelevant. Maybe I should look at the main part of the statute first, then the fair-use factors. Do my facts fit within the fair-use examples—criticism, comment, news reporting, teaching (including multiple copies for classroom use), scholarship, or research? I understand all these factors, so I don't need to look them up. Well, maybe not; terms in the law may have a different meaning. I should do some background reading. (I probably should have done this when I started.) I'll look in the library catalog for a copyright treatise. The reference librarian says that Nimmer is probably the best one. Here is the fair-use chapter. Now I have a general idea about the terms.

Criticism? No, our client isn't criticizing the passage. Comment? He isn't commenting on the passage, either. News reporting, no. It might be teaching. There is a little problem here because he put it in a book, but let's keep this one in mind. Scholarship? Yes, this seems to be scholarship. Research, no. OK, this helps, but I think we need to go on to the fair-use factors.

The four-factor test: are the four factors conjunctive or disjunctive? It says "the factors to be considered," so this is probably a weighing test, and the clarification at the end seems to support this.

Factor one looks at the purpose and character of the use, including whether such use is of a commercial nature or is for nonprofit educational purposes. I'll read about this factor in Nimmer before I go on. The statute says it is further defined by whether use is of a commercial nature or is for nonprofit educational purposes. This one's pretty clear. Because our client gave the pamphlet out for free, the use is noncommercial, and it is noncommercial educational use. So, I guess we win on factor one. But Nimmer also asks whether the use is transformative. I don't see this in 107; I guess the courts added it. Our client used the paragraph verbatim, so it's not transformative. On this factor, we win on the noncommercial educational part, but it's not transformative. I would think that since the noncommercial part is in the statute, it's the most important part. Anyway, I think our client wins on this factor.

Factor two is the nature of the copyrighted work. Our client's work is nonfictional, and nonfictional works receive less protection. Oh, it's not talking about our client's work, it's referring to the copyrighted work, Professor Famous's treatise. This makes sense. Factor one concerns the use, factor two the copyrighted work. The copyrighted work is nonfictional. Since a nonfictional work receives less copyright protection than a fictional one, this factor favors our client.

Factor three is the amount and substantiality of the portion used in relation to the copyrighted work as a whole. I remember from property that "amount" means raw percentage. Nimmer says basically the same thing. Our client used only a paragraph out of a five-hundred-page treatise, which is less than 1 percent. Now, substantiality. Doesn't it mean the same thing as amount? No, they wouldn't have put two words here if one would have conveyed the meaning. According to Nimmer, substantiality refers to the quality of the use—whether the user has taken the essence or heart of the work. Although our client's use was verbatim, it is unlikely that a single paragraph from a five-hundred-page book would be the essence or the heart of the original. Accordingly, our client probably wins on this factor.

The final factor is the effect of the use on the potential market for or value of the copyrighted work. It is unlikely that our client's use will fail either part of this factor. Taking only one paragraph is unlikely to cause potential readers not to buy a five-hundred-page book, and it should have no effect on the copyright. [What type of legal reasoning did I use here?]

All four factors favor our client, so our client probably has a fair-use defense. Any reservations? Just the transformative part, but I would say that in light of the strong case for our client, it probably isn't important. [An engaged problem solver would go back and reevaluate all the steps, but this is enough for now. Of course, in the real world, the problem would also involve case law research.]

The example in Chapter Four concerning Chin's will is another example of a think aloud. Many of my answers also involve think aloud.

Below you will find three think-aloud problems for your own use. Because these are statutory analysis exercises, you don't need to do any outside research. You can also use old exam questions as think-aloud questions. Finally, Schwartz and Riebe have several think-aloud exercises in their contracts book.[25]

EXERCISE IX-14

Ed Weaver, a firm client, was fired from his job at the Jack Beam Brewery in Hunnington, Hysteria, because he was an alcoholic. His boss had read in the paper that Ed had been convicted of drunk driving. Although the charges were later dropped, Ed admitted to his boss that he had a drinking problem, but he was going to Alcoholics Anonymous meetings and had not had a drink for over six months. Ed's alcoholism had not affected his job performance.

Your boss, Angela Smith, has asked you to write a memo on whether Jack Beam's dismissal of Ed violated the Hysteria Disabilities Act of 1990 (the "Act"). The Act states:

> No covered entity shall discriminate against a qualified individual with a disability because of the individual's disability in regard to job application procedures, the hiring or advancement of employees, employee compensation, job training, and other terms, conditions, and privileges of employment.

The Act defines disability:

> The term "disability" means with respect to an individual—(a) a physical or mental impairment that substantially interferes with a major life activity, (b) a record of such impairment, or (c) being regarded as having such an impairment.

The Act explicitly excludes drug addicts from its protection. The legislature added this exclusion five years after the Act's enactment because the Hysteria Supreme Court had held that drug addicts were protected by the Act. The Act does not mention alcoholism.

The legislative history states that the Act's purpose is "to provide a clear and comprehensive mandate for the elimination of discrimination against individuals with disabilities." The legislative history does not specifically mention alcoholism.

In *Smith v. Doe*, the Alabama Supreme Court held that the Alabama disability statute, which is similar to Hysteria's, did not apply to alcoholics. The court stated that the legislative history clearly demonstrated that the legislature had not intended the statute to protect alcoholics.

Hysteria is a highly religious state. More than 95 percent of its citizens belong to the Hysteria Orthodox Church, which strictly forbids the consumption of alcohol.

Think aloud the above problem with a professor or classmate.

EXERCISE IX-15

John Moyer was recently appointed a U.S. attorney in Rhode Island. Mr. Moyer believes in family values and that it is the duty of federal prosecutors to uphold public morality.

A strip club, owned by James Griffith, recently opened in Bristol, Rhode Island. (You may assume it is a strip club and nothing more.) Mr. Moyer believed that this strip club contravened the public morality, and he searched for law to use to shut it down. After an exhaustive search, the only statute he found that might be applicable was the Munn Act, a statute that Congress had passed in 1910.

The Munn Act states:

> Any person who shall knowingly transport or cause to be transported . . . in interstate commerce, . . . any woman or girl for the purpose of prostitution or debauchery, or for any other immoral purpose, . . . shall be deemed guilty of a felony, and upon conviction thereof shall be punished by a fine not exceeding ten thousand dollars, or by an imprisonment of not more than five years, or both.

Mr. Moyer thought that the Munn Act might apply to the strip club because Mr. Griffith recruited his strippers from Massachusetts, and he drove them from Massachusetts to Bristol in a bus every evening. (Mr. Griffith was not able to recruit strippers in Rhode Island, probably due to the fact that it is a very moral state.) Mr. Moyer obtained an indictment against Mr. Griffith for violation of the Munn Act. A federal court in Rhode Island convicted Mr. Griffith of five counts of violating the Munn Act, fined him $50,000, and sentenced him to five years in a federal prison.

Mr. Griffith is appealing his conviction to the U.S. Court of Appeals on the ground that the Munn Act does not apply to his conduct. (You may assume that there is no other issue than the question of the statutory interpretation of the Munn Act.) Your senior partner has asked you to analyze this issue and write up that analysis.

In your research you have come across the following relevant materials. A few months before the passage of the Munn Act, a newspaper printed a series of articles claiming that young women were being kidnapped and forced into prostitution both in the United States and foreign countries. The Senate committee report stated that the legislation was needed "to put a stop to the villainous interstate and international traffic in women and girls." Senator Jackson of Utah spoke against the bill because he thought it might be used to prosecute polygamy. Senator Johnson of New York stated that the bill was not intended to deal with polygamy. Senator Dooley, another opponent of the bill, declared that he was aghast at the statute's broad language.

You have also found some cases from your jurisdiction interpreting the bill that date from the first ten years after the bill's passage, but all these cases concerned prostitution. You did find one case from the Ninth Circuit from 1933 that held the statute was applicable to a situation where a married man took a seventeen-year-old girl from California to Nevada to have sexual relations with her. There is *no* other relevant case law.

Think aloud the above problem with a professor or a friend.

EXERCISE IX-16

On October 22, 1997, several conspirators bombed the U.S. courthouse in Portsmith, Oregon. Ten people were killed, including a federal judge. Jack Cooper was convicted of conspiracy and other charges in connection with the bombing and sentenced to life in prison. The U.S. Court of Appeals for the Ninth Circuit reversed Mr. Cooper's conviction on the ground that the court should not have allowed the testimony of one of the witnesses because the prosecutor had violated the Federal Anti-Bribery Statute of 1990 when she offered leniency to the witness in exchange for his untruthful testimony. The case is now before the U. S. Supreme Court on the ground that the statute does not apply to federal prosecutors.

Section 2 of the Federal Anti-Bribery Statute states:

Any person who, directly or indirectly, gives, offers, or promises anything of value to another person for or because of testimony under oath, or affirmation given or to be given by such witness upon a trial, shall be fined up to $10,000 or imprisoned for no more than two years, or both.

The following materials are relevant to the interpretation of this statute. The Dictionary Act in the U.S. Code states:

> When used in the United States Code, the term "person" means natural person, corporation, partnership, association, or governmental entity, unless the context indicates otherwise.

The Senate committee report stated that the purpose of the comprehensive anticrime bill that contained the Federal Anti-Bribery Statute was to "give federal law enforcement officers and prosecutors more tools to fight crime." The report also stated that the purpose of the section at issue in this case was to "guarantee the integrity of the judicial process." Senator Scallon, the bill's sponsor, was asked during the debate whether the bill would hinder a prosecutor's ability to do his job, and she said that it would not.

In the trial court, the prosecutor cited several cases and a statute relevant to the practice at issue. "From the common law, we have drawn a long-standing practice sanctioning the testimony of accomplices against their confederates in exchange for leniency."[26] Similarly, "no practice is more ingrained in our criminal justice system than the practice of the government calling a witness who is an accessory of a crime for which the defendant is charged and having that witness testify under a plea bargain that promises him a reduced sentence."[27] In addition, the Sentencing Reform Act of 1986 allows courts to reduce sentences for individuals who provide substantial assistance in the investigation or prosecution of a federal crime.

Think aloud the above problem with a classmate or a friend.

EXERCISE IX-17

1. What can you do to continue to improve your learning skills? (Brainstorm, then criticize)
2. What can a law student do to improve legal education? (Brainstorm, then criticize)
3. What can a law firm or an attorney do to improve legal education?

CHAPTER WRAP-UP

Has this chapter changed the way you think about legal problem solving? If so, how? What approaches do you use for legal problem solving other than the ones given earlier in this chapter? How can you improve your problem-solving skills? Do some problem-solving skills work better in solving personal problems rather than legal ones? If so, which ones? Think about this again. Can you modify those problem-solving strategies for the law?

Do you have problems dealing with ambiguity? If so, how can you learn to deal with ambiguity better? Why is ambiguity important in the law? How can attorneys use ambiguity? Do you have problems overcoming your prejudices and preconceived notions? Can you think from someone else's viewpoint? What can you do to improve these skills?

What legal problems have been solved by creative solutions (like the use of strict liability in products liability to solve problems of proof)? Think of a problem in your life. Can you come up with a creative solution? Does brainstorming help you come up with ideas? Can you effectively criticize your own ideas?

Can you apply your problem-solving skills to different types of problems? Does thinking aloud help you see the steps in solving a problem? Does it help you develop your problem-solving abilities?

How would you improve this book? (Brainstorm, then criticize) Should I have given more answers? Did I give too many answers? Was this book effectively organized? Could you organize it better?

CONCLUSION

Learning is a lifelong process. Instead of just absorbing content, you need to learn how to be a self-regulated learner. I hope this book has helped you accomplish that.

Concluding thought: "Critical thinking has to include assessing one's own thinking."[28]

Answers
EXERCISE IX-1

I hope most of these were easy. Just in case: opus is a work, such as an opus of Beethoven, and also the name of a cartoon character; a piston is a part of a car or a Detroit basketball player; the rest should be in the dictionary. Of course, many of these have several meanings. The point of this exercise is that it is difficult to tell the meaning of many words out of context. For example, is era a time period, a baseball statistic, or a proposed constitutional amendment? One who eliminates the possible meaning of a word too quickly shows a lack of flexibility. Doing crossword puzzles helps with your word flexibility because there is no context for a clue.

EXERCISE IX-2

English. "Hard work and hard play lead to happiness." To get this problem right, you need to abandon your preconceived notion about spacing.

EXERCISE IX-3

Example: The legislature of Utopia has proposed an affirmative action bill that provides for racial quotas. (Don't worry about constitutional issues.) View one, white male: I believe in equal opportunity for all, but the bill goes too far. It will cause reverse discrimination against whites who have had nothing to do with discrimination against blacks. View two, black male: I support the bill. Quotas are necessary to make up for past discrimination. View three, white female: The bill does not go far enough because it deals only with racial discrimination. Women have been discriminated against, too.

Other possible topics: abortion, Jackie Robinson's entry into baseball, laws against pornography, the next election, flag burning, the erection of a creche (manger scene) on a court house steps, hair styles, the importance of *Brown v. Education*, this year's hemlines, prayer in school

EXERCISE IX-6

I hope you concluded that the problem was poorly or wrongly designed. Answers B and D are equally good. If you answered B or D, you decided because you felt restricted by my direction—"Choose the *best* answer." In real life, problems are not neatly set out in a package. Always question your assumptions.

EXERCISE IX-7

The first reaction of most people is that the surgeon is the boy's stepfather or that the driver of the car was. However, the problem did not say that either party was the stepfather. The correct answer is that the surgeon was the boy's mother. Those who still think of surgeons as being men will have difficulty in coming up with the right answer. This problem was not used to show that sexism remains in our society, but rather to try to get the reader to stop thinking in limited ways. Many problems can be solved by rejecting ways of thinking that really don't apply. (I got this problem from an episode of *All in the Family*.)

EXERCISE IX-8

One of the women is the child's natural father. He had a sex change operation shortly after the boy's birth.

EXERCISE IX-9

1. The solution to this problem is very simple: let some air out of the tires. This will make the bus slightly shorter. If you had difficulty coming up with this answer, it is because you were concentrating on how to push or pull the bus out. The key is to make the bus shorter and let the bus drive out under its own power. (One of my high school teachers told me this one.)

2. November 4, 2012, was the day we turned back the clocks to standard time. Jack was stopped by the policeman at 1:15 a.m. daylight savings time. At 2 a.m., the clocks were turned back to 1 a.m. Jack then committed the murder at 1:30 a.m. standard time. There was plenty of time for him to drive the thirty miles.

EXERCISE IX-10

1. Use it to prop open a door. 2. Use it to steady a table with uneven legs. 3. Kill flies with it. 4. Tear it up and burn it to keep warm in the winter. 5. Use it as a weapon against muggers. 6. Stand on it to reach a high shelf. 7. Drop it in the Grand Canyon to see how deep the canyon is. 8. Read it

before going to bed to save on sleeping pills. 9. Let a little girl cut paper dolls out of it. 10. Cut it up and use it to line a bird cage. (There are numerous other correct answers.)

EXERCISE IX-11

1. Carve it into an art object. 2. Use it as a bookmark. 3. Use it as a weapon. 4. Take out the lead and poison your enemy with it. 5. Use it to scratch your back. 6. Use it to clean out the garbage disposal. 7. Use it as a pointer. 8. Wear it in your hair. 9. Use it as a toothpick. 10. Stick it in the ground as a marker. (There are numerous other correct answers.)

EXERCISE IX-12

1. The plaintiff consented. 2. The plaintiff provoked the defendant. 3. Self-defense. 4. The plaintiff had it coming to him. 5. Privilege. 6. The plaintiff insulted the defendant's mother. 7. The plaintiff was unconscious at the time of the battery. 8. The defendant was a police officer acting in the line of duty. 9. The statute of limitations for battery has expired. 10. The plaintiff was not injured. (There are many more possibilities. The reader will note that some of the preceding examples are not good defenses. However, the point of this exercise is to list all possible examples. The list can be critically pared down later.)

EXERCISE IX-13

1. The first creative answer is to try to get the contract invalidated based on unconscionability. This is a possible defense, but it may not succeed; Joe knew what he was signing away. He took the risk that he wouldn't have much of a football career. There is a more creative answer. The contract is invalid because it is illegal; it is an attempt to create or continue a monopoly. (See Section 2 of the Sherman Act and statutes in many states.) Note that the facts state that ABZ is trying to sign up all rookies and is the largest manufacturer of football cards. More research needs to be done before one can say for sure whether there is a violation

of antitrust laws (one especially needs to look at ABZ's market share), but illegality of contract is certainly a defense that needs to be explored.

2. This is an easy question, at least to those who are familiar with tax and corporate law. The only person who should have any difficulty with this question has listened too closely to the clients' desire to set up a partnership. The correct solution is to set up an S corporation. An S corporation would give Jo and Mary the limited liability of a corporation or a limited partner in a limited partnership, but an S corporation is taxed like a partnership. A creative person might have also suggested that Jo and Mary set up a regular corporation and draw a salary instead of taking dividends. However, from the facts, it appears that Jo and Mary are not going to do the work, so this solution may not be practical.

3. The first issue is which state's law applies. This is an easy question, because all the relevant connections are with Hysteria. Based on this determination, you will apply the Hysteria rule. Since breaking off the engagement was not Polly's fault, she should be able to keep the ring. The other side might try to argue that Polly's cutting her hair caused the breakup, but it is doubtful that any court would accept this as justification.

EXERCISE IX-17

1. You are on your own.
2. Here are some ideas to get you started.
   A. Learn about the issues in legal education. Regularly read the *Legal Skills Prof Blog* and the website Educating Tomorrow's Lawyers. Read *Best Practices for Legal Education* (free download from website) and *The Carnegie Report*.
   B. When choosing a law school, look for law schools that stress the connection between theory and practice (legal skills courses, clinics, doctrinal courses with skills exercises). One place to look is the Educating Tomorrow's Lawyers Consortium.
   C. Take as many skills courses and clinics as you can. If students take more skills courses and clinics, your law school will have to hire more skills professors and offer more skills options.

D. Suggest to your professors that they adopt textbooks that have skills exercises. Carolina Academic Press has published a number of casebooks, the Context and Practice Series, that include legal skills and professionalism exercises. Similarly, LexisNexis has published a series of supplemental books, the Skills and Values Series, that include skills exercises. Similar books will come out in the near future.

E. When your dean has an open forum, go! Don't be afraid to express your views (respectfully, of course). Let your deans know what courses you want. Work for change in the law school curriculum. Encourage law school transparency. Talk to faculty members about what you want from your law school. Participate in law school organizations, and if your law school has students on faculty committees, volunteer for those committees.

F. Show as much respect to your legal writing, clinic, and other skills teachers as you do to your doctrinal teachers. Meet with these teachers frequently. Legal writing teachers and clinicians love to interact with students. It is the best part of our jobs. Value your professors for their teaching ability, not their rank.

G. Be an engaged, active learner; be curious. Don't just sit passively and observe in the classroom—participate. Question what you read in your textbooks. Consider the implications of what you read in your textbooks and what your professors say. Don't settle for easy answers. Talk with your classmates about legal issues. Become excited about the law.

H. Take care of yourself. Don't let law school get to you. If you are having a problem, discuss it with someone.

3. Law firms and attorneys can play a significant role in legal education reform. If students are better prepared for practice, law firms will have to do less training of new lawyers. Also, students who have taken practical courses better know what type of law they want to practice. Most important, clients will grow to trust lawyers who have had more practical training and produce a better product. Here are a few suggestions on what law firms can do.

A. Interview at law schools that have strong skills programs. A place to begin is the law schools that are members of the Educating Tomorrow's Lawyers Consortium.

B. When interviewing prospective hires, ask about the skills courses they have taken and what skills they developed in those courses.

C. When hiring, put more stress on a student's preparation to practice law than on *U.S. News* rankings.

D. If you are a hiring partner, let the law schools you hire from know that you want practice-ready attorneys. Compliment those law schools that have strong skills programs.

E. If you are an alum, let your law school know that you want it to produce practice-ready attorneys.

F. Earmark donations to your alma mater for skills programs. Help set up chairs for legal writing professors, clinical professors, and other skills teachers.

G. Write articles in local bar journals advocating legal education reform.

It is time for legal education to change. Law schools need to prepare their students better for practice so that they can be better lawyers and fulfill their main function: serving the public.

NOTES

1. Quoted in Reza Zabihi & Mojtabe Pordel, *An Investigation of Critical Reading in Reading Textbooks: A Qualitative Analysis*, 4 INT'L EDUC. STUD. 80, 82 (2011).

2. PATRICIA L. SMITH & TILLMAN J. RAGAN, INSTRUCTIONAL DESIGN 132 (Wiley 2d ed. 1999). Kristen Holmquist describes the process in a slightly different way: "Cognitive psychologists define a problem, simply, as any situation in which the current state of affairs varies from the desired end point. And solving that problem entails a series of decisions and actions, each building on the last, in order to move the world closer to the goal state. In order to make these decisions, or encourage others to, we rely on stock stories, or schemas, familiar stories and arguments that act as heuristics and allow us to create meaning through narrative. . . . Lawyers as problem solvers rely on legal—and cultural—stocks in order to try to move the world

in directions that benefit their clients. This movement involves persuasion of one form or another—whether it's persuading a court to find for one's client, an opposing party in litigation to see one's settlement offer as a good deal, or a collaborative party to undertake some kind of a joint venture." Kristen Holmquist, *Challenging Carnegie*, 61 J. LEGAL EDUC. 353, 368–69 (2010). She adds, "On the most obvious level, legal precedent serves this function. . . . But lawyering involves appealing to stories and arguments that are relevant and persuasive for larger empirical, cultural, and social reasons, as well." *Id.* at 371. As I mentioned in Chapter Two, case briefs are schemas for understanding the law. When lawyers problem solve, they draw on these schemas.

3. Michael Hunter Schwartz, *Teaching Law by Design: How Learning Theory and Instructional Design Can Inform and Reform Law Teaching*, 38 SAN DIEGO L. REV. 347, 397 (2001).

4. *Id.*

5. This model is based on a model at About.com: Psychology, at http://psychology.about.com/od/problemsolving/f/problem-solving-steps.htm.

6. Tina L. Stark, *Thinking Like a Deal Lawyer*," 54 J. LEGAL EDUC. 223 (2004).

7. *Id.*

8. As one author has declared, a 21st-century worker must be "someone who can carry out multistep operations, manipulate abstract and complex symbols and ideas, efficiently acquire new information, and remain flexible enough to recognize the need for continuing change and new paradigms for lifelong learning." Diane F. Halpern, *Teaching Critical Thinking for Transfer across Domains: Dispositions, Skills, Structure Training, and Metacognitive Monitoring*, 53 AM. PSYCH. 449, 450 (1998). She adds: "If people cannot think intelligently about the myriad issues that confront them, then they are in danger of having all of the answers but still not knowing what the answers mean." *Id.* My ideas on thinking outside the box and creativity have been influenced by what teachers taught me in high school and college. The major thinker in this area is Edward de Bono. *See* LATERAL THINKING CREATIVITY: STEP BY STEP (Int'l Center for Creative Thinking 1970).

9. Halpern, *supra* note 8, at 453.

10. SUSAN A. AMBROSE, HOW LEARNING WORKS: 7 RESEARCH-BASED PRINCIPLES FOR SMART TEACHING 109 (Jossey-Bass 2010).

11. Halpern, *supra* note 8, at 453.

12. *Id.*

13. *Id.* The brain organizes information in data structures in long-term memory ("schemata"). *Id.* at 373 ("These structures contain slots, theoretically organized like a card catalogue, for each of a countless number of specific situations."). Schemata store information, procedures, and subprocedures. *Id.* (comparing schemata to computer programs).

14. *Id.* at 454.

15. *Id.* at 453.

16. Schwartz, *supra* note 3, at 419.

17. Professor Schwartz notes, "The more deeply information is processed, the more likely one is to remember it." *Id.* at 373. Accordingly, "overlearning" material will make recall easier. *Id.*

18. *Id.* at 419.

19. Teaching Excellence in Adult Literacy, Just Write! Guide, https://teal.ed.gov/resources at *29 (Teal 2012).

20. Michael Hunter Schwartz & Denise Riebe, Contracts: A Context and Practice Casebook 71-20 (Carolina Academic Pr. 2009); *see also* Stefan H. Krieger & Serge Martinez, *Performance Isn't Everything: The Importance of Conceptual Competence in Outcome Assessment of Experiential Learning*, 19 Clinical L. Rev. 251 (2012); Brian P. Coppola, *Progress in Practice: Using Concepts from Motivational and Self-Regulated Learning Research to Improve Chemistry Instruction*, 63 New Directions for Teaching and Learning: Understanding Self-Regulated Learning 87, 89–90 (1995).

21. Schwartz & Riebe, *supra* note 20, at 720.

22. Just Write! Guide, *supra* note 19, at 34.

23. Robin A. Boyle, *Employing Active-Learning Techniques and Metacognition in Law School: Shifting Energy from Professor to Student*, 81 U. Det. Mercy L. Rev. 1, 15 (2003).

24. Krieger & Martinez, *supra* note 20, at 255.

25. Schwartz & Riebe, *supra* note 20, at 720–30.

26. Hoffmann v. United States, 385 U.S. 211 (1966).

27. United States v. Cervantes, 862 F.2d 344 (5th Cir. 1988).

28. Andrew Revkin, *Daniel Kahneman on the Trap of "Thinking that We Know,"* N.Y. Times Blogs at http://dotearth.blogs.nytimes.com/2012/05/25/daniel-kahneman-on-the-trap-of-thinking-that-we-know/ (Mar. 25, 2012).

INDEX

A

activity restrictions, narrow versus broad, 115

affirmative defenses, 184

Aldisert, Ruggiero J., 189

ambiguity, 96
dealing with, 214–215
in persuasive analyses, 111

American law. *See also* law
common law basis, 121

analogical arguments. *See also* reasoning by analogy
conclusion, 66
model of, 65–66
reader-oriented, 67
reasoning, comparison of, 66
rule illustration, 65
writing, 65
writing practice exercises, 67

analogies. *See also* reasoning by analogy
acceptability of, 189–190
as support for rule-based reasoning, 80
backing up, 40
basis of comparison, 65

case discussion, 65
choosing, 50, 52–53
degree of similarity, 52, 65, 80, 175
distinguishing cases with, 187
facts, comparison of, 66
general, 50
legal, 52–53
premises, supporting with, 87
relation to case, 66
testing, 50
testing criteria, 189–190
understanding, 49–50
validity, 49

analyses
application of rule, 82
case analyses, 16–17, 33–34, 38, 185
critiquing, 110–111
of concurrences, 20
of dissents, 20
of factors, 115–116
of holdings, 18–19
rule-based reasoning framework for, 80
writing, 161–162

appellate cases, structure of, 180